Apocalypse in Australian
Fiction and Film

CRITICAL EXPLORATIONS IN SCIENCE FICTION AND FANTASY
(a series edited by Donald E. Palumbo and C.W. Sullivan III)

1 *Worlds Apart? Dualism and Transgression in Contemporary Female Dystopias* (Dunja M. Mohr, 2005)

2 *Tolkien and Shakespeare: Essays on Shared Themes and Language* (ed. Janet Brennan Croft, 2007)

3 *Culture, Identities and Technology in the* Star Wars *Films: Essays on the Two Trilogies* (ed. Carl Silvio, Tony M. Vinci, 2007)

4 *The Influence of* Star Trek *on Television, Film and Culture* (ed. Lincoln Geraghty, 2008)

5 *Hugo Gernsback and the Century of Science Fiction* (Gary Westfahl, 2007)

6 *One Earth, One People: The Mythopoeic Fantasy Series of Ursula K. Le Guin, Lloyd Alexander, Madeleine L'Engle and Orson Scott Card* (Marek Oziewicz, 2008)

7 *The Evolution of Tolkien's Mythology: A Study of the History of Middle-earth* (Elizabeth A. Whittingham, 2008)

8 *H. Beam Piper: A Biography* (John F. Carr, 2008)

9 *Dreams and Nightmares: Science and Technology in Myth and Fiction* (Mordecai Roshwald, 2008)

10 Lilith *in a New Light: Essays on the George MacDonald Fantasy Novel* (ed. Lucas H. Harriman, 2008)

11 *Feminist Narrative and the Supernatural: The Function of Fantastic Devices in Seven Recent Novels* (Katherine J. Weese, 2008)

12 *The Science of Fiction and the Fiction of Science: Collected Essays on SF Storytelling and the Gnostic Imagination* (Frank McConnell, ed. Gary Westfahl, 2009)

13 *Kim Stanley Robinson Maps the Unimaginable: Critical Essays* (ed. William J. Burling, 2009)

14 *The Inter-Galactic Playground: A Critical Study of Children's and Teens' Science Fiction* (Farah Mendlesohn, 2009)

15 *Science Fiction from Québec: A Postcolonial Study* (Amy J. Ransom, 2009)

16 *Science Fiction and the Two Cultures: Essays on Bridging the Gap Between the Sciences and the Humanities* (ed. Gary Westfahl, George Slusser, 2009)

17 *Stephen R. Donaldson and the Modern Epic Vision: A Critical Study of the "Chronicles of Thomas Covenant" Novels* (Christine Barkley, 2009)

18 *Ursula K. Le Guin's Journey to Post-Feminism* (Amy M. Clarke, 2010)

19 *Portals of Power: Magical Agency and Transformation in Literary Fantasy* (Lori M. Campbell, 2010)

20 *The Animal Fable in Science Fiction and Fantasy* (Bruce Shaw, 2010)

21 *Illuminating* Torchwood: *Essays on Narrative, Character and Sexuality in the BBC Series* (ed. Andrew Ireland, 2010)

22 *Comics as a Nexus of Cultures: Essays on the Interplay of Media, Disciplines and International Perspectives* (ed. Mark Berninger, Jochen Ecke, Gideon Haberkorn, 2010)

23 *The Anatomy of Utopia: Narration, Estrangement and Ambiguity in More, Wells, Huxley and Clarke* (Károly Pintér, 2010)

24 *The Anticipation Novelists of 1950s French Science Fiction* (Bradford Lyau, 2010)

25 *The* Twilight *Mystique: Critical Essays on the Novels and Films* (ed. Amy M. Clarke, Marijane Osborn, 2010)

26 *The Mythic Fantasy of Robert Holdstock: Critical Essays on the Fiction* (ed. Donald E. Morse, Kálmán Matolcsy, 2011)

27 *Science Fiction and the Prediction of the Future: Essays on Foresight and Fallacy* (ed. Gary Westfahl, Wong Kin Yuen, Amy Kit-sze Chan, 2011)

28 *Apocalypse in Australian Fiction and Film: A Critical Study* (Roslyn Weaver, 2011)

29 *British Science Fiction Film and Television: Critical Essays* (ed. Tobias Hochscherf, James Leggott, 2011)

30 *Cult Telefantasy Series: A Critical Analysis of* The Prisoner, Twin Peaks, The X-Files, Buffy the Vampire Slayer, Lost, Heroes, Doctor Who *and* Star Trek (Sue Short, 2011)

31 *The Postnational Fantasy: Postcolonialism, Cosmopolitics and Science Fiction* (ed. Masood Ashraf Raja, Jason W. Ellis, Swaralipi Nandi, 2011)

Apocalypse in Australian Fiction and Film
A Critical Study

ROSLYN WEAVER

CRITICAL EXPLORATIONS IN SCIENCE FICTION AND FANTASY, 28
Donald E. Palumbo *and* C.W. Sullivan III, *series editors*

McFarland & Company, Inc., Publishers
Jefferson, North Carolina, and London

LIBRARY OF CONGRESS CATALOGUING-IN-PUBLICATION DATA

Weaver, Roslyn, 1979–
    Apocalypse in Australian fiction and film : a critical study / Roslyn Weaver.
      [Donald Palumbo and C.W. Sullivan III, series editors]
        p.   cm. — (Critical explorations in science fiction and fantasy ; 28)
      Includes bibliographical references and index.

    ISBN 978-0-7864-6051-9
    softcover : 50# alkaline paper ∞

    1. Australian fiction — 20th century — History and criticism.
    2. Australian fiction — 21st century — History and criticism.
    3. Motion pictures — Australia — History. I. Title.
    PR9612.5.W43   2011
    823'.91409382 — dc22   2010050274

British Library cataloguing data are available

© 2011 Roslyn Weaver. All rights reserved

No part of this book may be reproduced or transmitted in any form or by any means, electronic or mechanical, including photocopying or recording, or by any information storage and retrieval system, without permission in writing from the publisher.

Cover images ©2011 Shutterstock

Manufactured in the United States of America

McFarland & Company, Inc., Publishers
  Box 611, Jefferson, North Carolina 28640
    www.mcfarlandpub.com

Table of Contents

Acknowledgments ix

Preface 1

Introduction 3

ONE • An Apocalyptic Map: New Worlds and the Colonization of Australia 23

TWO • The Shield of Distance: Apocalypse in Australian Literature After 1945 54

THREE • An Apocalyptic Landscape: The *Mad Max* Films 83

FOUR • Children of the Apocalypse: Australian Children's Literature 108

FIVE • (Re)Writing the End of the World: Apocalypse, Race, and Indigenous Literature 135

SIX • The End of the Human: Apocalypse, Cyberpunk, and the Parrish Plessis Novels 159

Conclusion 186

Chapter Notes 191

Bibliography 201

Index 219

Acknowledgments

Projects such as this are often largely solitary endeavors but I am very grateful to several people for their support and encouragement of my research along the way. These include Professor Gerry Turcotte for his advice, guidance, and time invested in this project from its genesis, Dr. Richard Harland for his time and feedback, Dr. Kimberley McMahon-Coleman for shared research interests, and Professor Van Ikin for his comments on the original thesis. I would also like to acknowledge and thank the staff of the Faculty of Arts in the University of Wollongong, as well as the staff at the University of Western Sydney, where parts of this research were undertaken. I am grateful as well to the audiences at various conferences where I have presented my work in progress, and to journal reviewers and editors for their feedback on my earlier work in this field. All feedback I have received along the way has, I hope, been used to develop and refine the ideas and arguments in the research.

I am above all indebted to my parents, David and Kay, for instilling in me a love of literature, and I thank all my family: my parents, and Carolyn, Michael, and their families, for their unfailing support, encouragement and motivation throughout the course of this research. Thank you also to my aunt, Margaret Steinberger, not only for being a great encouragement throughout my research in literature but also for her always brilliant editorial advice, and for her time and energy in editing this book.

Finally, I want to thank several groups for granting me permission to use images and previous work: the National Library of Australia and the National Archives of Australia, who gave permission to use the maps referred to in Chapter One; and Marianne de Pierres, who gave her time in answering questions and providing an image. Parts of this book were published as earlier, shorter versions, and while much has since been revised, updated, and repositioned in the larger context of Australian apocalypse, I do thank the publishers for granting permission to use parts of those works in this book.

"At the End of the World: Australian Adolescent Literature and Apocalypse." *Journal of the Fantastic in the Arts* 17.2 (2006): 155–68.

"'The Four Horsemen of the Greenhouse Apocalypse': Apocalypse in the Science Fiction Novels of George Turner." *Apocalypse Now. Spec. issue of Forum: The University of Edinburgh Postgraduate Journal of Culture and the Arts* 5 (2007).

"The 'Sacred Heart': Sam Watson's *The Kadaitcha Sung*." *Studies in Australian Weird Fiction* 2 (2008): 39–48.

"'The Shadow of the End': The Appeal of Apocalypse in Literary Science Fiction." *The End All Around Us: Apocalyptic Texts and Popular Culture.* Ed. John Walliss and Kenneth G. C. Newport. London: Equinox, 2009. 173–97. (c) Equinox Publishing Ltd 2009.

"The Shield of Distance: Fearful Borders at the Edge of the World." *Terror Australis Incognita? Spec. Issue of Antipodes: A North American Journal of Australian Literature*, 23.1 (2009): 69–74.

"'Smudged, Distorted and Hidden': Apocalypse as Protest in Indigenous Speculative Fiction." *Essays on Postcolonial Literature and Film. Science Fiction, Imperialism, and the Third World.* Ed. Ericka Hoagland and Reema Sarwal. Jefferson, NC: McFarland, 2010. 99–114.

Preface

This book explores the enduring theme of apocalypse in Australian speculative fiction and film. Australia has been a frequent choice as the location for narratives about disaster and the end of the world, including some of the most famous apocalyptic texts, such as Nevil Shute's *On the Beach* and the *Mad Max* films. Australian apocalypse appears in narratives of nuclear war, ecological disaster, invasions, and colonization; in science fiction and fantasy; in literature and film; and in works for adults and children. Although apocalypse is a growing field of research internationally, with studies that examine apocalypse in specific national contexts such as the U.S. and Canada, the area of Australian apocalypse has not been explored in detail to date.

The focus of this book is on literary and cinematic Australian texts that adopt and adapt a secular version of the Biblical apocalypse. Apocalypse means revelation, but the popular imagination often associates it with destruction, and texts that reveal a catastrophic future or past Australia. While the case studies are primarily from the last fifty years, this work begins with a survey of early utopian and dystopian approaches to Australia to provide a historical context. The popularity of apocalypse in Australian fictions has its origins in pre-colonial European speculation about the *terra australis incognita*, the unknown south land. For hundreds of years prior to the British colonization of Australia, European cartographers and writers imagined the south land in many different ways. Speculation about this new land ranged from hopes of a new world — the apocalyptic New Jerusalem — to a secular place of wealth and fortune to a place of horror and dystopia, the end of the world. This perpetual and persistent speculation established an apocalyptic map of Australia before colonists even experienced the land, and has resulted in a tradition of imagining the nation in apocalyptic terms ever since.

The case studies in this book demonstrate a range of agendas that motivate authors to use apocalypse. These texts undermine complacency, warn of future environmental disasters, and act as a language of resistance and protest for minority groups. Despite the different scenarios, many Australian apocalypses display similar anxieties about the nation and its vulnerability to its neighbors, and construct the landscape as a dystopian space, a place of exile and punishment. Such fears remain as a shadow to more optimistic visions of the south land. Other fictions use apocalypse to imagine new worlds, to present spaces of hope and utopia in the future. Together, these narratives imagine Australia as, and at, the end(s) of the world, both geographically and psychologically. These recurring and pervasive associations suggest that there is a significant relationship between Australia and apocalypse.

Introduction

> But the day of the Lord will come like a thief. The heavens will disappear with a roar; the elements will be destroyed by fire, and the earth and everything in it will be laid bare. Since everything will be destroyed in this way, what kind of people ought you to be? You ought to live holy and godly lives as you look forward to the day of God and speed its coming. That day will bring about the destruction of the heavens by fire, and the elements will melt in the heat. But in keeping with his promise we are looking forward to a new heaven and a new earth, the home of righteousness.
>
> 2 Peter 3:10–13

Imagining Australia in apocalyptic terms has long been of interest to writers and filmmakers. Many speculative texts narrate Australia's complete destruction in the future or envisage a chaotic post-apocalyptic society. Apocalyptic scenarios and themes are found in works by writers (Nevil Shute's *On the Beach*, Gabrielle Lord's *Salt*) and filmmakers (*Where the Green Ants Dream*, *Until the End of the World*); in texts for adults (Tess Williams's *Map of Power*, Simon Brown's *Winter*) and for children (Lee Harding's *Waiting for the End of the World*, John Marsden's *Tomorrow, When the War Began*); and in works by authors of both genders and varying cultural backgrounds.

Apocalyptic texts do not provide a comprehensive picture of Australia's cultural scene, of course, for much of the nation's fiction is confident and optimistic in outlook. Yet apocalypse nonetheless forms one important strand of the overall fabric of the country's cultural identity. Australian apocalyptic texts cover a broad range of issues and scenarios. They reveal disastrous effects of white colonization on Indigenous groups (for example, B. Wongar's works, Sam Watson's *The Kadaitcha Sung*). Futuristic dystopias such as George Turner's Ethical Culture series (*Beloved Son, Vaneglory, Yesterday's Men*) narrate the devastating effects of genetic tampering, while in Turner's *The Destiny Makers* and Erle Cox's *Out of the Silence* there are plans to annihilate particular races. Ecological thrillers such as Andrew Sullivan's *A Sunburnt Country* and Ian Irvine's *The Human Rites Trilogy* foreground environmental issues by imagining a future of natural disasters. Nuclear films (*On the Beach, The Chain Reaction*) warn against imprudent use of weapons. Outback and bush nightmares (Kenneth Cook's *Wake in Fright*, Joan Lindsay's *Picnic at Hanging Rock*) recognize an unease and horror felt by inhabitants of this land. Young adult apocalyptic narratives use totalitarian motifs and disaster to portray adolescent issues (Penny Hall's *The Paperchaser*, Caroline Macdonald's *The Eye Witness*, the film *Dead End Drive-In*), while prison-themed films offer dystopian future Australian settings that invoke penal colony associations and arguments about law and order and attitudes to authority (*Ghosts ... of the Civil Dead, Turkey Shoot*). Some writers have used religious scenarios, such as Robert Potter in *The Germ Growers* and Helen Simpson with *The Woman on the Beast*, while others create post-disaster medieval futures, as in the *Mad Max* films and Sean McMullen's *The Greatwinter Trilogy*. Other novelists such as Andrew McGahan employ narratives of vast, apocalyptic, abstract natural disasters (*Wonders of a Godless World*) or specific local disasters, such as the imagined destruction of Canberra (*Underground*). British comic illustrators and writers Jamie Hewlett and Alan Martin located *Tank Girl* in a post-apocalyptic Australia, films such as *The Matrix* and *Dark City* used an unidentified Sydney to represent simulated environments hiding a dystopian reality, while cinema (*Salute of the Jugger, Pitch Black*) and television (*Farscape, Thunderstone*) have utilized the Australian landscape to show threatening, alien environments.

Despite the remarkable number of works that imagine Australia in apocalyptic terms, there has been little critical work about the subject. Much of the relevant research available involves discussions of particular texts rather than considerations of the broader national context. This is matched by a relative lack of critical attention given to Australian speculative fiction in general. The genre as a whole has received growing interest

Introduction 5

internationally, due in no small part to popular films and books such as *The Lord of the Rings* trilogy, J.K. Rowling's *Harry Potter* series, and Stephenie Meyer's *Twilight* novels, but Australian speculative fiction has yet to command much of this interest, despite its own critical and popular successes. Of the work that has been done, bibliographic surveys of the field have included detailed works by Graham Stone, Paul Collins (*MUP*), and Donna Maree Hanson, among others, while many critical essays and articles explore different facets of Australian speculative fiction. Few works, however, examine the genre as a whole in sustained, critical explorations, although a notable exception is *Strange Constellations: A History of Australian Science Fiction*, co-authored by Russell Blackford, Van Ikin and Sean McMullen.

The field of apocalyptic theory is large, yet there is a need for more research into specifically Australian aspects of apocalypse, as the majority of the key research to date (for example, Bull; Cohn; Dellamora; Kermode; O'Leary; Seed; Wagar) highlights particular features or uses of apocalypse with less emphasis on its applications to nation. Studies on national apocalypse usually focus on texts from the Americas, including most notably the United States (for example, Ketterer; Berger) and to a lesser extent Canada (for example, Goldman) or South America (for example, Zamora). Some critics, of course, have acknowledged the presence of dystopia and apocalypse in Australian literature. For example, Andrew Milner notes in an essay that Australia is appealing for apocalyptic scenarios because the nation has a persistent "sense of itself as unusually exposed to the threat of invasion and extinction" and that fears of invasion, particularly from Asia, were "peculiarly conducive to the genesis of dystopian collective fantasies of racial extinction" (37). Russell Smith has published an article examining apocalyptic narratives about Australia's capital city, Canberra, while Lyman Tower Sargent has explored utopias and dystopias in the Australian context. In an essay on *Mad Max: Beyond Thunderdome*, Paul Williams points out that there is a significant number of post-nuclear apocalyptic Australian texts. However, the nuclear setting is simply one more episode in a long apocalyptic tradition that imagines the end of the world in Australia in various ways. In an overview of the history of children's speculative fiction in the country, Maurice Saxby identifies dystopia as one of the dominant traditions in children's literature; Bradford, Mallan and Stephens similarly point to a dystopian trend in children's literature. John Stephens also acknowledges the large number of post-apocalyptic novels in Australian writing; however, he writes that the disaster scenario is particular to children's literature and not evident in adult fictions (126) whereas I demonstrate that apocalypse is a significant tradition in both adult and children's literature in Australia.

The end(s) of the world has been imagined so frequently in an Australian setting that more study into Australian speculative fiction seems warranted in general, and particularly more research into the enduring theme of apocalypse in Australian fiction and film. This book provides a sustained discussion of the apocalyptic scenarios that continually inspire Australian writers and filmmakers, with a focus on texts after 1950. It becomes evident that there is a significant tradition where writers and filmmakers repeatedly enact the end of the world in an Australian context. This serves to reinforce a sense that there is an inherent connection between the nation and apocalypse. The present work explores the ways in which Australian speculative fictions draw on the apocalyptic paradigm and its themes and imagery for different agendas. For example, some authors use disaster to attack the complacent belief that Australia's isolated geographical position protects the nation from danger, while others use catastrophe to symbolize colonization and imperialism, to undermine dominant groups, or to draw attention to the dangerous landscape. Other texts adopt apocalypse for utopian ends, to suggest new approaches for particular goals such as harmonious multicultural societies. Apocalypse, in the Australian context, proves flexible for a range of purposes.

Apocalypse and Speculative Fiction

Speculative fiction denotes the wide array of forms in which apocalypse can appear, including science fiction, fantasy, magic realism, horror, gothic, science-fantasy, and cyberpunk.[1] The setting may be a real or imagined past, present, or future. This book favors an inclusive approach that understands speculative fiction as a text that violates reality in some way, but that nonetheless describes what is or may be possible. This approach aligns with W. Warren Wagar's definition of speculative fiction as a literature "that specializes in plausible speculation about life under changed but rationally conceivable circumstances, in an alternative past or present, or in the future" (*Terminal* 9). This definition of speculative fiction in some ways favors science fiction over fantasy texts because, as W. R. Irwin points out, fantasy narrates what is impossible, while science fiction is concerned with what is improbable and amazing (99). Most of the works discussed in the following chapters would thus be classified as science fiction, but as my criterion is apocalypse within speculative fiction, the boundaries are fairly large and thus encompass a range of subgenres.

The relationship between apocalypse and speculative fiction is close, for apocalyptic writing essentially is speculation. Speculative fiction reveals imagined glimpses of a different past, present, or future, straying from the status quo and the world readers know in order to disclose something new. Van Ikin and Terry Dowling have suggested that science fiction can alter the reader's perception, for "we are made to see the world, our lives, our blinding reality, with new eyes" (xv). Similarly, Kathryn Hume explores the uses of fantasy in that writers can employ the genre to look at real-life issues and even attempt to influence readers' perspectives (55). This parallels the revelatory aspect of apocalypse, for apocalyptic literature also reveals new perspectives to the reader. David Ketterer similarly notes this shift in perception in his description of apocalyptic, fantastic, and mimetic fictions. Apocalypse sits between mimetic fiction, which reflects the real world, and fantastic literature, which depicts "escapist worlds": "Apocalyptic literature is concerned with the creation of other worlds which exist, on the literal level, in a credible relationship (whether on the basis of rational extrapolation and analogy or of religious belief) with the 'real' world, thereby causing a metaphorical destruction of that 'real' world in the reader's head" (13). Ketterer suggests that apocalyptic literature has a transformational aspect in that "an apocalyptic transformation results from the creation of a new condition, based upon a process of extrapolation and analogy, whereby man's horizons — temporal, spatial, scientific, and ultimately philosophic — are abruptly expanded" (16).

George Turner, whose novels are discussed in Chapter Two, describes science fiction as "a logically derived presentation of activities and their consequences taking place under conditions which, while scientifically admissible, represent life and the universe not as we know them but as under changed circumstances they could be" ("Some Unreceived Wisdom" 16). For Turner, science fiction should extrapolate reality and be credible and possible. The depicted futures should be the realistic projected outcomes of contemporary political and social conditions, and in this way the genre can operate as a literature of prophecy, acting as a commentary or even warning on issues facing current society. This is, of course, an apocalyptic function, the idea of the prophetic author having special knowledge about the future and telling others.

The works discussed in the following chapters are apocalyptic speculative fictions, for despite their differences in medium and genre (film, novel, science fiction, fantasy, cyberpunk) they share apocalyptic elements, whether revealing catastrophe or new worlds. These texts depart from the accepted version of reality in significant ways, through their futuristic settings, technologies, or revised histories. However, readers can interpret the fictional events as possible and logical extrapolations of reality.

Biblical Apocalypse

When apocalypse is used in popular culture, the term usually means a widespread disaster of particularly catastrophic or horrific proportions. Yet even secular apocalyptic texts retain significant connections to Biblical apocalypse. Many themes and images from both the Old and New Testaments of the Bible reappear in and inform secular fictions. While the Bible is not the sole source of apocalyptic thought, it is the most influential on secular apocalyptic writing in the Australian and Western context, and it is therefore worth summarizing both Biblical and secular versions of apocalypse as a preface to the case studies.[2]

The literal meaning of apocalypse is revelation, discovery, or disclosure. The word derives from the Greek *apokalypsis* (uncovering) and *apokalyptein* (to uncover). Apocalyptic writing aims to show; to reveal; to disclose something hidden. The most popular association of apocalypse is with the Book of Revelation — Apocalypse — in the Bible. Although many people link apocalypse with Revelation, there are other apocalyptic texts in the Bible, such as Daniel and Zechariah, as well as the prophecies in Isaiah that speak of revealing "new things, of hidden things unknown to you" (Isaiah 48:6).

There is a consistent pattern across apocalyptic books such as Revelation and Daniel. According to L. L. Morris, apocalypse in the Bible includes several key features:

> Characteristic of apocalyptic is the thought that God is sovereign, and that ultimately He will intervene in catastrophic fashion to bring to pass His good and perfect will. He is opposed by powerful and varied forces of evil, and these are usually referred to symbolically, as beasts, horns, *etc.* There are visions; angels speak; there is the clash of mighty forces; and ultimately the persecuted saints are vindicated [1093].

Norman Cohn similarly argues that there is a paradigm in apocalypse that foretells the eventual overthrow of tyranny, leaving the persecuted group the ultimate victors in a supernatural conflict:

> The world is dominated by an evil, tyrannous power of boundless destructiveness — a power moreover which is imagined not as simply human but as demonic. The tyranny of that power will become more and more outrageous, the sufferings of its victims more and more intolerable — until suddenly the hour will strike when the Saints of God are able to rise up and overthrow it. Then the Saints themselves, the chosen, holy people who hitherto have groaned under the oppressor's heel, shall in their turn inherit dominion over the whole earth [21].

In the Bible, dreams and visions of the future predict invasions and oppression from powerful, corrupt rulers seeking to persecute God's people, with beasts and creatures symbolizing human empires and kingdoms. The visions reveal a cosmic conflict between God and figures representing the Antichrist, and give numerical accounts of when the events will occur. There will be great trials, judgment for those who defy God, the second coming of the messiah, the Christ, in all his glory, the promise of "everlasting life" (Daniel 12:2) and deliverance from pain and sorrow for the faithful in a renewed, remade world; God himself will "wipe every tear" away (Revelation 21:4).

Biblical apocalypse shows that the hope for this renewed world follows a time of disaster. The "day of the Lord" is a refrain throughout both the Old and New Testaments, in books of letters and books of prophecies (for example, Joel 2:31, Zechariah 14:1, 2 Thessalonians 2:2). This perspective gives God's faithful a sense that human history is approaching a significant rupture, for "the end of all things is near" (1 Peter 4:7):

> At that time ... there will be a time of distress such as has not happened from the beginning of nations until then. But at that time your people — everyone whose name is found written in the book — will be delivered. Multitudes who sleep in the dust of the earth will awake: some to everlasting life, others to shame and everlasting contempt. Those who are wise will shine like the

brightness of the heavens, and those who lead many to righteousness, like the stars for ever and ever [Daniel 12:1–3].

Andrew McNab writes that in New Testament texts "the coming of the Lord which would mark the close of the age was believed to be imminent" (1140). Apocalyptic discourse in the Bible insists that a time is rapidly approaching when God will judge all. He will reward those who are faithful to his rule—those "whose name is found written in the book"—while those who have rejected God will face the consequences of their rebellion. Wagar describes the destruction in Revelation as "a warehouse catalogue of calamities" with its "natural disasters, such as earthquakes, storms, and droughts. Pestilence does its worst, along with monsters" (*Terminal* 53). It seems clear that the Biblical scenes of environmental destruction have provided contemporary fictions with a template for imagining disaster, for as Revelation reads, "There was a great earthquake. The sun turned black like sackcloth made of goat hair, the whole moon turned blood red, and the stars in the sky fell to earth, as late figs drop from a fig tree when shaken by a strong wind. The sky receded like a scroll, rolling up, and every mountain and island was removed from its place" (Revelation 6:12–14).

Yet not all interpretations of Biblical apocalypse emphasize destruction and some readers treat the language as symbolic. Leonard L. Thompson writes that Revelation in particular has "highly metaphoric, poetic language" (5) that requires considerable attention to be properly understood. L. L. Morris suggests that there are four common interpretations of Revelation. The preterist perspective interprets the text in terms of the historical context, viewing "all the visions as arising out of conditions in the Roman Empire of the 1st century A.D.," while the historicist view considers that the visions offer a "continuous story" of history from the time of writing until Christ's return (1094). Futurist interpretations relate the events to the future, although this can be problematic in that such readings "removed the book entirely from its historical setting" (1095). The fourth interpretation, Morris writes, is the idealist or poetic reading, an approach that understands Revelation's imagery purely in symbolic terms as representative of God's victory and "insists that the main thrust of the book is concerned with inspiring persecuted and suffering Christians to endure to the end" (1095). Morris suggests that an accurate reading of Revelation takes all four views into consideration.

Moving beyond a simple association of Biblical apocalypse and destruction, therefore, we can see that apocalypse can be a language for the oppressed faithful of past and present times, a discourse that foretells disaster in the future yet nonetheless offers hope and the promise of better things to come. God will ultimately reward the faithful who persevere and endure with future glory in the new world: New Jerusalem, Zion. One of the main purposes of these revelations is therefore encouragement, for the writings and prophecies often occurred during times of oppression. The context of future blessing and restoration gives meaning to the destruction and catastrophe:

> Then I saw a new heaven and a new earth, for the first heaven and the first earth had passed away ... I saw the Holy City, the new Jerusalem, coming down out of heaven from God.... And I heard a loud voice from the throne saying, "Now the dwelling of God is with men, and he will live with them. They will be his people, and God himself will be with them and be their God. He will wipe every tear from their eyes. There will be no more death or mourning or crying or pain, for the old order of things has passed away" [Revelation 21:1–4].

In the Biblical narrative, the visions of disaster focus on the promise of a new world for believers, as seen in the concluding sections of apocalyptic texts, which emphasize the expectation of the new heavens and the new earth (for example, Isaiah 65:17–19, Revelation 21:1–4). The focus is on the "new": new creation, new testament, new life, new commandment; the "old world" with its troubles and persecution will pass away. John W. Martens makes the crucial point that apocalypse celebrates the end of evil rather than the end of life; its concerns are "hope and justice, not destruction and threat" (226).

It is worth noting some key motifs in Biblical apocalypse and prophecy. Throughout the Bible there is a coherent dichotomy that gives secular apocalyptic writing much of its resonance. God gives his faithful, obedient people a fruitful, secure land, and those who turn from his ways and mistreat others are exiled. When the nation of Israel rebelled against God, surrounding nations and empires invaded and colonized and exploited the land, for national vulnerability to invasions was a judgment on the nation. The desert wilderness is often a place of testing and judgment[3] while the verdant, abundant land is the promised home to those who walk in God's ways.

These apocalyptic motifs, as seen in Revelation, Daniel, and other parts of the Bible, are important themes for the background of this book, for some of the main tropes in Australian speculative fictions reflect the images and discourse of Biblical apocalypse, specifically the themes of punishment, exile, invasion and wilderness. This suggests that there is a vital relationship between apocalypse and Australian fictions. The language and imagery of Biblical apocalypse resonate in secular depictions of the Australian environment and outback, creating a place of testing and punishment that is far removed from the fertile and fruitful promised land of European scenery. The country's designation as a penal colony further reinforced the motif of punishment and dread.

With these key characteristics of Biblical apocalypse in mind, then, one can briefly summarize it in the following ways. Firstly, apocalypse in the Bible is a revelation about the world, a new perspective uncovering what was previously hidden. Secondly, the revelation often concerns the future, and this knowledge enables the readers to see their present circumstances more clearly and in context. Thirdly, the revelation is intended to provoke a response; the vision of the messiah's coming in the future served as encouragement to the faithful as well as inspiring a response of right living in the present. The revelation includes a darker side of warnings of judgment, seen in terms of global catastrophes that signal the end of the present world. The apocalyptic vision thus reveals not only the future hope for the faithful but also a warning of the destruction awaiting those who do not turn to God. Finally, Biblical apocalypse includes a promise of a new and better world after the disaster. Apocalypse offers a voice for those who suffer, giving hope of their restoration. In this book, then, I use apocalypse in a way that recognizes both the positive and the negative features of the term, the utopian and dystopian, that appear to various extents in literary texts.

Secular Apocalypse

While there are some contemporary apocalyptic texts that explicitly adopt Biblical themes, many profess and display little or no interest in Biblical apocalypse. Yet there are many intersections between Biblical and secular apocalypse. Secular apocalyptic literature often follows the pattern of Biblical apocalypse yet also digresses from the origins of the genre. The images and themes from Biblical apocalyptic writings permeate secular apocalypse, demonstrating a lasting legacy even while non-religious writing usually excises the supernatural elements. If contemporary fictions diminish or reject the religious overtones of Revelation, they nonetheless frequently evidence Biblical imagery in their portrayals of the future.

Commentators have often noted this reliance on the Biblical paradigm. Northrop Frye suggests that "the Biblical Apocalypse is our grammar of apocalyptic imagery" (141), while Jacques Derrida argues that the apocalyptic tone or discourse that intimates the end is near "always cites or echoes (*répercute*) in a certain way John's Apocalypse" ("Apocalyptic Tone" 25). Jennie Chapman points out that there is a "long-standing reciprocity of Christian and secular forms of the apocalyptic imagination" (168); Ketterer writes that even the most secular of apocalyptic fictions retains the "religious element," no matter how "displaced, [or] disguised" (333), and Wagar also notes that the symbols of Christian apocalypse have left a legacy in secular fictions (*Terminal* 61). This might mean, for example, that a nuclear war might be a secular substitute for a Biblical Judgment Day (Brians 54). Ketterer argues that the basic plot of science fiction disaster narratives follows the sequence of events in Revelation, with four stages: dystopia; the warning or experience of a disaster; life post-disaster; and the establishment of a new world (123–24). He writes that the revelatory aspect of apocalypse occurs because the new worlds envisioned leave the reader's viewpoint challenged and "expanded" (16), thereby revealing "the *present* world in new or other terms" (38).

While there are similarities between Biblical and secular apocalypse, some critics suggest that this inheritance can be problematic, particularly in science fiction. For instance, Brian Stableford has suggested that the "religious imagination echoes in the literature of the scientific imagination as a series of apparitions" (101). This creates a conflict in the literature, Stableford argues, for the secular use of words such as apocalypse, Armageddon and millennium is "coloured with echoes of religious mythology" and associations with religion, in apparent contradiction to the scientific world view of the contemporary apocalyptic fictions that use them (101). Robert Galbreath notes that these competing discourses result in ambiguity:

> These examples of unorthodox Messiahs, gospels, theologies, and Antichrists, together with those discussed earlier, indicate a fundamental ambivalence.

On the one hand, there is a fascination with traditional images of the End, both for their continuing power and for their accessibility as a familiar structure of otherworldliness and radical discontinuity; on the other, there is a tendency to disconnect these images from formal belief and, indeed, to place them in contexts of ambiguity, skepticism, or heterodoxy [68].

Galbreath suggests that there is thus a double and contradictory message of apocalypse: "simultaneously that humanity can and must rise above its own limitations and that humanity deeply wishes for salvation by something greater than itself" (55).

Even as secular fictions may disregard the divine, they nonetheless demonstrate the influence of the imagery and themes of Biblical apocalypse. Secular apocalyptic authors often locate their stories in the future, almost functioning as prophets who warn of a forthcoming event. Much as Revelation foretells future judgment to elicit appropriate responses, apocalyptic fictions can depict grim futures intended to provoke action now. Writers may canvass social and environmental issues, using dark futures to critique current policies. For example, environmentally-themed films and documentaries about catastrophic global warming, such as *The Day After Tomorrow* or *An Inconvenient Truth*, can foretell the future in order to call for action in the present. Alternatively, minority groups may use apocalypse to highlight injustices and reject dominant ideologies and instead imagine a new and better world. Discussing the genre's Biblical influences, Ketterer insists "the fulfillment of the apocalyptic imagination demands that the destructive chaos give way finally to a new order" (14). This occurs in secular visions that imagine post-apocalyptic worlds that are superior to the pre-disaster setting.

Despite their shared features, Biblical and secular apocalypses diverge in two key ways. The first major change is that some secular narratives subvert the original context of apocalypse as a language for the oppressed to instead use apocalyptic rhetoric to dominate and justify the persecution of minority groups, a problem explored in Chapter Five. The other key difference is that secular versions of Revelation frequently over-emphasize disaster and judgment, ignoring or minimizing the themes of blessing and mercy that are of great significance in the Bible. Such visions of apocalypse, that is, often conclude with the end of the world with authors unable or unwilling to anticipate a new world. Far from being a literature of encouragement, such tales often display pessimism about the world, although authors can channel this negativity into critiques of society. Krishan Kumar notes that contemporary apocalypse is often missing this vision of a new world, and questions why the modern "sense of an ending [is] so flat, so lacking in *élan*? Why have we truncated the apocalyptic vision, so that we see endings without new beginnings?" (212). Kumar argues that "we need both millennium and utopia" (212), for millennium offers hope while utopia provokes desire: "The one tells us that change is possible, the other why we need to make the change, what we might gain if we do so" (214). Often, however, there is no hope of a new world in secular apocalypses, which promise the destruction without the new heaven and new earth and imagine not utopia but dystopia.

Secular apocalypse, then, magnifies the aspect of destruction as the primary interest. Hence the most popular use of the term apocalypse, meaning not revelation but widespread destruction. Ketterer suggests that secular fictions frequently adopt the "negative aspect" of apocalypse "with its emphasis on destruction, Hell, and chaos" (94), while Edward James notes that despite the preponderance of secular references to Armageddon or Doomsday, in most contemporary fictions such terms are "not even a token reference to the Book of Revelation, but merely a common shorthand for a man-made catastrophe, particularly a devastating war" (50).

The language and imagery of Biblical apocalypse are pervasive and they recur in contemporary apocalyptic fictions, even if with different motivations and from secular perspectives. Revelation's four horsemen of the apocalypse, the seven seals, plagues, scrolls, the woman and the dragon, the heavenly city and its garden containing the tree of life, and especially the notion of a promised land, a new world, are references that can appear in disaster narratives without any of the divine meaning of the original visions. Indeed, even those texts that do explicitly use Biblical figures do not always succeed; some critics dismiss them for their "cheesy" portrayals of characters such as the Antichrist (Quinby, "The Days Are Numbered" 100). Most secular apocalypses, however, do not reference God in serious or sustained ways. Yet it should be no surprise that secular writers with no interest in God often adopt and adapt apocalypse, for the natural disasters of Revelation in particular lend themselves to secular appropriation even if the authors ignore the divine foundations of the apocalypse. Wagar suggests that "stories of man-made catastrophes continue the ancient tradition of prophetic warning, by which sinful man is reminded of his disobedience and the wrath to come that his wrong-doing has earned" ("Rebellion of Nature" 170). Authors might construct the catastrophe as a judgment of humanity, such as apocalyptic events that are, for example, nuclear or technology-themed, in which the disaster that befalls humans is clearly the result of their own corruption and greed for power, even if God is absent from the text.

Given the origins of apocalypse as revelation and this common identification of apocalypse as disaster, the term is used broadly. For Derrida, the identification of catastrophe as apocalypse creates an "apocalypse without apocalypse, an apocalypse without vision, without truth, without revelation" ("Apocalyptic Tone" 34). The fact that one can understand the term in many different ways suggests a flexibility of definition. Malcolm Bull, for instance, argues against too narrow or restrictive a definition of apocalypse because "the terminology of apocalyptic is, or at least appears to be, meaningfully used in other contexts" (*Seeing* 48). Commentators have used apocalyptic terms to describe events ranging from the advent of atomic weapons to the 9/11 terrorist attacks in the U.S., from the World War II Holocaust to the 2004 Asian tsunami and the 2010 snow storms in the U.S.[4] James Berger writes that people often consider apocalypse as a break in history where "historical events are often portrayed apocalyptically—as absolute breaks with the past, as catastrophes bearing some enormous or ultimate meaning: the Holocaust, for example, or Hiroshima, or American slavery, the American Civil War, the French Revolution, the war in Vietnam and the social conflicts of the 1960s" (xii). Gary K. Wolfe has argued that many fictional holocausts and real-life apocalypses (e.g., concentration camps, the industrial revolution) refer not to the literal end of the world but rather to the end of ideologies, beliefs, or ways of life (1–2).

Current use of the term apocalypse most often describes a catastrophic event of any kind, usually involving human deaths and widespread destruction of land and the urban environment. The disaster might be natural (environmental or geological); or it might be deliberate and of human origin (a war, a chemical weapon such as a virus, or, often, nuclear weapons). The destruction might be local, but it is usually global and the effect on humans catastrophic. The concept can also refer to a danger to humankind, a cataclysmic event that threatens the continued existence of humans. Regardless of the context and the background, people often view the resulting destruction as apocalyptic. Of the secular texts in the following discussion, many narrate disaster as well as emphasizing the potential for progress in the future after the catastrophe. It is clear that writers and readers understand and use apocalypse in a multitude of ways, each of which reflects parts of the original Biblical apocalypse, whether that part is the destruction, the vision of the future, or the new world.

Case Studies

In a project such as this, it is difficult to include every relevant text without sacrificing room for any analysis. Indeed, the present work makes no attempt to provide a definitive catalogue or bibliography of every Australian apocalyptic or speculative work. Instead, it offers a critical analysis of one particular trend in Australian culture and uses case studies to elucidate specific points of interest. Given the current popularity of apocalyptic texts, new novels and films are always adding to the field, which inevitably means our critical understanding of the area is always developing and being refined. However, these particular case studies exemplify certain recurring themes in Australian apocalypse, cover a broad range of texts and times, and together contribute to our ever-evolving understanding of both apocalypse generally and Australian speculative fiction specifically.

The criteria for the case studies included are an Australian setting and the presence or threat of a disaster. Most of the texts chosen were released in the last fifty years, although Chapter One outlines earlier works in order to provide a socio-historical and imaginative context. In line with the secular, popular association of apocalypse with disaster, many of these texts use apocalypse in its negative sense, focusing on disaster and destruction, while others deploy apocalyptic imagery and themes in positive ways, and still others negotiate a path between the two extremes. While a large number of these apocalyptic fictions adopt a dystopian setting, depicting catastrophes and horror without any accompanying hope, there also exists the potential for writers to use apocalypse to generate positive meanings.

The case studies represent different textual visions of Australian apocalypse and illustrate some of the approaches to apocalypse by local writers and filmmakers working within the genre. The selected texts contribute in their own way to an Australian apocalyptic discourse and reveal the different facets of the apocalyptic imagination that are significant in the nation's fictions. Authors and filmmakers use apocalypse to critique environmental and racial policies, media technologies, nuclear proliferation and inequities between white and Indigenous groups. Yet throughout the texts, points of special significance emerge time and time again, revealing an ongoing preoccupation with issues of invasion and anxieties about European colonization and white inhabitation of Australia, as well as an ambiguous relationship with the distinctive Australian landscape. In this respect, then, whether authors adopt, adapt, or even reject these apocalyptic tropes, their texts participate in an ongoing apocalyptic tradition that had its beginnings in pre-colonial times.

Chapter One surveys the historical background of the apocalyptic tradition and discusses what we might label an "apocalyptic map." This map is based on the speculation about the south land before and also during British settlement, using Jean Baudrillard's discussion of maps and territories as one approach to understanding Australian apocalypse. When Europeans speculated and created fictions about parts of the world they had not yet seen or colonized, they either imagined that great treasures, wealth, and utopian tribes or civilizations awaited them in new lands, or, alternatively, foretold that the new land would be a place of grotesque monsters and alien beings. Explorers also often anticipated discovering "New Worlds." They similarly imagined that the Australian continent would be a utopia but there was another line of thought that never expected the country to be a paradise. The earlier idea of a utopian south land competed with the dystopian tradition but gradually abandoned Australia as a likely location. This early speculation about Australia preceded and ultimately superseded the actual experience itself, creating an apocalyptic map that has proved a powerful way for contemporary writers to imagine Australia.

Chapter Two explores apocalypse in the post–World War II period. The decades after 1945 saw a general rise in apocalyptic literature of all kinds, although there was a special anxiety surrounding the genesis of the nuclear age. Australia's speculative fiction reflected these global concerns, and this chapter analyzes Nevil Shute's *On the Beach* and George Turner's science fiction novels. One of the main ideas in these texts, and others since, is a "shield of distance." This inverts the popular idea of a "tyranny of distance" in that the nation relies on a shield of distance as protection from the outside world, yet writers reveal this shield to be nonexistent.

The fear of outside influence or invasion has a long history in Australian literature. Shute adapts apocalypse to reject the idea of renewal after destruction; disaster is the end of all things and there is no hope or promise of a better world. Turner, meanwhile, imagines post-apocalyptic worlds where there are survivors, but he warns about environmental problems and his dark visions most often see only dystopian futures following catastrophes rather than renewal. The works of Shute and Turner insist that complacent, utopian images of Australia are false.

Chapter Three focuses on apocalyptic depictions of land in Australian speculative texts. Literature and films often present the Australian landscape in gothic terms, depicting the land as actively menacing and hostile to humans. Australian culture frequently imagines the outback in particular as the "dead heart," a place of punishment and death where people vanish or die in mysterious circumstances. This chapter argues that such constructions find their origins in the Old Testament, where the wilderness was at times a place of punishment and testing for the nation of Israel. The three *Mad Max* films give audiences a bleak and uninspiring landscape. Hope for the future, for a better world, is always far away from the interior. The desert is "the nothing" and it consumes humans who attempt to traverse it. The films use the apocalyptic paradigm of destruction followed by a new world but subvert this hope by rejecting the existence of the promised land. The films turn around the images of coastal cities and beaches as paradise to suggest that they are mere illusions or unreliable dreams, while the desert offers no hope or refuge either.

Chapter Four similarly explores apocalyptic landscapes, this time in children's literature, but investigates concerns over colonization, identity, land and belonging. Lee Harding's *Waiting for the End of the World*, Victor Kelleher's *Taronga* and *Red Heart*, and John Marsden's *Tomorrow, When the War Began* series all demonstrate significant anxieties, particularly in regard to the vulnerability of Australia to outside attack, as well as an ambivalent attitude to the Australian landscape. While the novels of Kelleher reinforce a sense that white people do not truly belong in Australia because they do not have the rightful claim of Indigenous inhabitants, Harding's text attempts to argue that Europeans do actually have a mystical right to be there, and Marsden's series appears to position the white protagonists as the new Indigenous people, staking their claim on the country as their own. Kelleher's *Red Heart* is particularly concerned with the issues of colonization, articulating an apocalyptic discourse that condemns the violence inherent in imperialism.

Apocalypse has been claimed as both conservative and radical by different critics. Chapter Five examines the use of apocalypse to rewrite the end of the world in an Indigenous context. Although post-apocalyptic scenarios can facilitate racism in that non-white populations are often suspiciously absent from tales of the future, politically committed writers can use the disaster narrative to subvert this tendency by using the end-of-the-world motif to demonstrate injustice or by constructing a post-catastrophe scenario with a new society and a different approach to problems. This chapter looks at how two writers use an apocalyptic scenario to show the devastating effects of European colonization on Indigenous peoples and cultures in Australia: namely, Sam Watson's *The Kadaitcha Sung* and Archie Weller's *Land of the Golden Clouds*. If the concept of the "dead heart" of the Australian land is a popular trope in apocalyptic fiction, Indigenous writers have reworked this theme to suggest that the land is instead a "sacred heart," needing to be restored from the damage that white colonization and brutality caused the land and its original inhabitants.

If apocalypse can be a useful tool for critique, there is one genre where it is nonetheless claimed as irrelevant and meaningless: cyberpunk. Chapter Six turns its attention to technologies to explore why commentators have claimed that cyberpunk is an essentially anti-apocalyptic genre that refuses national and ethnic identities in favor of a globalized culture. The genre, therefore, presumably provides freedom from the apocalyptic tropes that have permeated so much Australian literature, and this chapter examines what happens to the sense of location and the Australian apocalypse in Marianne de Pierres's Parrish Plessis series, *Nylon Angel*, *Code Noir*, and *Crash Deluxe*. The novels demonstrate that there is an underlying anxiety about the end of the human in a technological world, and they reflect the apocalyptic trope of false utopian images of Australia hiding a darker reality. More than this, the texts adopt an anti-apocalyptic nonchalance towards disaster and prophecies yet they ultimately reinforce apocalypse both by framing the protagonist, Parrish, as a messianic figure with a destiny of salvation for those around her, and by articulating fears about the end of the world. It appears that even when writers use an apparently anti-apocalyptic genre, an Australian apocalyptic discourse nonetheless intrudes.

These chapters and case studies are roughly chronological, and also representative of some key ways in which various writers and filmmakers have used the apocalyptic scenario. Investigating these areas should not only offer some insight into the genre of apocalypse generally but also highlight an important tradition in Australian speculative literature. In these apocalyptic texts, several themes keep emerging as ongoing anxieties, particularly regarding the consequences of colonization and the vulnerability of the nation to both foreign invasion and internal attack from the hostile landscape. A survey of these fictions shows several reasons for these themes. European speculation had already established Australia as a place of apocalypse prior to colonization, variously as a utopian new world of promise and hope or a dystopian space of judgment and suffering. As a colonized country, moreover, there were substantial underlying anxieties surrounding white existence, Indigenous rights, and fears of invasion from other countries. The unusual and seemingly hostile environment reinforced the popular depiction of Australia as an apocalyptic space. These factors contributed to a long tradition in which the nation is often dystopia and sometimes utopia, making the location of apocalypse in Australia — and apocalypse *as* Australia — an appropriate expression of the cultural imagination.

• ONE •

An Apocalyptic Map
New Worlds and the Colonization of Australia

> Today abstraction is no longer that of the map, the double, the mirror, or the concept. Simulation is no longer that of a territory, a referential being, or a substance. It is the generation by models of a real without origin or reality: a hyperreal. The territory no longer precedes the map, nor does it survive it. It is nevertheless the map that precedes the territory —*precession of simulacra*— that engenders the territory ... today it is the territory whose shreds slowly rot across the extent of the map. It is the real, and not the map, whose vestiges persist here and there in the deserts that are no longer those of the Empire, but ours. *The desert of the real itself.*
> Jean Baudrillard, *Simulacra* 1

The persistent linking of apocalypse and Australia both in direct and subtle ways emerged before British colonization in 1788, for there was a tradition that already inscribed the land with noticeably apocalyptic qualities. European speculation about *terra australis incognita* variously depicted the Antipodes as the site of great wealth and riches, or, alternatively, as a hellish place harboring odd creatures. An apocalyptic dialectic therefore emerges between utopian visions of a land of promise and bounty — the "lucky country"[1]— and a dystopian lens that sees the antipodean land mass as the end of the world both geographically and psychologically. In this context, we can read Jean Baudrillard's proposition that it is "the map that precedes the territory" (*Simulacra* 1) in terms of Australian colonization because a "map" existed before Europeans ever settled the land, and colonial experiences did little to change the perceptions already in place from the apocalyptic map. After colonization, the unusual landscape defied attempts to conquer it and render it homelike in European terms.

This chapter examines the map that preceded, and eventually superseded, the territory of Australia, in order to demonstrate that early maps of the south land established an apocalyptic tradition that still resonates in contemporary fictions. If one reinterprets Jean Baudrillard's comments in the context of colonization and Australia, it is possible to see how European imagination delineated an apocalyptic map of the country before explorers and settlers even arrived, a map that located Australia as a tabula rasa, a blank slate where heaven and hell might equally be feasible. This chapter surveys the dialectic emerging from these conflicting visions.

The Map That Precedes the Territory

We can turn to Baudrillard for one useful way to understand the apocalyptic strand in Australian film and fiction. In *Simulacra and Simulation*, Baudrillard discusses the relationship between image and reality, between the simulacrum and the original. While commentators have noted that Baudrillard's writing can be at times inaccessible (Detmer 97) and nihilistic (Heffernan 171), his work nonetheless offers one starting point to articulate and comprehend the process by which the early speculation about Australia created an apocalyptic map that preceded colonization. Baudrillard refers to the "hyperreal," a concept he uses to describe the conflation of the real and the imaginary (124). He suggests that the proliferation of models and simulacra have degraded the sense of a dichotomy between reality and fiction. Veronica Hollinger points out that Baudrillard's observations have been "repeated often enough to have become sufficiently banal, and ... sufficiently obvious. In an age configured by late capitalism, the circulation of simulacra, and the cyborging of the human body, experiential reality feels less and less connected to the 'natural' world and more and more like science fiction" ("Future/Present" 219).

Baudrillard proposes three categories of simulacra: the utopia, science fiction, and models. In each category, the distance varies between the real and the image or imaginary. In the first, the utopia, the distance is large, and the simulacrum is an imaginary world removed from reality. The second category, science fiction, minimizes the distance and the image reflects an extrapolated construct that is not essentially different to reality. In the third, there is no distance between the simulacrum and the real:

> This projection is totally reabsorbed in the implosive era of models. The models no longer constitute either transcendence or projection, they no longer constitute the imaginary in relation to the real, they are themselves an anticipation of the real, and thus leave no room for any sort of fictional anticipation — they are immanent, and thus leave no room for any kind of imaginary transcendence. The field opened is that of simulation in the cybernetic sense, that is, of the manipulation of these models at every level (scenarios, the setting up of simulated situations, etc.) but then *nothing distinguishes this operation from the operation itself and the gestation of the real: there is no more fiction* [122].

Baudrillard's declaration that there is no more fiction has apocalyptic overtones, and Hollinger has noted the "unabashedly apocalyptic rhetoric and imagery he scatters throughout writings.... Baudrillard's apocalypticism may be sublimely ironic, but French irony cannot erase the sheer eschatological *affect* of his reports from the trenches of hyperreality" ("Apocalypse Coma" 165). Baudrillard's models, or simulacra, anticipate and precede the "real" and we cannot easily differentiate between fiction and reality; indeed, simulacra become "imitations of nothing" (Attebery, "Metaphors" 93).

The simulacrum, or representation of the reality, can thus become more important than the reality. In the terminology of maps and territories, referencing the philosophical debate, Baudrillard speculates that the precession, pre-existence, precedence of the map has in an important way diminished the significance and reliability of the territory itself. He also theorizes that the complete mapping of a territory produces a negation of reality, for "when there is no longer any virgin territory, and thus one available to the imaginary, *when the map covers the whole territory, something like the principle of reality disappears*" (123). Reality depends on a corresponding imagination to give the term its weight and meaning, and when that imagination exhausts itself because all places have been imagined, so too reality disappears. Baudrillard focuses on reality, representation and the complicated negotiations between the two, particularly the ways the image intrudes on reality.

Hollinger writes that Baudrillard uses "science fiction as a field of discourse and image to offer a theoretical representation of the reality of current highly technologized life in the West" ("Future/Present" 222). Yet we can also apply his work to colonization. There is a correlation between the issues of representation that Baudrillard notes and the images and imagination surrounding the colonial world. If one transfers and reads Baudrillard's proposition in the context of the European imagination, the pre-colonial literary and cartographic speculations about new lands essentially — in some cases literally — delineated a map by which authors charted and knew the countries before Europeans discovered and experienced the real territories. These maps and simulacra covered the entire globe, imposing fantasies onto distant lands and places that explorers had not yet found. In the Australian situation in particular it is possible to view apocalypse as a map that inscribed a particular tradition on the country, where the fictions and speculations prior to European settlement became the reality.

Baudrillard's discussion of doubles and shadows offers a further approach to understanding the importance of the early speculations about Australia. He writes that "the double" of a subject is "an imaginary figure" (*Simulacra* 95); it is a likeness, reflection, or even a shadow of reality. The double poses a threat to the integrity of the original subject because "the shadow, the mirror image, haunts the subject like his other, which makes it so that the subject is simultaneously itself and never resembles itself again, which haunts the subject like a subtle and always averted death" (*Simulacra* 95). Baudrillard's terminology resonates when one reads it in the colonial context. The "double" of Australia is its representation at the hands of cartographers and writers speculating what the land might be like. This double, the pre-colonial speculation, haunts the reality of experience and casts a permanent shadow, destabilizing the coherence of national identity. These images have continued to infect and inform depictions of the nation.

Apocalypse, New Worlds and Colonization

While others have addressed the history of speculation about Australia in detail elsewhere,[2] in this book I read the speculation in terms of apocalyptic expectations of a new world, whether heaven or hell. Like other European colonies, there was a sense that Australia could be a "new world," a space with the apocalyptic potential of being the New Jerusalem. The Introduction noted a number of key points related to Biblical apocalypse, and these concerns are evident in many secular Australian fictions. These points include the promise to God's faithful that they will inherit an abundant and safe territory while those who reject God will live in exile. There is a dichotomy between the fruitful promised land and the desert wilderness, with the latter frequently a place of trials and judgment. When the Israelites were unfaithful to God, they were susceptible to invasions from neighboring nations, although repentance saw new hope. These themes resonate in Australian apocalypses, albeit secularized, for the portrayals of the south land prior to and after colonization demonstrate very similar ideas of the new heavens and the new earth, punishment and exile in the wilderness, as well as vulnerability to invasion, which indicates that a significant apocalyptic discourse exists in many Australian fictions.

As Ketterer points out, there are both utopian and dystopian aspects of the apocalyptic paradigm because both are "exercises of the apocalyptic imagination" (93). In apocalyptic writing, he argues, "a dystopian situation and the end of the world go hand in hand as thematic aspects of the same 'bad scene'" (133). Indeed, utopia and dystopia are important concepts in this discussion of apocalyptic writing. Lyman Tower Sargent has defined dystopia — a "negative utopia"— as "a non-existent society described in considerable detail and normally located in time and space that the author intended a contemporaneous reader to view as considerably worse than the society in which that reader lived" ("Three Faces" 9). Dystopia offers a glimpse of the future that is bleak and negative, acting as a counterpoint to utopianism.[3] Fredric Jameson proposes that apocalypse writing warrants its own category, distinct from utopia and dystopia:

> If it is so, as someone has observed, that it is easier to imagine the end of the world than the end of capitalism, we probably need another term to characterize the increasingly popular visions of total destruction and of the extinction of life on Earth which seem more plausible than the Utopian vision of the new Jerusalem but also rather different from the various catastrophes (including the old ban-the-bomb anxieties of the 1950s) prefigured in the critical dystopias. The term apocalyptic may serve to differentiate this narrative genre from the anti–Utopia as well, since we do not sense in it any commitment to disabuse its readership of the political illusions an Orwell sought to combat, but whose very existence the apocalyptic narrative no longer acknowledges. Yet this new term oddly enough brings us around to our starting point again, inasmuch as the original Apocalypse includes both catastro-

phe and fulfillment, the end of the world and the inauguration of the reign of Christ on earth, Utopia and the extinction of the human race all at once [*Archaeologies* 199].

Kumar notes apocalypse's connection with utopia and argues that one aspect of apocalypse is "a sense of hope, of something constructive emerging from the ruins" (205), and that this parallels the expectation in utopianism that "a great disaster ... must precede the emergence of the millennial kingdom or the good society" (205). Yet he suggests that modern apocalypse does not tend to exhibit this hope for a better future. Instead, the contemporary "low-keyed" apocalypse (211) constitutes what he calls a "debased millenarianism, without a compensating utopian vision" (212). Kumar considers that this debased millenarianism is evident in declarations of the end of history, such as Francis Fukuyama's *The End of History and the Last Man*, because any belief that modern society has achieved progress and "peace and plenty" (205) lacks genuine pleasure in such developments and is instead "profoundly negative" (215).

Facets of apocalypse, utopia and dystopia are seen in the colonial experience. Biblical texts that describe the new heaven and earth inform the secular exploration of "new worlds," both expressing the hope of finding and inhabiting a better place. The association between new worlds and apocalyptic thought is important. In Isaiah, this new land is a paradise:

> Behold, I will create new heavens and a new earth. The former things will not be remembered, nor will they come to mind. But be glad and rejoice forever in what I will create, for I will create Jerusalem to be a delight and its people a joy. I will rejoice over Jerusalem and take delight in my people; the sound of weeping and of crying will be heard in it no more [65:17–19].

Isaiah's prophecies about the new world to come, echoed in Revelation 21, promised a place of security and blessing, a place free from persecution and pain and oppression. As other critics have remarked, European imperialist powers often imported Biblical discourse into their colonial exploits, framing the new countries as possible sites of the new heavens and a new earth. Even in secular thought, the expectations of utopia and dystopia remained strong, for it was a common perception in Europe that colonization might yield a utopian paradise. David Ketterer points out that naming colonial locations as "new" reinforces the apocalyptic belief in the new heavens and the new earth. Place names such as New York and New Hampshire are examples of locations that "might be new in the ideal sense of the

New Jerusalem" (27). Explorers named other colonies throughout the world in similar ways: New Zealand, New Holland, New South Wales, New England, Nova Scotia, New Caledonia and others.

The earlier experience of the Americas gives us a point of comparison for the Australian situation. Europeans discovered the American "New World" in 1492 and they positioned it as a utopia, a veritable new heaven. Lois Parkinson Zamora writes that "explorers, statesmen, and clergy alike viewed the events of geographical exploration and colonization of America as the fulfillment of the prophecies of Revelation — that is, as necessary prerequisites to the end of the world" (8). Zamora notes that the explorations took place in the context of "the apocalyptic aspirations imposed upon the New World by Europeans, beginning with Christopher Columbus":

> To convey to his royal patrons his conviction that his mission represented the fulfillment of apocalyptic prophecy, Columbus referred in letters and in his diary to passages from Revelation and Isaiah which describe the new heaven and new earth. So he immediately initiated what was to become a perennial imaginative association of America with the promise of apocalyptic historical renewal [7].

Colonists explicitly linked the exploration of the "New World" of the Americas with apocalypse, therefore, and Zamora points out that some colonists interpreted the Native Americans as being the new Jews, the lost tribes of Israel described in Revelation 7:4–9 (8).

Berger argues that this initial promise of America met with disappointment because the American utopia did not always meet expectations:

> The American apocalyptic sense, however, always encountered conflict. The vast American wilderness could be seen as Edenic but also as demonic. And the non–Christian inhabitants made implausible the premise that a New Jerusalem could simply be placed onto a virgin land. The American sense of apocalypse was from its beginning split into two contradictory senses: first, that the apocalyptic break from Europe had successfully been achieved; second, that an apocalyptic struggle with native, or natural, powers was still to come [133].

American frontier narratives outlining border wars suggested a "violent terror of some darkness that both loomed outside and dwelled within" (134). Berger writes that the experience of disappointment following the anticipation of perfection produced "an explosive ideological coexistence" while later negative experiences such as slavery and Vietnam compounded this disillusion and created "great difficulty" in maintaining "a narrative of national perfection" (134). Ketterer argues that apocalypse is vital to the American story of nation (332) because "America has always been a land of promises" (23). Ketterer proposes that "Exodus provides a convenient paradigm of a fallen America with the Promised Land as an elusive goal" where "the curse of slavery" ended the nation's Edenic idyll (3). He notes that "American society is, in fact, a projected utopia that now seems to have turned into a dystopia" (23). Colonists, then, strongly linked America with utopian hope that ended in disappointment, an early tradition that provided, and provides, the standard against which to measure experience.

The Unknown South Land

Cartographers had imagined the *terra australis incognita*—unknown south land—in various ways prior to European colonization. Some of the utopian ideals apparent in early speculation about the south land have remained in popular culture, and these images depict Australia as the blessed, lucky country, while other approaches focused on the dystopian aspects of apocalypse, envisioning only disaster in the new land and no promise of heaven. As one of the last lands in the world that Europeans colonized, there was a particularly strong tradition of imagining what the south land would be like (Bird 22). For instance, in a work from 1618, *le Relationi Universali*, Giovanni Botero described nations and regions around the world, yet wrote that the south land, "that great Globe Commonly termed *Australie*," was still unknown and he could only speculate about what it might be like (19):

> Terra Australis: This Land was lately found out, and by our latest cosmographers, for the great and spacious circuit thereof, as comprehending many large Regions ... described for the sixth part of the world. But what people inhabit them, what fashions they use, or what profitable commodity fit for the life of man they afford, it hath not yet beene by any man discovered [643].

Europeans had not yet discovered the south land and were thus able to imagine it in many different ways. Botero wrote that in general "people of the North [are] more courageous [*sic*], taller, and stronger" (10) compared to people from nations in the "south," such as Africa and India, who are intelligent, but physically weak as well as cruel — South Americans, Botero alleged, "bathe their children in the gore of their slaughtered enemies" (12–13). Such descriptions thus contributed to an implicit belief that the *terra australis* might be equally strange, if not more so.

Australia thus operated as a tabula rasa, a blank slate upon which one might inscribe any images. Ross Gibson argues that uncharted space demands imagination because "inevitably, when a new world is opened up, the dreamer in a writer stirs to supply felicitous images of unlimited potential in an unexploited realm" (*Diminishing* 65). Robert Holden notes that the images of the south land spanned every conceivable idea: "Ideas of a great southern landmass, and a 'South Sea,' occupied a remarkable duality in the European imagination over many centuries. This duality pictured the unknown as either the site of a Utopia or as a bizarre realm where the natural order was inverted. It inspired satires, fantasies, even downright hoaxes, and an ever expanding repertoire of imaginary creatures" (26).

Early speculative maps of the *terra australis incognita*, such as Abraham Ortelius's "Typus orbis terrarum" from 1570, depicted the south land as a supercontinent, spanning half the globe. Paul Longley Arthur suggests that the speculations performed a "political role" in that they functioned as "models for actual colonisation in the Antipodes" (191). Here it is not difficult to read Arthur's use of "models" in the sense of Baudrillard's models and simulacra discussed earlier in this chapter. Arthur argues that these tales of the Antipodes effectively acted as a "'control' over the Antipodes because they enacted colonial voyages and staged scenes of colonial encounters in a way which made them appear natural, routine and desirable, even (and often especially) to the *colonised*" (191). These early literary and cartographic maps of the territory not only exerted European "control" and modeled future colonization as natural, as Arthur argues, but they performed another important role. The maps also constructed "knowledge" of the territory, for their depiction of monsters or vast riches engendered certain images about the land even if the maps were admittedly fictional. In *Inventing Australia*, Richard White suggests that there were several different images of Australia prior to settlement, and these images included a land of scientific discoveries, a place of odd flora and fauna, and also "a primitive land in a perfect state of nature" (14). These prior images inevitably created particular expectations.

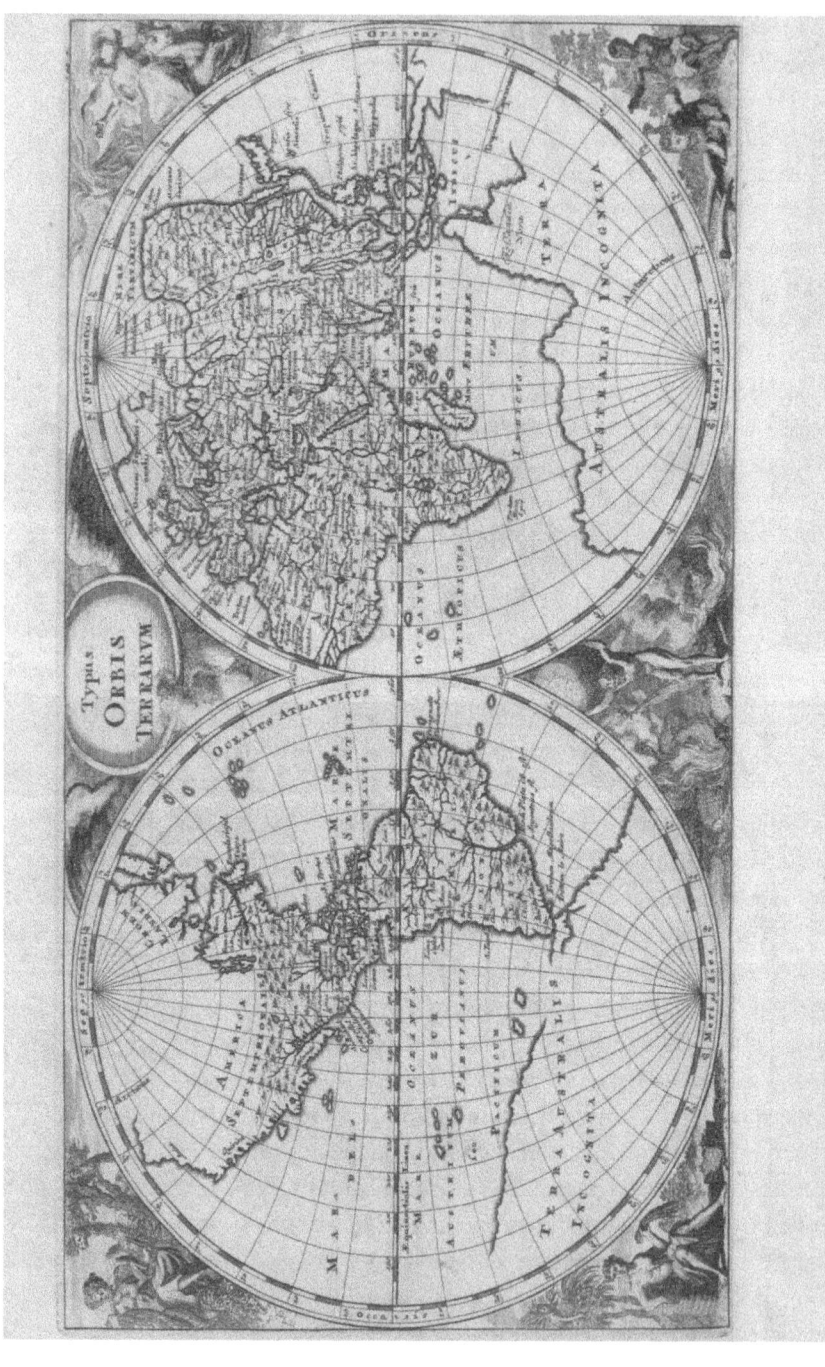

Australia as Utopia

The Spanish explorer Pedro Fernandez de Quiros imagined the south land as an apocalyptic space with the potential to usher in the new heavens and the new earth. Arriving in 1606 to a place that he initially believed to be the long-anticipated south land (mistaking Vanuatu for Australia), the explorer renamed *terra australis* Austrialia del Espiritu Santo, that is, the south land of the Holy Spirit, claiming it as a place where the gospel would spread, a land set apart and dedicated to God (Kotlowski 7–8): "I take possession of all this part of the South as far as the pole in the name of Jesus, which from now on shall be called the Southern land Austrialia of the Holy Spirit and this always and forever to the end that to all natives, in all the said lands, the holy, sacred Evangel may be preached zealously and openly" (qtd. in Coman 60). B. J. Coman notes that Austrialia (a reference to Austria) was then translated wrongly as Australia and further confused by the long associations to *terra australis* (60). As Gibson points out, the title suggests that the country is "a land of the future, a paradise belonging to the final stage of history" (*Diminishing* 21). The potential for Australia, the south land of the Holy Spirit, to fulfill this hope of the new world, then, was clearly an apocalyptic expectation, although the fact that de Quiros was, in fact, in another country entirely is somewhat ironic. This association recurred much later; as Russell Smith notes, utopian plans for the capital city, Canberra, also saw it compared to the "Biblical Promised Land" (80).

Other visions anticipated a secular paradise, a place of bounty containing the treasures that explorers had discovered earlier in other countries. Some explorers believed that Australia's location near the South Pacific Islands was indicative of its potential for great wealth and abundance. One example of this is a map from 1744 by Emanuel Bowen, "A Complete Map of the Southern Continent," which joins a fairly accurate depiction of the Australian coastline in the western half of the country with Papua New

Opposite: Terra australis incognita, the unknown south land, was long depicted in European maps as a supercontinent, providing a space for endless potential. The large southern continent in Ortelius's "Typus orbis terrarum" (1570) is shown also in Cluver's map of the same name, from 1652, pictured here. Typus orbis terrarum, Philipp Cluver, 1652. Call Number: MAP RM 1880. National Library of Australia.

Guinea, while trailing off into nothingness elsewhere, creating a picture that is like, yet very unlike, the reality. The map labels the mass of land as both Terra Australis and Hollandia Nova, and in the empty spaces a caption outlines the exciting discoveries awaiting explorers:

> It is impossible to conceive a Country that promises fairer from it's [*sic*] Scituation [*sic*], than this of Terra Australis; no longer incognita, as this Map demonstrates, but the Southern Continent Discovered. It lies Precisely in the richest Climates of the World. If the Islands of Sumatra, Java, & Borneo, abound in Precious Stones and other Valuable Commodities; and the Moluccas in Spices; New Guinea and the Regions behind it must by a parity of Reason be as plentifully endowed by Nature. If the Island of Madagascar is so Noble and Plentiful a Country as all Authors speak it; and Gold, Ivory, and other Commodities are common in the Southern part of Africa.... If Peru overflows with Silver; if all the Mountains of Chili [*sic*] are filled with Gold, and this precious Metal, & Stones much more precious ... this Continent enjoys the benefit of the same position and therefore whoever perfectly discovers & settles it will become infalliably [*sic*] possessed of Territories as Rich, as fruitful, & as capable of Improvement, as any that have been hitherto found out.

This particular map exemplifies the kind of discourse that equated the exploration of new worlds with the discovery of riches and bounty. In the apocalyptic sense, the new lands brought the promises of a new heaven and a new earth.

Another note on Bowen's map admits that it is itself a simulation, a reproduction of the original: "This Map is very exactly Copied from the Original." However, the map's veracity is assured, for "the Reader is desired to observe that nothing is marked here but what has has [*sic*] been Actually discovered," although modern readers may not observe an entirely precise map. Bowen explicitly and repeatedly rejects the assumption that his map may be a fictional representation and not reality, and displays no small concern that people might confuse the imitation and the real:

> It is also requisite to observe that the Country discovered by Ferdinand de Quiros lies according to his description on the East Side of this Continent directly Opposite to Carpentaria which if Attentively considered will add no small weight to the Credit of what he has written about that Country and which has been very rashly as well as very unjustly treated by some Critical Writers as a Fiction; whereas it Appears from this Map of Actual Discoveries, that there is a Country where Ferdinand de Quiros says he found one: And if so why may not that Country be such a one as he describes?

Pedro Fernandez de Quiros's extravagant descriptions and Bowen's "Map of Actual Discoveries" ultimately turn out to be misrepresentations of the southern lands, albeit exhibiting a good deal more accuracy than other depictions.

Bowen's anxiety about the possibility of the loss of distinction between reality and fiction is a crucial point. If the explorers and cartographers who insist on the veracity of their descriptions are, in fact, mistaken, this confounds the relationship between truth and speculation. This cartographic uncertainty over the separation of fact and fiction thus relates back to Baudrillard's discussion of the hyperreal and the end of any clear boundaries between image and reality. The proliferation of images of the south land results in a convergence of truth and fantasy, and one may argue that the simulacra of Australia has in some ways superseded the actual experience. Arthur writes that fiction and reality often intermingled in early literary speculations, and indeed some readers even mistakenly accepted the fictions as genuine and accurate accounts (192): "Drawing upon the numerous first hand reports of travellers and colonists, European writers used this fictional genre to present the world of the Antipodes in highly 'realistic' terms at the same time as expressing popular European fantasies of the Antipodes, including fantasies of colonisation" (186). The boundaries between reality and speculation in these maps and early fictions are not clear. This compounds the idea that the maps of the south land that cartographers and writers imagined did precede the territory in a significant way that rendered the reality of subsequent colonization virtually meaningless, for in every important sense they already knew Australia because they had inscribed it beforehand.

The utopian perspective also imagined the potential for the new land to offer an alternative, more democratic way of life and society to the British system, presenting the opportunity for those who had failed in the old world to find hope and success in the new. Annagret Maack writes that Europeans sometimes depicted the southern inhabitants as "advanced" (124), while Manning Clark notes that there was a view that the forced journey for the convicts might result in their redemption in the new land where they may even become "the founders of an empire greater than that from which they were banished" (*History* 5). There was also utopian rhetoric evident in schemes that encouraged English people to migrate, with promises that "the adventurous, the needy, the failures and the misfits could start afresh in New South Wales or Van Diemen's Land" (Manning Clark, *History II* 13). In this discourse, the land was a place of rebirth.

Australia as Dystopia

The alternative to utopian speculations was to imagine the land in negative terms of apocalypse; that is, envisioning the new world as a dystopia. In one respect, the American experience might appear similar to that of other colonies such as Australia, which Europeans also anticipated in utopian terms. Yet for Australia, there was an alternative approach that never expected the land to be a utopia and always imagined it negatively. If settlers found the landscape frightening, if they saw the borders as vulnerable, or if life there proved far from paradise, there was a dystopian tradition that had already foreseen these problems and had previously envisioned a land of terrors. Indeed, Lyman Tower Sargent's work on utopias in "Australia as Dystopia and Eutopia" notes that "Australian utopian literature is among the most dystopian" of all nations he has researched (125), due to several factors:

> Dystopianism may be particularly important in Australia due to the perception of internal and external threat, given the country's following characteristics: a very harsh landscape with the constant threat of devastating fires, floods and drought; problematic relations with the indigenous population; and the perception of being a small population with the near North of Asia as a constant threat [125].

Optimistic expectations about the south land were far less pronounced than in American colonization — possibly because the American experience had already lowered expectations of new lands as utopias, as Ross Gibson notes (*Diminishing* 4).

As a counterpoint to Bowen's map, Cornelius de Jode's speculative art in his "Novae Guineae forma, & situs" map, from 1593, covers a similar area to Bowen's. De Jode's map appeared earlier than Bowen's utopian vision, and depicted mythical creatures dwelling in the southern lands. Mermen and mermaids inhabit the seas while pelican-fish creatures fly over the water and giant serpents and winged dragons prowl the space that is apparently Australia. These new lands offered a tabula rasa that enabled cartographers, artists and writers to inscribe the blank places of the globe

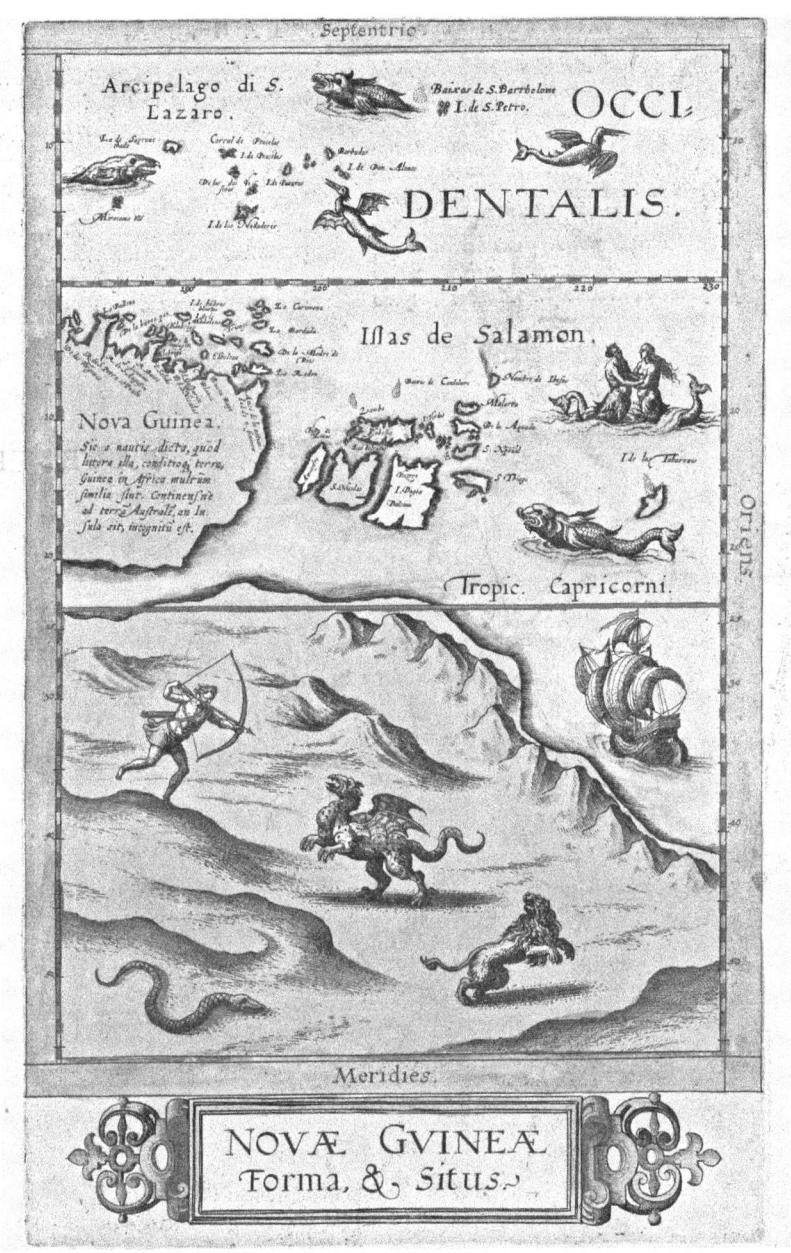

New and undiscovered lands offered the European imagination a blank space for fantastical speculation. In de Jode's map, mythical creatures inhabit the spaces around New Guinea, the Solomon Islands, and the imaginary Australian coast. Novae Guineae forma, & situs, Cornelius de Jode, 1593. Call Number: MAP RM 389. National Library of Australia.

with their fantastic imaginings. As Holden has noted, a "traveller using these maps was thus constantly reminded that along the route he followed and beyond the horizon lay monsters" (1).

Visions of the imagined inhabitants of the south land often verged on the grotesque or the strange. In Gabriel de Foigny's *La Terre Australe Connue*, from 1676, the land is a seeming utopia, although it also has a darker side: "All the Australians are of both sexes, or hermaphrodites, and if it happen that a child is born but of one, they strangle him as a monster. They are nimble, very active, their flesh is more upon the red than vermilion. They are commonly eight feet high" (qtd. in Carey 98). This speculation established Australia in apocalyptic terms even before British settlement in 1788, and early colonial experiences did not always counter this. Colonists and explorers saw the country as a "gargantuan curiosity" (Blainey *Land* 12) with little value. Discoveries of unusual flora and fauna — swans that were black rather than white, animals that traveled by hopping, unusual birds and lizards and trees — reaffirmed the concept that the country was different and strange, utterly unlike the British Isles homeland of the colonials. In this "land of oddities," being native was "almost by definition, freakish and bizarre" (White 6):

> A bizarre and unique real-life menagerie ... was a validation that in the Antipodes nature subscribed to an inversion of the natural order. Alongside these real-life anomalies, less tangible creatures eventually began to haunt a new and developing folklore which derived from Aboriginal lore, from the colonial imagination, and from literary sources and supposed "sightings" [Holden 2].

Holden notes that new fictional creatures such as bunyips, yowies, and hairy men replaced the monsters of European imagination (53) and he concludes that Australian folklore is "reinvested with an ongoing dimension of uncertainty and fear" (9).

The constant associations between the south land and utopia/dystopia created an apocalyptic discourse about Australia that was, and is, contradictory and ambiguous. The utopian tradition envisioned Australia as a space of potential for the fallen members of society but it competed with a negative perception that it might be hard to find any treasures and riches. Geoffrey Blainey writes that prior to settlement there were unfavorable attitudes to the south land because of the belief that the country lacked "rich minerals ... it seemed to offer no new timbers and spices or vegetables and fibres. It did not even offer a suitable port of call on the trade routes between Europe and more valuable lands" (*Land* 6). White suggests that disappointment at not finding the expected wealth for trade prompted William Dampier to denounce the south land in the late seventeenth century (3) and dismiss the Indigenous people as the "miserablest People in the world" (qtd. in White 2). Meanwhile, in 1623, Dutch explorer Jan Carstenz rejected Australia as "the most arid and barren region that can be found anywhere on the earth" (qtd. in Webb and Enstice, *Aliens* 21). Janeen Webb and Andrew Enstice note that the south land was such a disappointment that explorers actually continued looking, unable to believe that the place they had hoped for was, in fact, Australia (*Aliens* 21). These rejections of the country contributed to "the English vision of Australia as a waste land, a place of inhospitable landscapes and miserable savages" (Webb and Enstice, *Aliens* 26).

Colonial times reflected this perception that Australia lacked economic value. Blainey writes that the members of the First Fleet experienced disappointment when they arrived in 1788: "Joseph Banks in 1770 had seen Botany Bay and the surrounding country at its most flourishing but had imagined he was seeing it at its worst. [Governor] Phillip paid the price for Banks' opinion. He could not find the rich soil and the lush meadows. The soil was sandy and poor, the clearing of the tree-stumps and roots was heavy work" (*Land* 23). The experience of living in the country proved that the positive descriptions were too optimistic when the reality showed that the settlers could not produce enough food from the land for survival; Blainey notes that it is puzzling that the British maintained their colonial presence at all rather than simply giving up (*Land* 26).

Gibson explains the tension between the two opposing ideas of the south land as the real versus the ideal. For Gibson, the south land became a "diminishing paradise" when pre-colonial speculation about its superior qualities resulted in anti-climactic experience (*Diminishing* 3). The actual experience of the country negated the favorable first impressions, resulting in disillusion and disappointment. Despite its great size, the land was nonetheless vastly smaller than Europeans had imagined, and the discovery and experience of other colonies had already demonstrated that new countries were not without problems, often failing to live up to the high expectations (*Diminishing* 4). Contrary to the first optimistic hopes, there was a feeling that this new south land was instead "a hellish realm of suffering" (*Diminishing* 86).

Once the European convicts and settlers arrived, they already "knew" what to expect of the south land because of the wild speculations, and many initial experiences just confirmed the worst suspicions. The negative aspect of apocalypse was pervasive. The English government chose the country as a penal colony, a literal place of punishment, and this designation contributed to the dark images of Australia. England transported some of its convicts there as punishment for their crimes, and the reality for many was that to simply be in Australia was to be punished, and the colonists and settlers might hardly feel otherwise when confronted with an alien environment so dissimilar to their former home. White suggests that the placement of the convicts in Australia had "a terrible aptness"; the country was fitting as a "dumping ground" for "the lowest element of British society" because "nature itself was inverted ... thieves were to be condemned to a land where there was nothing at all of value" (16). White argues that the penal colony was "sheer brutality ... horror and depravity" (18), while Gibson notes that the colonists often portrayed the country as "a nightmarish realm of brutality and adversity" in their journals (*Diminishing* 38). Chapter Three discusses these ideas in the context of *Mad Max*.

While many of Australia's early British inhabitants were settlers rather than convicts, it does nonetheless seem that these were ideal conditions to encourage a sense of exile and isolation in a new environment that people considered to be the end of the world, literally and mentally. Colonization disconnected settlers from their homeland, who felt that their true home was elsewhere. This was a sentiment that would exercise an incredibly powerful hold on the cultural imagination. The character of the land itself compounded this dystopian picture. As Holden points out, Australia "was as far removed as possible from the centre of the Christian world and hence from the habitable realm which God had made for mankind" (2). While this meant writers could more easily locate monstrosity there (Holden 39), the land had another significance. In Biblical accounts, a nation's physical location, its geography, reflects its spiritual status. God promised the people of Israel a new land in Canaan:

> For the LORD your God is bringing you into a good land — a land with streams and pools of water, with springs flowing in the valleys and hills; a land with wheat and barley, vines and fig-trees, pomegranates, olive oil and honey; a land where bread will not be scarce and you will lack nothing; a

land where the rocks are iron and you can dig copper out of the hills [Deuteronomy 8:7–9].

The promised land contrasts starkly with the wilderness through which the Israelites wandered for forty years to make what should have been an eleven-day journey from Egypt to Canaan: "He led you through the vast and dreadful desert, that thirsty and waterless land, with its venomous snakes and scorpions" (Deuteronomy 8:15). Indeed, the word "Armageddon," which appears in both Biblical and secular apocalyptic texts to signify a great battle in the last days, derives from the word Harmagedon and its earliest definition, in Arabic, is a flat place — "the trodden, *level* place," "the Plain," although later interpretations include "mountain of Megiddo" or "his fruitful hill" (Sheriffs 505). The popularity of inscribing Australia's flat, level landscapes as apocalyptic wastelands in secular fictions might therefore in some way be said to owe a debt to early tradition, and texts such as *Mad Max* (see Chapter Three) exemplify this pattern.

The promised land prefigured the later new heaven and new earth in apocalyptic writings, as a place to anticipate. The "good land" is one that is fruitful and verdant while the desert wilderness is a place of alienation. The Australian continent is largely dry and unfruitful, with a vast desert, and it was thus possible for settlers to decry the Australian landscape as barren and a place outside God's blessing. Furthermore, writers refer to the Australian interior, the outback, as the "dead heart," an idea that suggests there is no life and no value in the wilderness. It was not merely that the land was hard to work or difficult to live in, for one of the recurring themes in Australian literature is the menace of the environment. Albinski identifies the theme of an "inhospitable land" as one of three key themes in Australian utopianism, along with an "optimistic, if qualified view of the future" and anxiety over invasion (23). In *The Country of Lost Children: An Australian Anxiety*, Peter Pierce documents that there was an ongoing fear of children lost in the bush and particularly vulnerable to the landscape, an idea that Chapter Four discusses further. The bush is not the sole place of terror, however. As Graeme Turner notes, some critics have tended to focus on the land while ignoring the city, even though the same ambivalence extends to urban life (31).

In *Images of Society and Nature: Seven Essays on Australian Novels*, Brian Kiernan discusses several modern mainstream literary Australian novels, including novels by Joseph Furphy and Patrick White, and argues that the writers are all in despair at the Australian situation, even "depressed" (178). Part of this depression is due to the unwelcoming landscape: "In all the novels, unsurprisingly, the image of society presented is that of European civilization and therefore something anomalous, alien, insecure that has failed to put down roots in this landscape" (174). The land prompts a dilemma difficult to solve, and the conclusions are dire: "in these novels, death or total alienation is the most frequent resolution of the individual's attempts to find some idyllic compromise between the conflicting forces of a society dehumanizing in its demands and a Nature that offers no refuge for the solitary" (181). Kiernan considered these works, incidentally, as "amongst the finest achievements of Australian fiction" (172).

An Apocalyptic Dialectic: A Dual Vision

There is, then, an apocalyptic dialectic evident here in two very different attitudes to Australia. One approach sees the land as a new world of potential and blessing, while the other sees it as a dystopia, a place of horror and disillusion. Nimon and Foster point to the "linking of 'beauty' and 'terror'" in Dorothea Mackellar's iconic Australian poem "My Country" and suggest that the doubled vision "exemplifies national attitudes to the Australian landscape, neatly presenting the binary oppositions by which Australians typically categorise the material world in which they live" (28), while White contrasts two visions of Australia as "Hell Upon Earth" (16) and "A Workingman's Paradise" (29). Judith Wright refers to this duality as a "double aspect" that encompasses the "reality of newness and freedom" and the "reality of exile" (xi). Graeme Turner discusses the dual vision in reference to Wright's quote and calls it a "hesitation before the reality of Australia" (25). These quotations from Wright and Turner highlight again the conflation of fiction and reality discussed earlier, in that imagination about the land contrasts, and in some places supplants, the reality. The earlier speculation about the continent before its colonization encourages a "double aspect," a "hesitation before the reality," for there is uncertainty over which of the two visions is actually correct.

Given the ambivalence of these dual visions, some critics have read the Australian imagination in terms of the uncanny and the gothic. As this chapter discussed earlier, Baudrillard has suggested that doubles haunt the subject, that the representation shadows and terrorizes the original (*Simulacra* 95). In his influential study "The Uncanny," Sigmund Freud defines the uncanny in terms of its ability to provoke two different feelings at once: an experience of something familiar being at the same time unfamiliar. Freud notes that the German word *heimlich* (homely), the opposite of *unheimlich* (roughly translated as uncanny), has a range of different meanings, including one definition that is actually "identical with its opposite, '*unheimlich.*' What is *heimlich* thus comes to be *unheimlich*" (224). What is homely and familiar, therefore, is also secretive and covert: "In general we are reminded that the word '*heimlich*' is not unambiguous, but belongs to two sets of ideas, which, without being contradictory, are yet very different: on the one hand it means what is familiar and agreeable, and on the other, what is concealed and kept out of sight" (224–25). This ambiguity contributes to making a text uncanny, because there is uncertainty as to whether a thing is one or the other. Freud links the ambivalent feelings to repressed memory, but it is the basic explanation of the uncanny as comprised of two opposite aspects that is relevant in the context of this study.

For Freud, the "uncanny" provokes some kind of hesitation in the minds of the readers. The application for the Australian context is clear. Australia was a place that colonial settlers and convicts viewed with uncertainty: it was "home" at the same time as being "not home," for their true land was very much still Britain. Ken Gelder and Jane M. Jacobs read the Australian landscape as uncanny because of the ambivalence that results from colonization, and they discuss the ambiguous effects of white inhabitation and "ownership" of a country of disputed land rights. They adapt the uncanny to comment on the issue of Indigenous land rights in Australia. They argue that the uncanny is a fitting description for "a modern Australian condition where what is 'ours' may also be 'theirs,' and vice versa: where difference and 'reconciliation' co-exist uneasily. In an uncanny Australia, one's place is always already another's place and the issue of possession is never complete, never entirely settled" (138). In a similar sense, in reference to early ghost stories Gelder has suggested that the ghost story, with its seemingly vacant places that ghostly inhabitants haunt, may have a postcolonial subtext (xii), a topic that Chapter Four examines further.

Other critics read this hesitation and uncertainty in terms of the gothic, a genre that they argue is a particularly appropriate expression for the Australian colonial experience. In reference to Freud's discussion of the uncanny, Gerry Turcotte notes that two colonial themes parallel gothic concerns: "the fear of separation and the terror of not belonging" ("Generous" 84). Turcotte argues that the gothic mode was especially apt for the colonial experience, offering a fitting framework to express the discomfort that coexistence with the "indigenous other" creates ("Generous" 78):

> The Gothic still appealed to the colonial writer as one of the most appropriate modes to express the New World experience. The Gothic is a literature that deals with alienation, disjunction, terror, and conflict; it frequently projects its protagonist into an alien place where the character is tried and tested; and this protagonist is almost always victimized by a powerful oppressor.... The colonist is uprooted, estranged, terrified, on alien territory, and pursued (if sometimes only in the imagination) by a daunting predator: which in Australia was alternatively perceived as the Bush, the convict past, bush rangers or the Aboriginal population ["Footnotes" 129].

Arthur has also suggested that the gothic mode has much in common with the pre-colonial speculation about the south land seen in fictional journeys to *terra australis*, in their "seductive combination of realism and fantasy" (195).

Critics argue that more recent texts also illustrate the close relationship between a gothic sensibility and attitudes to the Australian life and landscape. For instance, Susan Dermody and Elizabeth Jacka suggest that one can recognize the Australian gothic particularly in films from the early 1970s and 1980s such as *Wake in Fright* and *The Cars That Ate Paris*, and their description of the genre bears some resemblance to Freud's uncanny because of the convergence of the familiar and the unfamiliar:

> Their hallmark is dark, inward comedy.... "Normality"— of the Australian suburban and small town strain — is the hunting-ground for Gothic/comic hyperboles and motifs.... The normal is revealed as having a stubborn bias towards the perverse, the grotesque, the malevolent.... Few "sane" protagonists escape normality with their lives or sanity completely intact. And the stereotypes themselves are strongly flavoured with memories of popular trash culture ... the best examples of Australian Gothic are intuitive and bizarre mixtures of B-grade genres.... There is kinship to the horror film, hybridised by the generic mix which may include action, western, rock musical, sci-fi fantasy, teen film, bikie film [51–52].

Other commentators have addressed the Australian gothic in their work (for example, O'Regan) but later explanations tend to locate it closer to horror than black comedy:

> Instead of a genre, Australian Gothic represents a mode, a stance and an atmosphere, after the fashion of American Film Noir, with the appellation suggesting the inclusion of horrific and fantastic materials comparable to those of Gothic literature ... three thematic concerns which permeate all the films related to the Gothic sensibility ... are: a questioning of established authority; a disillusionment with the social reality that that authority maintains; and the protagonist's search for a valid and tenable identity once the true nature of the human environment has been revealed [Rayner 25].

Caryn James differentiates the Australian gothic from European and American gothic types, although her discussion is also about New Zealand:

> The Australian Gothic is not concerned with the way lightning hits the castle walls, as in Europe. And it is different from the American Gothic fear of the killer in the farmhouse.... The Australian Gothic begins with a sunnier disposition, with characters who at first seem to be garden-variety neurotics. Then at some point they turn a corner and explode in acts of horrific violence [n.p.].

This again reflects the idea of a dual vision, where the normal or "sunnier" surface hides a much grimmer reality.

Postcolonial Uncertainties and Romanticizing Australia

For the Europeans, Australia was the Antipodes, the opposite of their "homeland." This immediately contrasts Australia with its heat and desert with the more typical European landscapes of green mountains, rivers and fruitfulness.[4] For many settlers, the unusual Australian landscape suffered by comparison. Maureen Nimon and John Foster argue that this difference was not in Australia's favor:

> What was Australian was also defined by looking beyond Australia's shores and contrasting it with "England" and "Englishness" ... "England" and "Englishness" stood for codes of inherited culture which censured all things Australian as inadequate because they were not English. Since measures of normality are based on the familiar, the British inevitably judged Australian landscapes, climates and societies by the degrees by which they conformed with or diverged from those of England, and found them wanting [38].

Some colonists attempted to position the landscape in Romantic terms, to enforce European ideas of order on the new land, although such efforts often met with little success. For instance, British colonial women who settled in the land found it difficult to replicate English scenery in their new homes. Rachel Henning's letters are one example of a typical desire to impose English gardens on Australian rural properties. In 1861, Henning wrote of her plan to grow "English greenhouse plants" (75) even though others had told her that "English flowers do not grow very well there, but flowers of some sort must; at all events, I shall try them" (69). A. D. Cousins notes that an early attempt to produce a collection of Australian poetry in 1819 merely displayed the difficulties of transferring contemporary English views of the natural world to Australia. Compared to the sublime visions of nature in Wordsworth, Coleridge, and other Romantic poets, Australia's landscape proved hostile to efforts to suggest any kinship between nature and consciousness (Cousins). Arthur also writes that some attempts to render the landscape in Romantic terms resulted in the "Europeanising of Australian scenes" (188).

While it may have been difficult to look at this new landscape with the Romantic ideals associated with the English countryside, writers continued their efforts to romanticize the land, often by writing lost race romances based in the vast interior. Roslynn D. Haynes notes that colonists expected oases and "paradisal walled gardens" would exist in Australia's outback, based on prior experience of African and Middle Eastern deserts (25). Gibson writes that many settlers hoped that the interior would be a "reward-land" after the "hardships and disappointments" of the coastal experience (*South* 11). If the colonists could not always shape the landscape into a typically European ideal, they could nonetheless imagine it in better ways. European explorers had colonized Australia but hardly touched its interior, and writers found the vast unmapped areas an attractive space in which to rework the themes of the Australian utopia.

The lost race was a common theme in Australian speculative fiction, perhaps influenced by other writers such as H. Rider Haggard (for example, *King Solomon's Mines*). In their survey of Australian science fiction, Blackford, Ikin and McMullen discuss several early examples of lost race romances set in the outback, including the anonymously written *Oo-a-deen; or, The Mysteries of the Interior Unveiled*, published in 1847, and G. Firth Scott's *The Last Lemurian: A Westralian Romance*, from 1898, while later examples include M. Lynn Hamilton's *The Hidden Kingdom*.[5] Van Ikin points out that the "discovery of a 'lost race' or a 'hidden Kingdom' often prompted a speculation that this might be one of the lost tribes of

Israel" ("Dreams" 254). Blackford, Ikin and McMullen (23) point to a work from 1851 by Hannah Villiers Boyd, *A Voice from Australia; or An Inquiry into the Probability of New Holland Being Connected with the Prophecies Relating to the New Jerusalem and the Spiritual Temple*. The associations between Australia and Biblical prophecy strongly reinforce the "map" of Australia as the New Jerusalem, the new world. Despite de Quiros's mistaken proclamation of "Austrialia" as the south land of the Holy Spirit, the hope that the south land would be the promised new world of Biblical apocalypse did not cease with colonial experience; nor did the secular version of this idea, where Australia was a land of opportunity.

Critics have noted that the lost race romance made it possible to compensate for the absence of (European) history in Australia, by suggesting that the nation is "the site in which otherwise extinct traditions have continued (so that it becomes a land full of lost races and divergent civilizations)" and also "that Australia may be the summation of other histories and traditions: 'the Eldorado of Raleigh; the "Land of Gold" of which Cortez dreamed'" (Blackford, Ikin, and McMullen 7). Yet Ikin writes that by the late nineteenth century, situating utopias in Australia had lost much of its appeal ("History" xvii), while Nan Bowman Albinski highlights the fact that in the late nineteenth century few Australian authors envisioned their utopias in a future Australia, compared to American writers who almost exclusively used a future American state (16). Real-life widespread beliefs in the presence of a massive inland sea or a hidden garden in the interior also met with disappointment, resulting in "disenchantment" with the notion of utopia in the desert (P. Williams 303). In "Domesticating the Monster," Webb and Enstice note the tendency for Europeans to depict the Indigenous people in gothic, grotesque terms. They suggest that the lost race romances, in their conflation of science and fantasy, frequently depicted grotesque, bizarre creatures inhabiting the Australian interior. These depictions often evidenced racist attitudes to non-Europeans, as in one narrative that features "an extraordinary species of ovoid kangaroo-aborigines, developed from the unlikely primaeval union of the two groups" (93). The lost race romances of the Australian interior echoed the precolonial visions of grotesque creatures inhabiting the south land.

In *Writing the Colonial Adventure: Race, Gender and Nation in Anglo-Australian Popular Fiction, 1875–1914*, Robert Dixon argues that there were gendered and nationalist ideologies in Australian adventure romances, and writers sometimes adopted and other times contested them. He writes that during the 1870s, the British sociocultural scene underwent a change that saw a growing sense of uncertainty about Great Britain's dominance and position replace earlier pride and triumph in Empire. "Fears of racial decline and cultural decadence" (2), especially in Britain's cities, resulted in the construction and imagination of colonies as places of adventure that might restore masculinity; "the myth of the 'sick heart' was answered by the myth of the Coming Man" (3). Dixon's use of the term "sick heart" to denote fears about Britain's decadence compares with the construction of Australia's interior as the "dead heart" (discussed later in Chapter Three, while Chapter Five explores works that rewrite the land as a sacred Indigenous space).

Dixon points out that there was a growing conflict between Great Britain and its colonies because they occupied "divergent courses" (6), and this was reflected in various ways in adventure stories. This uncertainty over Australia's identity arguably arose because of the difficulty of negotiating an identity separate to Britain as well as distinct from the other (Asian) nations geographically close to Australia. Ikin has suggested that Australian science fiction "has mirrored the nation's apprehensive fascination with its own unexplored emptiness, and its fear of forfeiting its never-too-clear racial identity" ("History" xxxvii), and Webb and Enstice argue that the Coming Man notion was "a deeply racist version of social Darwinism" (*Aliens* 12). As Dixon puts it:

> In examples of imperial romance associated with Australia, anxieties about racial and cultural decline were exacerbated by a concern that the loss of an originary Englishness would not be replaced by a fully-formed colonial identity. The new discourse on nation required that Australian identity be different to Englishness, yet also distinct from those others — Women, Aborigines, Asia — against which that difference was measured [63].

John Rieder writes that the lost race narrative counteracts European anxiety about the presence of Indigenous inhabitants in Australia because the white explorers often discover remnants of their "own history lodged in the midst of a native population that has forgotten the connection," as if to reassure white readers that their inhabitation of Australia is legitimate ("Science Fiction" 376).[6] The growing power of German, Russian, and Asian nations generated fears of invasion in Britain, and adventure stories featuring invasions of Australia, particularly of Asian origin, reflected this dread (Dixon 136); often the invading nations defeat Australia (Blackford, Ikin, and McMullen 37). Albinski suggests that Federation and the sense of the country's "geographical vulnerability" (19) partly shaped the invasion narrative. Dixon writes that by the 1900s disillusionment with imperialism threatened to collapse the adventure genre; in Chapter Four I argue that the adventure story with its encoded imperial ideologies reappears in recent apocalyptic adventure narratives for children.

Istvan Csicsery-Ronay, Jr., characterizes the American experience as one of confidence and assurance. He writes that there was less uncertainty over the American geopolitical position than in other colonies because the issue of nationhood did not trouble American speculative fiction writers:

> The United States had largely resolved its national question with the expulsion of the European colonials from its territories, the near-extermination of its aboriginal population, and the establishment of economic hegemony over Latin America. Free of the anxiety about foreign invasions that marked English futuristic writing from 1871 on and enjoying the steady expansion of its territory, sf from the Gernsback era on displays a barely conscious American triumphalism [222].

Australia's "national question," on the other hand, was far from resolved. As Gelder and Jacobs suggest, Indigenous inhabitation of Australia prior to colonization made any white feeling of "ownership" problematic, while the country's Asian location, away from Britain, left a feeling of vulnerability.

We can look at historical literature and documents for evidence of fears of invasion and national vulnerability to non-white peoples. One example that demonstrates the anxiety is the "Million Farms" campaign of the 1920s, which included a series of maps, advertisements, and articles outlining the vulnerability of Australia's defense. Politician Joseph Carruthers initiated the campaign and it ran from 1919 to 1925, targeting the growth of Australia's population and production by encouraging the settlement of "a million families on a million farms." Documents from the campaign included maps that emphasized Australia's isolation from Europe and the threat of surrounding nations. One is a map of the world that reads "All Eyes on Australia" and depicts figures in each continent turning towards Australia as if in apparent intent to seize the country. The people all represent non-white populations from Africa, Asia, and Central and South America. A second document asks "Why not settle our idle lands

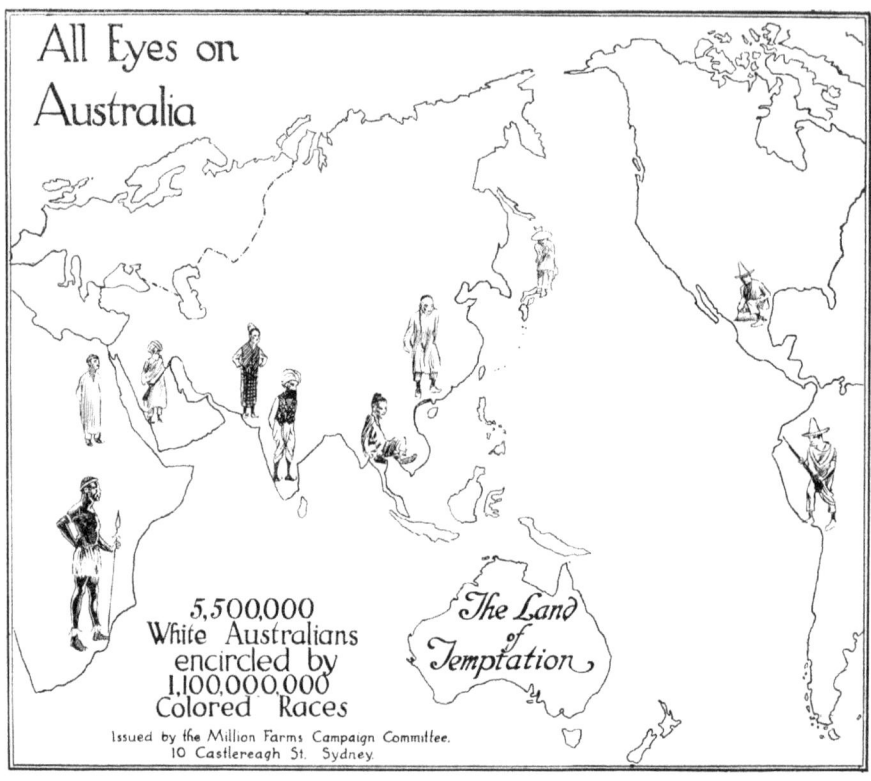

The threat of other nations, particularly non-white populations, to Australia's security and prosperity played a part in early invasion literature and continues to inform more recent Australian apocalyptic works. All Eyes on Australia. Immigration Encouragement. "Million Farms" Campaign. Sir Joseph Carruthers Scheme, 1921–22. National Archives of Australia: A457, I400/5 PART 2.

with white men?" and juxtaposes a map of Australia with Japan, listing their relative populations, size, and density. The implication is clear that Australia must populate itself with more (white) people if it is to defend itself against these hungry nations. Literature of the time — and since — mirrors these beliefs.

Yet other commentators highlight the optimistic aspects of the early postcolonial fictions. Melissa Bellanta has argued that surveys such as Dixon's overemphasize the anxieties and fears of the time, and fail to acknowledge the utopianism of such stories. Bellanta proposes that we should read the Australian lost race romances in terms of the utopian,

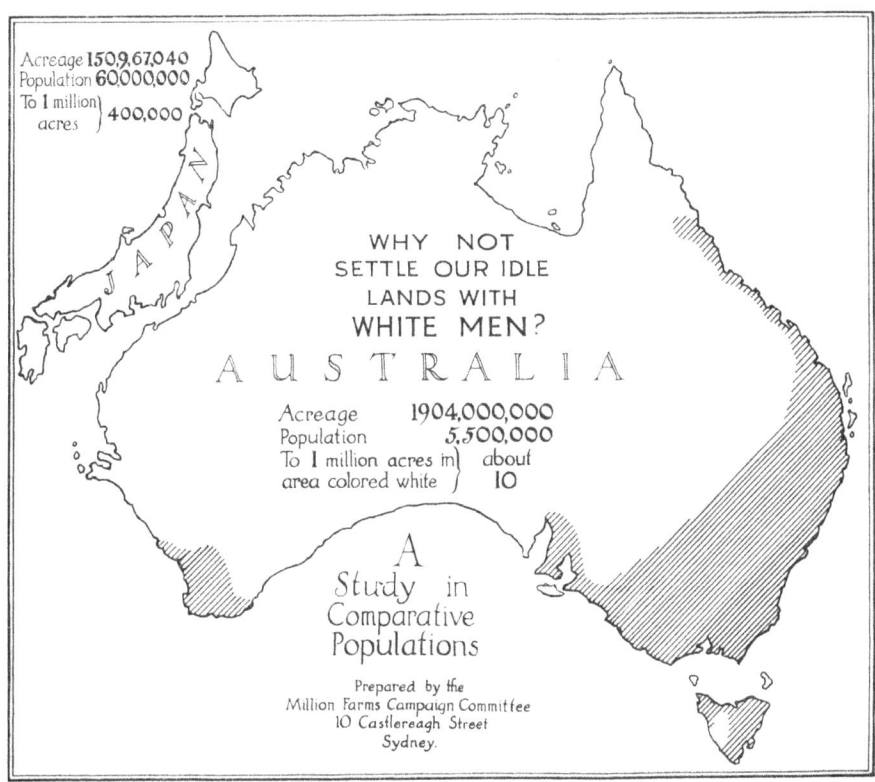

Part of the "Million Farms" Campaign, images such as this appeal to anxieties about the size and proximity of Asian nations to Australia. Why Not Settle Our Idle Lands with White Men? Immigration Encouragement. "Million Farms" Campaign. Sir Joseph Carruthers Scheme, 1921–22. National Archives of Australia: A457, I400/5 PART 2.

positive possibilities that they offer. She writes that the authors of the time often presented their bizarre depictions of the landscape as realistic, and suggests that just as writers could envision imaginary utopian societies in any number of ways, so too the Australian landscape allowed "fabulation" in that the utopists could imagine the interior as a place of potential for the future of the nation. Jacqueline Dutton has pointed out that the status of Australia as both desert and island means that the nation, as well as the other southern continent of Antarctica, was an apt place to situate utopian futures, for utopias frequently utilize desert and island motifs (285).[7] It is possible to detect in some lost race romances both fear and optimism, anxiety and celebration, doubt and hope. The apocalyptic status of Australia as one of the new worlds meant that some authors could imagine utopia and heaven there while others describe the south land as dystopia and hell.

European literature and art about other parts of the world prior to colonization therefore reveal a tradition of imagination and speculation ranging from idyllic dreams of paradise to nightmares of monstrosity. Cartographers created fanciful maps depicting the new worlds, while writers set tales of lost races or advanced civilizations in the undiscovered lands. The speculative maps merged reality and fiction, with some illustrating coastlines and country locations with accuracy while others joined continents together to form super land masses in maps wildly unlike modern cartography. These early images of new lands were powerful, and have retained a significant place in the cultural imagination. In a crucial sense, the images that speculation rather than experience generated eventually inscribed a discourse on countries that in some ways took precedence over the reality that followed. Even when the actual experience of exploration belied the early visions, they exerted an influence hard to counter.

The dualities and anxieties in Australian culture discussed in this chapter form an important backdrop to the discussion of an Australian apocalypse. Fears of invasion and anxieties about the nation's geographical position recur in the country's speculative fictions that construct the national situation as unstable and vulnerable, far from a place of security and safety. Some key aspects of Biblical apocalypse correlate to the secular apocalypse that characterizes Australia, for many of the themes found in Revelation and other Biblical texts parallel the concerns that recur in Australian writing, including punishment, exile, invasion and wilderness. At the same time, these negative images worked against the utopian ideals of explorers who had imagined Australia as a place of fortune and promise. The associations between apocalypse and nation that writers have repeatedly made in Australian fictions suggest that there is an inherent relationship between the two.

The pre-colonial ideas and speculation of the unknown south land proved powerful, for despite preceding the territory itself, the early maps exercised a dominant influence over the construction of Australia. The European imagination imposed an apocalyptic map onto the south land, a map that either offered the utopia promised by Revelation or alternatively, and frequently, focused on the negative aspects of apocalypse and imagined the land as a place of punishment and dystopia. These images contributed to an apocalyptic tradition in the early period, before the English even colonized the country, which would later play a significant role in the nation's imagination. The apocalyptic ethos would recur in Australian fiction, appearing in the guise of nuclear war, invasion, technological or environmental catastrophes. The early maps would also, hundreds of years later, result in some of the most famous Australian apocalyptic texts, which the following chapters will discuss.

• Two •

The Shield of Distance
Apocalypse in Australian Literature After 1945

"I won't take it," she said vehemently. "It's not fair. No one in the southern hemisphere ever dropped a bomb, a hydrogen bomb or a cobalt bomb or any other sort of bomb. We had nothing to do with it. Why should we have to die because other countries nine or ten thousand miles away from us wanted to have a war? It's so bloody unfair."

Nevil Shute, *On the Beach* 39

The northern hemisphere, we were told, suffered more than the southern. That had always been true, the palaeontologists said. In the southern hemisphere we remained the Lucky Country. Was it so? Really so?

George Turner, *Drowning Towers* 137

The previous chapter discussed the apocalyptic "map" in which explorers had already inscribed the territory of Australia with themes and images before its colonization, and this map appears to influence many speculative texts. One of the major themes of the Australian apocalyptic discourse is the nation's vulnerability to outside influence. In a sense, Australia's position on the edge of the globe not only excludes it from the world and its advantages but also shields the country from crises as a kind of utopian space free from harm, whereby the end of "the world" can occur even if Australia still exists.

In the case studies in this chapter, the nation initially appears to be a relatively utopian setting while war has destroyed the rest of the world, and the country's remote location seems to have protected it from the disaster elsewhere; yet this proves to be a false hope. Australia cannot escape catastrophe, and the authors suggest social and political complacency and indifference as the main reasons for collapse. In this way the novels function as warnings, using crisis to reveal dystopian futures. The associations these case studies make between disaster and Australia ultimately work to reinforce the concept that the nation is an apocalyptic space.

Australian apocalyptic writing does not, however, exist on its own. It is part of a global body of literature, and this chapter first explores the appeal and development of apocalypse internationally to contextualize the case studies. In the latter half of the twentieth century there was a growing number of apocalyptic works worldwide and Australian literature reflected this. This chapter surveys the movements in apocalyptic fiction in this period and then examines several Australian texts in the decades after 1945, including one of the most famous apocalyptic texts, Nevil Shute's *On the Beach*, and George Turner's science fiction novels. Apocalyptic literature worldwide increased following the various catastrophes that characterized World War II and after, including dictatorships such as Hitler's Third Reich and Mussolini's fascist Italy, the Japanese attack on Pearl Harbor, the Kokoda Trail campaign, invasions and occupations, the genocidal implications of the Holocaust, and the detonation of nuclear bombs on the Japanese cities Hiroshima and Nagasaki. After World War II, the American-Russian Cold War maintained a sense of crisis with its underlying threat of total annihilation, while terrorism continues to contribute to apocalyptic fears. The Australian case studies, while reflecting international concerns, also demonstrate the particularities of the Australian geopolitical situation.

The Appeal of Apocalyptic Scenarios

Before surveying apocalypse after World War II, it is worth briefly discussing the genre's appeal to writers and readers. One of the reasons for its ongoing popularity is its flexibility and resilience. Frank Kermode argues that apocalypse is a resilient mode because its meanings are fluid and open to interpretation and it gives sense and meaning to people's lives (4–7).

Kermode points to the continued popularity of apocalyptic fictions — a "perpetual crisis" (28) — and he notes that while there may be less belief in an "imminent" end of the world, there is now a sense that it is all around us:

> Our end-determined fictions ... are placed at what Dante calls the point where all times are present, *il punto a cui tutti li tempi son presenti*; or within the shadow of it. It gives each moment its fullness. And although for us the End has perhaps lost its naïve *imminence*, its shadow still lies on the crises of our fictions; we may speak of it as *immanent* [6].

The resilience of apocalypse lies chiefly in its ability to withstand false predictions and erroneous interpretations; this skepticism is one of the features of apocalypse (10):

> The great majority of interpretations of Apocalypse assume that the End is pretty near. Consequently the historical allegory is always having to be revised; time discredits it. And this is important. Apocalypse can be disconfirmed without being discredited. This is part of its extraordinary resilience. It can also absorb changing interests, rival apocalypses.... It is patient of change and of historiographical sophistications. It allows itself to be diffused, blended [8].

The genre proves so resilient, in fact, that even when time shows that various interpretations and guesses about Christ's return are incorrect, people can dismiss the calculations (not apocalypse itself) as "error" and develop new interpretations (9).

In contrast, James Berger argues that Kermode's "sense of an ending" has in fact "given way to visions of after the end, and the apocalyptic sensibilities both of religion and of modernism have shifted toward a sense of post-apocalypse" (xiii). He writes that life continues even after real-life apocalypses have occurred, which leaves a perspective of post-apocalypse, post-catastrophe (xiii). However, other critics argue that apocalypse remains relevant for our society. John W. Martens suggests that apocalypse points to "the fragile conscience of the West" (83) and our desire for future hope and restoration; apocalypse represents our "yearning for the love of God, a time of perfection, which we instinctively know our own behavior cannot achieve" (85). In contrast, W. Warren Wagar claims that apocalypse appeals to our sense of inhabiting end times; it is "one way in which a dying culture — in this case, the national-bourgeois culture of the post–Christian West — has chosen to express the loss or decline of its faith in itself" (*Terminal* xiii).

Some commentators have linked this loss of faith in ourselves to the increasing knowledge of humanity's ability to cause global disaster, rather than divine intervention alone. David Ketterer writes that apocalypse is particularly relevant after the advent of nuclear weapons, for atomic power enables humanity to "be the instigator of a do-it-yourself apocalypse" (4). Susan Sontag argues that science fiction reflects this shift of responsibility: "Recent science fiction films have a decided grimness, bolstered by their much greater degree of visual credibility, which contrasts strongly with the older films. Modern historical reality has greatly enlarged the imagination of disaster, and the protagonists — perhaps by the very nature of what is visited upon them — no longer seem wholly innocent" ("Imagination" 215). Mervyn F. Bendle points out that recent apocalyptic texts depict a loss of community and more conflict between humans, who become so desperate to survive that they attack each other.

Stephen D. O'Leary argues that part of the appeal of apocalypse is its perceived status as a solution to the "problem of evil" (14). Apocalypse is, he argues, essentially a rhetoric designed to persuade its audience; a rhetoric that is made up of three themes: time, evil, and authority. The construction of time is one of the crucial elements of apocalyptic discourse because rhetoric must convince its hearers that they are, indeed, living at the end of history, and if people see themselves as at the "end" they are reassured that there will be a final conclusion to evil. Apocalyptic rhetoric attempts "to situate its audience at the end of a particular pattern of historical time; to the extent that people adhere to apocalyptic claims, their perception of time is altered" (13). The authority theme is significant in that apocalyptic discourse must be convincing to its audience (51), constructing the prophecies as logical, feasible extrapolations of the current state of society.

Sontag offers a further explanation for the appeal of disaster scenarios. In "The Imagination of Disaster," Sontag asserts that there is an "aesthetics of destruction" (213) that proves attractive for audiences, who enjoy the spectacle and "sensuous elaboration" (212) of destruction. Sontag also claims that "there is absolutely no social criticism, of even the most implicit kind, in science fiction films" (223), although Mick Broderick asserts that some films can be very critical of nuclear war, for example ("Surviving Armageddon"). For some theorists, the appeal of disaster is psychological. Disaster scenarios "normalize what is psychologically unbearable, thereby inuring us to it" (Sontag "Imagination" 225). Rosemary Jackson similarly notes that the fictional expression of anxiety may alleviate that fear. Jackson argues that fantastic fiction contains transgressive or "anti-social" (9) elements and they can be neutralized by their very articulation, the reader's vicarious experience of them through the text. Thus, as both Sontag and Jackson observe, the textual expression of disturbing images and events may work to mitigate the feeling of anxiety rather than maintain it.

Apocalypse After World War II

In the decades following World War II, dystopian and apocalyptic visions of the world became dominant in speculative works, according to several critics. While much earlier "'classic' science fiction ... is optimistic about the future of human beings" (Hollinger "Future/Present" 216), science fiction gradually became bleaker over time:

> In the 1940s science fiction had promoted itself as prophetic and inspirational. In the 1950s it had been diagnostic and critical, but typically provided some sort of happy ending. But in the 1960s the dominant mood of much of the best writing could only be described as nihilistic. At last science fiction found a fictional voice appropriate to the nightmare of nuclear war [Brians 22–23].

Wagar claims that real-life world wars and the Cold War had a "profound effect ... on the apocalyptic imagination" (*Terminal* 110), while Tom Moylan argues that the growth of dystopian fictions competed with and eventually overshadowed a revival of utopia in the 1960s and 1970s (xii).

Some critics have suggested that the dystopian downturn in speculative fiction began specifically with the nuclear bomb. Many apocalyptic fictions offer worst-case futures, extrapolating contemporary fears to cataclysmic endings. The possibility of nuclear war is a frequent theme of post-apocalyptic literature, giving rise to many texts outlining bleak futures. I. F. Clarke writes: "After Hiroshima and Nagasaki that proposition [of nuclear war] became the key text for the greatest outpouring of warning stories in the history of this apocalyptic fiction" (22). Sontag suggests that the first use of the nuclear bomb, which she describes as a "trauma," heightened the fears underpinning many science fiction films: "it became clear that, from now on to the end of human history, every person would spend his individual life under the threat not only of individual death, which is certain, but of something almost insupportable psychologically — collective incineration and extinction which could come at any time, virtually without warning" ("Imagination" 224). David Seed notes that the bombing of Hiroshima can be considered both the "end of one period or the beginning of another"— that is, the atomic age ("Dawn" 88) — essentially creating an overlap of the old and new. The conflation of ending and beginning in the event of nuclear warfare is, of course, apocalyptic. In his introduction to *Postmodern Apocalypse*, Richard Dellamora points out that "World War II has been understood to signify a moment of rupture that permanently devalues the principles and aspirations associated with Euro-American tradition. The war signifies the end of the grand narratives that have shaped Western civilization for the past two hundred years" ("Introduction" 2). The *Bulletin of Atomic Scientists* created the Doomsday Clock in 1947, and the clock approaches midnight in times of crisis, as in the 1950s when Cold War nuclear testing saw the clock move to two minutes to midnight. In January 2007, the *Bulletin* moved the Doomsday Clock closer to midnight, from 11.53 P.M. to 11.55 P.M., because of environmental fears and nuclear development throughout the world ("Doomsday Clock").

Jacques Derrida has argued that the proliferation of texts and fantasies surrounding the nuclear issue has in an important sense diminished the actual danger of nuclear war, for there is no precedent of an actual nuclear war and hence no reality ("No Apocalypse" 23). In "No Apocalypse, Not Now (Full Speed Ahead, Seven Missiles, Seven Missives)," Derrida argues that nuclear criticism has so relentlessly discussed and imagined the idea of nuclear war that it has virtually become a "fantasy" (23); there is no longer an apocalypse because there is no real basis for it: "no truth, no apocalypse" (24). This is not unlike Baudrillard's contention that "apocalypse is finished" (*Simulacra* 160). In "The Anorexic Ruins," Baudrillard suggests that apocalypse is irrelevant because it has already occurred. Given that the "two great events" of revolution and the atomic age have already happened, it is "useless to hope" for anything else:

> The pole of reckoning, dénouement, and apocalypse (in the good and the bad sense of the word), which we had been able to postpone until the infiniteness of the Day of Judgment, this pole has come infinitely closer ... we have already passed it unawares and now find ourselves in the situation of having overextended our own finalities, of having short-circuited our own

perspectives, and of already being in the hereafter, that is, without horizon and without hope ["Anorexic" 33–34].

Yet as Derrida notes in "Apocalyptic Tone," those who announce that there is no more apocalypse are still using apocalyptic language, albeit an "apocalypse *without* apocalypse" (35), in the same way that pronouncements on the death of God, the end of history, and so on, are also using an apocalyptic tone (20–21). As Stephen D. O'Leary points out, Derrida's efforts in "Apocalyptic Tone" to proclaim the "end of all programs and philosophies that purport to reveal the ultimate End" (O'Leary 260) essentially do little more than confirm the fact of apocalypse's enduring status, for such a pronouncement "demonstrates that apocalypse is a discourse that is inherently self-refuting, one that bespeaks continuity with every utterance of closure" (219).

Baudrillard also dismisses fears of nuclear war and proposes that the fact of nuclear proliferation actually works to diminish the risk of nuclear war rather than heightening apocalyptic scenarios as many have argued:

> Entry into the atomic club, so prettily named, very quickly effaces (as unionization does in the working world) any inclination toward violent intervention. Responsibility, control, censure, self-deterrence always grow more rapidly than the forces or the weapons at our disposal: this is the secret of the social order. Thus the very possibility of paralyzing a whole country by flicking a switch *makes* it so that the electrical engineers will never use this weapon: the whole myth of the total and revolutionary strike crumbles at the very moment when the means are available — but alas *precisely because* those means are available. Therein lies the whole process of deterrence [*Simulacra* 39].

Where nuclear war becomes irrelevant, however, other catastrophes become more real. As Brian Stableford notes:

> The advent of atomic weapons did more than confirm a growing suspicion that the modern world possessed the means to bring about a man-made catastrophe of awesome dimensions. It helped bring about a consciousness of the future as a kind of *continuing* catastrophe — a mess which we had already made and would have to take special measures to escape. The lesson of Hiroshima was that *it was already too late* to avoid the dark and hostile future which had earlier been feared; the world was locked on course [126–27].

The fact that other anxieties have taken the place of nuclear war indeed suggests that there is a "continuing catastrophe." Sontag writes that disasters such as AIDS, Third World poverty, overpopulation, and environmental problems constitute a "long-running serial: not 'Apocalypse Now' but

'Apocalypse From Now On' ... catastrophe in slow motion" (*AIDS* 88). The accumulation of disasters has negative effects in that catastrophe becomes expected, ordinary: "That even an apocalypse can be made to seem part of the ordinary horizon of expectation constitutes an unparalleled violence that is being done to our sense of reality, to our humanity" (*AIDS* 93). However, Russell Smith suggests that there is a "destructive impulse" at the heart of utopia, whereby the desire for utopia always requires the end of one society to create another one (82): we cannot begin utopia without ending something.

In 1974, David Ketterer suggested that environmental and pollution concerns in fictions inferred that humans are guilty (133). Over the years, these same visions of ecological catastrophe have only deepened and are possibly at their highest point in current texts, where high-profile politician- and celebrity-endorsed documentaries receive as much attention as Hollywood blockbusters, such as *An Inconvenient Truth*, *2012*, *The Day After Tomorrow* and *The Core*, to the point that the prospect of widespread environmental disaster appears to have replaced nuclear war as the dominant fear in society.

Australian Apocalypse After World War II

Australian apocalypse reflected worldwide developments to an extent, by producing nuclear-themed texts (Shute's *On the Beach* and films such as *One Night Stand*), as well as ecological disaster scenarios of overpopulation (Turner's science fiction novels). In one sense, one can understand Australian fictions as mimicking a global pattern of apocalyptic discourse that the explosion of the first nuclear weapon inaugurated. Yet in another significant sense these Australian fictions were not imitating worldwide trends but were in fact operating within a long-established tradition of their own by engaging in a discourse that frequently associated the nation with the end of the world. Such texts merely adopted contemporary apocalyptic concerns such as nuclear weapons or eco-catastrophe while nonetheless continuing to reflect the thread of apocalypse that shadows the country's fictions. The early European speculation about *terra australis* created an apocalyptic map that influenced these fictions centuries later and provided a template for an apocalyptic dialectic about the promise of paradise against the fear of a dystopian place outside the new heavens and the new earth.

In the decades following the end of World War II, several important themes in Australian speculative texts emerge. These texts often depict a future Australia that appears to be the "lucky country" because distance removes it from the troubles faced by the rest of the world. This has its origins in the apocalyptic discourse about pre-colonial Australia that positioned the great south land as a utopia. It is a secularized version of the Biblical apocalypse where the new world replaces the old one with its troubles, and it is a paradise secure from the dangers of the outside, former world. These authors, however, reveal a reality where Australia is far from utopian. Instead, the nation's people are so indifferent to reality that their complacency leads to disaster. For instance, M. Barnard Eldershaw's *Tomorrow and Tomorrow* critiques capitalist political and social systems.[1] The novel is set four hundred years into the future after the World War III bombing of Sydney, a city that is a "promised land [that] was a mirage" (46). The future Australia is a "Golden Age" with "peace and plenty" (19), but discontent is evident and power belongs to the elite few. Yet when some people attempt to establish a more democratic system of government, their efforts meet with indifference and apathy. *Tomorrow and Tomorrow* displays several of the themes that recur in Australian fiction, especially in the work of Shute and Turner, by engaging with a tradition that reveals the utopian image of Australia to be a façade, a mirage that hides the true reality of a dystopia. This mirage is often a shield of distance that fails those who trust in it, and the following case studies exemplify this.

Nevil Shute: On the Beach *(1957)*

Nevil Shute's *On the Beach* is one of the most famous examples of nuclear fiction worldwide. Filmmakers have adapted the novel more than once, the most successful of which was Stanley Kramer's 1959 film starring Gregory Peck and Ava Gardner, while a telemovie appeared in 2000. Brians, in his comprehensive survey of nuclear fiction, rated *On the Beach* as the most influential novel of its kind for decades following its publication (19) and "one of the most compelling accounts of nuclear war ever written" (20). While other Australian texts have used a nuclear storyline, including the films *The Chain Reaction* and *One Night Stand*, *On the Beach* remains the best-known nuclear fiction.

Shute sets his novel in Melbourne after a nuclear war takes place in the Northern Hemisphere. The characters discuss the events, but nobody is certain of the causes or course of the conflict. Radiation fallout from the nuclear war is gradually spreading south and will lead to the death of all human life on the planet. As one of the southernmost countries, Australia is one of the last places with life. In the last few months of their lives, the characters engage in long-term activities in apparent denial of the reality of their situation: enrolling in courses of study, and planning farming and gardening for the following years. The American character, Dwight, makes plans for his family in the U.S., who are dead, and refuses to become involved with another character, Moira, because he considers himself to be still married. Towards the end the characters' pursuits become more short-term and indulgent, such as racing cars and fishing. By the conclusion of the novel the radiation has reached Melbourne and the characters take suicide pills rather than succumb to radiation sickness. Presumably people are still alive at this point in Tasmania, New Zealand, or even in Antarctica, and despite their inevitable death, one character says, "It's not the end of the world at all.... It's only the end of us. The world will go on just the same, only we shan't be in it" (79).

Novels such as *On the Beach* exemplify the pessimistic extreme of attitudes to nuclear war, and Stephen R. L. Clark suggests that in the 1950s, nuclear fiction imagined scenarios with "nothing living, or nothing that we could consider worth living" (34). Shute's work certainly offers its readers little hope. For I. F. Clarke, dystopian fictions are not only nihilistic but also didactic because the discovery of the "new-found human capacity for creating the most genocidal instruments conceivable ... transformed the tale of the Last Days into a most admonitory form of fiction that centres on the dangerous pursuit of super-weapons" (21). Apocalypse can therefore be an appropriate mode for writers keen to protest against complacent political systems, harmful environmental policies, and reckless technological and scientific experimentation; the form allows authors to extrapolate from current events and imagine a terrible future should society take certain actions. Even if writers do not intentionally offer social criticism, their disaster scenarios function as a warning regardless, particularly when humans cause the catastrophe. In this way, readers may construe politics, technologies, ecological issues and science as significant causative factors in either the end of the world or a world very much worse than it is now.

Brians describes the warning or didactic function of apocalypse, particularly nuclear fiction, as an "admonitory effect" (ix) yet argues that most writers of such literature are not actually against war. It might seem that novelists depicting the end of the world are utilizing the genre in order to make a stand against war or nuclear weapons, but Brians insists that this is not the case and the opposite may indeed be true; most writers of nuclear fiction are not pacifists but instead use nuclear war in their writing as a justification for retaliation, violence, and resistance (44). Shute's work does not appear to be intentionally didactic. Whatever an author's motivation, however, their apocalyptic novels do give their readers "a permanent question mark over the shape of tomorrow's world" (Clarke 23), perhaps in line with Kermode's declaration that the "shadow [of the End] still lies on the crises of our fictions" (6).

Edward James, however, has suggested that "holocaust novels are far more frequently novels about post-holocaust survival and perhaps revival" (52), rather than genuine end-of-the-world propositions. Certainly, it is rare to find apocalyptic and disaster texts without at least a band of survivors, which suggests that *On the Beach* is rather unusual. Brians, who considers the novel "inferior" to the 1959 film, attributes its power to "its insistence on the relentless, inescapable advance of the zone of radioactivity, removing all trace of human life from latitude after latitude on its way south ... its almost unique insistence that everyone — without exception — is going to die" (20), the "elimination of one hope after another" (57). Other critics, however, have argued that the film adaptation negates the idea of total annihilation and in fact suggests survivalism. Jerome F. Shapiro has written that there is a sense that life goes on because the camera point of view encourages the audience to identify with it, and the camera continues to film after the characters have died or gone out of the frame (133–34). Yet as far as the novel is concerned, Australia is, quite literally, the end of the world.

Characters offer various accounts of the causes of the catastrophic war, but an air of uncertainty accompanies such accounts.[2] Shute simply describes it as a "short, bewildering war ... of which no history had been written or ever would be written now, that had flared all round the northern hemisphere and had died away with the last seismic record of explosion on the thirty-seventh day" (9). Warring nations detonated more than 4700 nuclear bombs in the Northern Hemisphere (73). The participating countries in the conflicts are from almost every continent, confusing culpability and emphasizing that all people share responsibility.

Shute's use of the apocalyptic paradigm focuses on disaster and rejects the possibility of a new world for the characters, who cannot avoid the approach of death. Brians sees the novel's Australian perspective as "ideally situated to address the fears about fallout" (19). There is no escape for the characters, no way of preventing or postponing the inevitable. There is only waiting for the end. Shute prefaces his novel with T. S. Eliot's words: "This is the way the world ends/ Not with a bang but a whimper" (5), and certainly its bleakness and lack of hope reflect this. The importance of Shute's work, according to Brians, is that the historical context of fallout concerns and the novel's everyday settings and ordinary characters compelled readers to focus on the danger of nuclear war to their own existence (20).

Andrew Milner argues that "both Australia and Melbourne were indeed ideal locations for a film or a book about the end of the world" (36) because of Australia's sense of vulnerability to outside attack and invasion (37). Moreover, Milner claims that this dystopian attitude was essentially Australian until Hiroshima made end-of-the-world themes relevant globally—at this point, "the whole of the West finally had Australianness thrust upon it" (37), although this may be overstating the case given that apocalyptic scenarios were not limited to Australia prior to World War II by any means. Milner links this "Australianness" to what he terms the "apocalyptic hedonism" in *On the Beach*, which he describes as "the peculiar frisson of a textual erotics deriving from the simultaneous juxtaposition of the terrors of imminent extinction and the delights of hedonistic affluence" (36). Milner writes that the coexistence of hedonism and dystopia is particularly Australian because of the country's affluence as well as its fear of attack or extinction (37). The mix of attitudes is evident in one character's car racing: "They're all going to be dead in a couple of months' time anyway.... So am I, and so are you. I'm going to have a bit of fun with this thing first" (Shute 191).

Wagar has suggested that Shute's imagined society in *On the Beach* is a "utopian" one, with "an intimacy of wholeness and goodness unattainable in the everyday present" (*Terminal* 74). Yet rather than celebrate a utopia or hedonism, the novel undermines complacency and satisfaction. Graeme Davison contrasts the breakdown of morality in the novel with earlier media and public perceptions of Melbourne as conservative: "The 'sober,' 'stable,' 'prim' Melbourne observed by visitors and local journalists becomes a city of fatalistic libertines, eating, drinking and making merry in the knowledge that they are soon to die" (159). Helen Grace, however, writes that what is present in the novel is not hedonism but "poignancy in the continuing belief that life will go on" (296). Yet the attitudes present in *On the Beach* appear to be less poignant than willfully ignorant, for the characters subscribe to a belief in the security of Australia's geographical position that is founded — and foundered — on denial.

Shute identifies complacency as one of the main causes for the disaster. Indifference and denial are constant themes in the novel, evident in society's love of its utopian façade. This complacency in the face of grim reality has grave consequences: "'No imagination whatsoever,' remarked the scientist. 'It's the same with all you service people. "That can't happen to *me*."' He paused. 'But it can. And it certainly will'" (79). One of the main characters, Peter, suggests that if people had put aside their superficial interests, educated themselves, and engaged with political and social problems, they might have averted the end of the world. "You could have done something with newspapers. We didn't do it. No nation did, because we were all too silly. We liked our newspapers with pictures of beach girls and headlines about cases of indecent assault, and no Government was wise enough to stop us" (258). Dwight suggests that "we've been too silly to deserve a world like this" (79). The key factors behind the collapse are ignorance, denial, and poor governance, although Shute does not offer any specific solutions to "silly" behavior.

The critique of complacency in *On the Beach* is a common refrain in Australian speculative fiction, and its recurrence suggests that it is an ongoing Australian preoccupation. Charles E. Gannon has argued that a nation understands nuclear war in terms of its geography, and his survey of British and American fiction serves as a useful start for understanding the Australian perspective in texts such as *On the Beach*. British fictions, for instance, are likely to imagine nuclear war as the end of the world, because of the small size of the country. Previously Britain's size and island location proved an advantage against attack, with the sea an effective barrier against the enemy. However, in nuclear attack the small size of the nation becomes "claustrophobic vulnerability" (108): people cannot escape an atomic explosion. Gannon writes that in U.K. films and literature "the dominant British image is that of the crushed city" (107).[3] This is because the British cultural identity, so tied up in its capital city, London, means that any attack on a British city operates as one against London and therefore a strike at the heart of England; the destruction of "the sheer concept of 'city'—is the nexus of national and social terror" (107). Recent works such as *Children of Men* or *28 Days Later* and its sequel *28 Weeks Later* are examples of Gannon's point; the cities depicted in *Children of Men* are violent and disintegrating while the *28* films linger on an empty, ravaged London after a "rage" virus has decimated the country. Brians notes also that "a sense of terror and despair usually lacking in the works of their transatlantic colleagues" tends to characterize British nuclear fiction (16).

Gannon contrasts this with the different "geopolitical perspective" (109) of the U.S., which literally has room for nuclear war. He argues that "no single city or region in the U.S. has ever been comparably central to the national consciousness, governance, and history [as is London to Britain]" (107).[4] Rural settings become more important in U.S. nuclear fictions either as the sites of nuclear attacks along with cities or the location of post-nuclear narratives, for "much of the post-blast action ... takes place away from urban centers" (108). Gannon cites American texts such as Walter M. Miller, Jr.'s *A Canticle for Leibowitz* and the film *The Day After* as examples of this tradition; to these texts, one may add more recent American apocalypses such as Cormac McCarthy's *The Road* and its cinematic version, the films *The Postman*, *Waterworld* and *The Book of Eli*, and the television series *Jericho*.[5] American cultural identity is thus not necessarily limited to the city, but is spread across many places, from urban centers such as New York, Chicago, and Los Angeles, to rural settings such as the prairie lands, New England villages, and southern deserts.

Brians argues that American nuclear fiction also tends to be more optimistic than British fiction because its authors "were often bent on demonstrating that the impending holocaust could be survived, averted, or even turned to profit" (16–17). George Slusser has identified survivalism as one of the key features of American apocalypse because it "defines the traditional way America has dealt with its sense of an ending" (118) with a belief in its readiness for post-holocaust life. Gannon suggests that a survivalist tendency in U.S. nuclear literature exists both because of the country's large size and also its "frontier mentality" (109)—Americans can survive an apocalypse because if enemies bomb one part of the nation people can simply go elsewhere; there will always be "a new land beyond the horizon, a new mountain beyond which to start a new life, an undiscovered country ready to welcome the determined and the industrious" (109).

One version of American apocalyptic survivalism is evident in the *Terminator* films. While the first two films suggest that the future can be changed—"the future is not set" (*Terminator*), "there's no fate but what we make for ourselves" (*Terminator 2: Judgment Day*)—the third and fourth films abandon this optimism in favor of promoting the apocalypse as inevitable. Apocalypse can no longer be stopped, but it can be survived. In *Terminator 3: Rise of the Machines*, the American survival ethos is obvious when the main character, John Connor, concludes that "our destiny was never to stop Judgment Day. It was merely to survive it." Connor again repeats "There is no fate but what we make" at the conclusion of the fourth film, but by now it is clear that the only hope is winning (not preventing) the war against the machines to keep surviving. While the films have always borrowed from Biblical apocalypse (Judgment Day, the messianic status and initials of John Connor), the fourth film seems to invest more heavily in religious motifs. There is a voiceover of Psalm 23, an opening text history that tells us: "Some believe one man holds the key to salvation. Others believe he is a false prophet," and the title: *Terminator Salvation* (promoted with the tagline: "The End Begins"). These are but motifs in what is otherwise a work focused on human survival. Commercial motivations aside, the film sequels and a television series, *Terminator: The Sarah Connor Chronicles*, places the *Terminator* franchise as part of an American apocalyptic trend that continually enacts, and reenacts, apocalyptic disaster and post-apocalyptic survival.[6]

In contrast to these British and American attitudes to apocalypse, I would suggest that the Australian apocalyptic imagination is shaped by a perception of being at the edge of the world. This reflects Australia's geopolitical position of looking on while major world events take place at a distance, for other nations are always writing history somewhere else. "World Wars" occur elsewhere and Australia's involvement is more often due to ties of Empire or alliances than geographical considerations. All other countries are "overseas" and Australia is the "Antipodes"—in opposition to Europe. Psychologically, therefore, the end of the world may occur when catastrophes destroy the dominant forces across the globe — the U.S., U.K., Europe. This appears to be the attitude prevalent in *On the Beach*. Australia may escape the (immediate) disaster, but in the schema of the novel, the "world" has ended.

For the characters of *On the Beach*, there is a sense that Australia's distance from the rest of the world should result in isolation from remote wars and conflicts. This discourse positions Australia as the promised new world of apocalypse that would offer a utopian space sheltered from the influences of the outside world. In this line of thought, there should be an automatic reduction or even elimination of the dangers that create unease in other societies, because of Australia's removal from close proximity. This is the opposite side to the "tyranny of distance" idea, where Australia's position in the world so often incurred penalties in economic and political terms (see Blainey's *Tyranny* for his work on this theme). Instead, we could label this belief a "shield of distance," a sense that if there are disadvantages to a remote position there are also benefits whereby what endangers the rest of the world need not threaten Australia. This attitude recurs in apocalyptic literature in Australia. Davison writes that in the Cold War, "Australians, living far from the cockpit of cold war conflict, may have felt safer from such threats than their European or North American contemporaries" (158), while Nimon and Foster point to a loss of security in children's novels: "Formerly many Australians serenely assumed that 'the tyranny of distance' protected them from other countries' problems. National institutions were unassailable, surrounded by a vast moat of encircling seas. Our shrinking world has reduced Australia's safety exclusion zone to a membrane-thin guard" (68). This translates in Australian fictions to a sense of optimism and belief that there is a utopian space because of the country's position in the world.

Yet *On the Beach* insists that utopia is a false image, for the shield of distance invariably fails and optimism is unjustified and unrewarded. Rather, there is a belief — and a sense of injustice — that Australians cannot hope to escape the nightmares and anxieties that persecute the rest of the world. In *On the Beach*, Moira complains that Australia's position in the Southern Hemisphere should have ensured its security: "People were saying once that no wind blows across the equator, so we'd be all right. And now it seems we aren't all right at all..." (38). If Australia was not involved in the conflict throughout the rest of the world, this distance should have offered protection. Moira perceives this as "unfair": "Why should we have to die because other countries nine or ten thousand miles away from us wanted to have a war?" (39). Other speculative texts reflect this attitude, such as *Tomorrow and Tomorrow*, in which Australia is "helpless, because, despite Canberra, despite the illusions of independence, despite the confidence of success and merit it advertised, she was bound with chains of gold to the world overseas" (95). Similarly, in *One Night Stand*, the characters wonder why a war between countries in the Northern Hemisphere affects them. The American sailor insists Australia will be safe because it is not of "strategic importance"; his theory is soon disproved when enemy forces bomb Australia, although apparently only because their real targets were U.S. bases in Australia. Such texts always disprove the belief in a shield of distance; the country's remote location cannot protect the land from the disasters that overtake the rest of the world. The apocalyptic dream of a safe new world always fails.

While Gannon argues for the importance of the city in British fictions and rural areas in U.S. texts, it is harder to categorize *On the Beach*. Shute's novel uses both city and rural settings, which may suggest that apocalypse is pervasive across Australia, rather than tied to a particular place. Many Australian texts do, of course, use a city setting for apocalyptic narratives. For example, catastrophes ruin Sydney in not only *Tomorrow and Tomorrow* but also many other texts, such as *Mad Max: Beyond Thunderdome*, *One Night Stand*, *The Girl From Tomorrow: Tomorrow's End*, and also on the cover of George Turner's *Down There in Darkness*. The last text is perhaps the most mystifying given that the cover shows the ruins of Sydney yet Turner sets his work in Melbourne. And, of course, the media reported Ava Gardner's apparent comment that Melbourne is remarkably appropriate for a film about the end of days: "It's a great place to make a film about the end of the world" (Davison 159).[7] Smith, meanwhile, analyzes several literary attempts to destroy Canberra, arguing that the capital city functions as a "failed utopia" (92) and a "city of the dead" (84) both in the national consciousness and several novels.

Yet the dominant images of Australia that sell the country overseas and to its own inhabitants tend to be rural and natural settings: beaches, wilderness, and outback. In terms of its large size, Australia should logically be optimistic about a catastrophic event; as in the U.S., a nuclear bomb does not have to mean the end. If war destroys the cities, people can simply

The ruins of the Sydney Harbour Bridge and Opera House are common images in Australian apocalypse, pictured here on the cover of *Down There in Darkness*. *Down There in Darkness*, George Turner. New York: Tor-Tom Doherty Associates, 1999.

move elsewhere to start again: the outback offers a vast scope for opportunity. Yet because the outback already substitutes as a hostile post-apocalyptic wasteland in popular texts such as *Mad Max* and *Tank Girl*, it would seem there is nowhere to go. The outback offers no refuge or future, because civilization is in the cities, rather than the virtually uninhabitable interior. Even in post-apocalyptic works such as those by Turner or the *Mad Max* films, the prevailing atmosphere in these survivalist texts is not optimism but a sense of continued apocalypse because surviving the catastrophe still means enduring life in a dystopian world until death. The characters of *On the Beach* have nowhere to go to escape the radiation, and there is no sense of survivalism to offer optimism to readers.

George Turner's Science Fiction Novels (1978–1999)

George Turner's science fiction novels offer a rich vein of dystopian, post-apocalyptic images of a future Australia. While *On the Beach* concludes with disaster, Turner's works more closely follow the apocalyptic paradigm of disaster followed by a new world. His novels, indeed, often begin with the idea that Australia has survived the disaster better than other nations. However, Turner frequently interrogates this new world to show that the façade of utopia or progress hides serious social and political problems. Although Turner's work received attention internationally — *Drowning Towers* "had enormous impact" (Buckrich 170) — he is less well known in Australia, yet his novels remain key examples of the Australian apocalyptic tradition. Several of his works are interconnected, such as the trilogy *Beloved Son*, *Vaneglory*, and *Yesterday's Men*, as well as *The Destiny Makers* and *Down There in Darkness*, while others are independent novels, such as *Drowning Towers*; together they present similar warnings of a dark future. Frank Kellaway has suggested that Turner's shift from mainstream fiction to speculative novels develops his earlier work because his science fiction texts allow him "to make a more general philosophical comment on human life than he has previously done" (13). Turner's science fiction, published over a twenty-year period, is explicitly visionary in its concerns, which range from scientific and genetic manipulation and catastrophic ecological issues to class problems. His work also shows familiar concerns about Australia's vulnerability to the external world. The other major difference from

On the Beach worth noting is the subject matter, for Turner's works show little interest in the prospect of nuclear war. In his postscript to *Drowning Towers* he writes that the nuclear threat is "unlikely" if only because nobody would remain to "loot the losers" (318). Andrew Milner notes that "global environmental catastrophe comes increasingly to substitute for large-scale nuclear warfare" (37), and Turner usually links chaos in his imagined worlds with the environment, particularly the exploitation of resources.

Turner uses science fiction to warn his readers about the catastrophic problems facing society and the dire consequences of inaction, and his works explore the problems of class, wealth, race and politics that cause disaster. For example, his first science fiction novel *Beloved Son* imagines life in 2032 when the crew of the space shuttle Columbus returns to Earth from a forty-two year journey to discover that the world has suffered a cataclysm. During their absence there was an event called the "Five Days," which was "a short week of vast airstrikes, and whole cities dissolved in dust and fire" (101). The wars were caused by overpopulation, pollution and resource exploitation. In a deliberate attempt to curtail the population, biochemists engineer a "final solution" (99) where mutating crops and diseases have "genocidal" results (100) and much of the world starves and dies. Westerners suffer in particular because they prove unfit for the new "Stone Age" lifestyle (101); Asian populations die because of disease (102); and people with experience or knowledge of Indigenous "tribal methods of survival" fare better, including in Australia, "one of the world's harshest lands" (104). England and "a dozen such areas around the planet" become "uninhabitable" for a century or more (56). The changes lead to the creation of a communist America, the New York Soviet, while religious fanatics take over Russia. In contrast, the disaster barely affects Australia, which only experiences "a few bombs ... famine and disease" (*Vaneglory* 128) because of its shield of distance from the rest of the world, "the luck of isolation" (*Beloved* 100).

Yet Australia's utopian position, escaping the worst of the calamities that befall the rest of the world, is equivocal in *Beloved Son* because there is some suggestion its inhabitants may have been the perpetrators of the scheme to murder the populations of other countries (100). At first this future society appears to be utopian: people live peacefully, crime is rare, and governments run the world by adherence to the ethics of non-interference and the "freedom to seek and perfect their own systems" (47).

With its skyscrapers and business district, Melbourne proves impracticable for this new world, so it is demolished, along with other "monster cities" (77), in favor of a newer, more economical environment. The citizens have "destroyed it, smashed it down, taken what they wanted and left the rest in rubble, forty city blocks of shapeless and heartless trash heaps of brick and concrete, plaster and tile and splintered glass" (214).

Turner makes it clear that pursuing the ideals of this ethical society does not work, and that the utopian surface of this future Australia hides a darker reality. Although people adhere to the ethical system, this is a world that Security controls tightly, where authorities suppress news stories and brainwash dissenting citizens into "robots" (224) and where youth suicide is unusually high: "Security was only another stop-gap preservation of a status quo eternally unbalanced by the same powers as were marshalled for its equilibrium; it would go the way of all attempts at regulation — Marxism, Victorian morality, religious persecution, dictatorship — as inner change rendered it obsolete" (*Vaneglory* 192). The reader sees this new world through the eyes of Raft and Lindley, two of the returned travelers, and their impressions are highly critical. In *Beloved Son*, Lindley claims that it is a world developing into "totalitarianism" (361) that Hitler would have admired (142), while Raft denounces it as "drugs, hypnotism, spy gadgets, computer records and Security ready to spring on any individuality that doesn't toe the ethical line!" (251). Powerful groups target Raft himself as part of an experimental cloning program to create a race of "supermen" (296) with improved life span, skills and physical regeneration; ultimately, a "virtually immortal" body (307). Genetic experimentation, however, results in grotesque, monstrous beings that haunt scientific progress with the reality of their disturbing presence. Cloning has dire consequences because the potential exists for it to "ruin a civilisation and rule the ruins" (62). Biologists and geneticists have acted irresponsibly and dangerously:

> The bomb we've learned to live with and pollution we will handle. But biologists! What they have achieved since the sixties is enough to put the fear of hellfire into Jehovah himself. Artificial inovulation, the gerontological drugs, brain regrowth and the mechanics of gene manipulation — these are already with us, imperfect and unready but with us. They are only the beginning. Consider the implications, and retch [25].

Raft and Lindley's criticism of the new world results in Raft's brainwashing to become one of the cloned "zombies" (345), and as the novel concludes, authorities capture Lindley to brainwash him too; he escapes this threat only to be killed at the conclusion of the sequel to *Beloved Son*, *Vaneglory*.

The idea that Australia's isolation, its shield of distance, protects it from the rest of the world recurs in these novels only for Turner to undermine such complacency. The quote that opened this chapter from Turner is in one of his later works, *Drowning Towers*, and bears repeating:

> In the Lucky Country we had no disasters. None, that is, in public. We had incidents, bushfires that were "contained," torrents that "subsided," droughts whose effects were "minimized." Other continents existed in permanent catastrophe, stalked by calamity, starvation and death as ruined ecologies reeled.... The northern hemisphere, we were told, suffered more than the southern. That had always been true, the palaeontologists said. In the southern hemisphere we remained the Lucky Country. Was it so? Really so? [137].

Even if Australia escapes the worst of disasters, doubt remains about just how utopian a space it truly is. *Drowning Towers*, published outside the U.S. as *The Sea and Summer*, again describes a future, utopian Australia after apocalypse. In *Drowning Towers*, a character is writing a history of the time before a disaster changed the country, and this earlier period is the major focus of the book with the story taking place from 2041 to 2061 in the Old City, Melbourne, before global warming when rising sea levels flooded all coastal cities. A rigid class system divides the nation into two main groups representing the extremes of wealth and poverty: Sweet (the rich) and Swill (the poor), the latter of whom makes up ninety percent of the Australian population. There are also Fringers, former Sweet who have lost their position. Only the Sweet enjoy the advantages of living in Australia because catastrophes have affected their lifestyles less than the Swill, who live in extreme poverty. For the Swill, Australia's status as the Lucky Country is false because it is a fortunate place only for the Sweet:

> "You've seen triv pictures of Calcutta and Shanghai and South America and Africa — all shanties and lean-tos, no sewers, no taps, no way to distribute food, only street mud to walk on. We're better off than those." So I found myself defending the State everyone knew to be a failure. "They did the best they could."
> "So we're still the Lucky Country!"
> That phrase had come down the years to haunt us, seeming to mean that we always escaped the worst of the world's troubles by luck or distance, but in Arry's mouth it was a Swill curse [166].

The State encourages class divisions and attitudes in order to "preserve an economically manageable status quo" (157) and authorities also experiment on a virus to decrease the population. Indeed, the Swill do not oppose the situation in the belief that resistance would worsen their lot (237), and their indifference and complacency in the status quo stymie any chance of revolution.

Turner uses apocalypse to highlight and critique social inequities and racist policies. He suggests that human reactions to catastrophes prove to be opportunities for radical programs of depopulation that demonstrate the hidden racist or fascist desires of the ordinary person. In Turner's works, scientists and politicians build their new worlds for a chosen people. The crisis of overpopulation leads to population "culling," usually of particular groups. The authorities use science or simple neglect to annihilate populations based on age or color or gender. Society abandons the aged to die in *Beloved Son* to make way for the youth, an idea that the older groups actually promote because they are "wrecked by hunger and disease and they carried the old ideas with them like poison; they were a dead weight on an emerging world" (110–11). In *Drowning Towers*, authorities engineer and test a sterilizing infection on the poor, and then they appear to select women as the chosen victims of a suspected experimental disease that slowly kills them. Meanwhile, governments target non-white populations in *The Destiny Makers*, set in 2068. In this novel, Turner highlights the sinister possibilities of choosing particular races:

> It became necessary to decide who should be preserved and who wiped out.... Of course each alliance had different ideas about that. Blacks would dispose of whites with some sense of justice done, and who would blame them? Islam would have little mercy for the non–Mohammedan, while Hindus and a few others would cheerfully see Islam to the devil. Religion and race are only part of the problem; political persuasions enter, too [260].

A group of mostly Western nations — Australia, the U.S., U.K., Canada, New Zealand and Israel — votes on whether or not to produce a genetically engineered sterilizing virus that will target and annihilate non-white populations, and they also consider the idea of "preserving carefully monitored numbers of nonwhites for the sake of the gene pool ... [or] that reasonable numbers be preserved to form a serving and laboring caste" (269). Australia is the last country to vote and Victoria has the deciding vote of the states. Some of the characters denounce this plan as racist and evil and attribute its existence to a corrupt and unjust political system.

Eventually, people carry out the culling scheme in the sequel *Down There in Darkness*, although the dominant groups choose their targets based on adaptability to the new world rather than ethnicity. *Darkness* begins in 2070 and continues a hundred years later after the release of a virus that sterilized all but the desirable populations. In the decision about who would populate the new world: "Race and color were ignored. The true demographic distribution was not by nation but by environmental suitability; physical types could be divided into geographically based groups characterized roughly as coastal-dwellers, plainsmen, mountainmen, tropical foresters, and so on" (196). Yet the ordinary citizen is inherently racist. When Ostrov and his friend Kostakis have the opportunity to represent the ordinary working class vote, both protest the racist plan, yet during a drug-induced interrogation that reveals a person's real thoughts and beliefs, Kostakis recommends that they should kill everybody, while Ostrov says: "We should make a white man's world. No slaves, no servants; just us. We can talk to each other; we understand the same things" (*Destiny* 283–84). Turner shows that the veneer of civilization that ordinary people wear hides a core of racism and rage against others.

Unlike Turner's other novels that end in bleak dystopia, *Down There in Darkness* takes the apocalyptic paradigm further to more fully imagine a remade, better world. Perhaps fittingly for a novel in which the future world has narrowly escaped being exclusively white, *Darkness* focuses more strongly on Australia's Indigenous inhabitants and suggests hope for a multiracial future, unlike Turner's earlier works.[8] Brian Attebery points out this optimism in *Darkness* where Turner envisions "a future in which Aboriginal genes and culture contribute to a new Australian identity" ("Aboriginality" 395). Certainly Turner describes Indigenous groups in *Darkness* as superior in many ways; they are morally superior in this novel, treating all people the same (224), and demonstrate sustainable living in action: "They have developed a tribal system based on living with the land rather than simply inhabiting it, so that everything is used but nothing is destroyed—a far cry from the culture of greed and ruthless development practiced by our own Last Generations" (236–37). In some ways, though, Turner's depiction of Indigenous groups is stereotypical. For instance, there is a clear opposition between Western science, technology, rationality and Aboriginal spirituality, mystery, secrecy: "white science had bypassed the Koori's need for intense inward searching" (239). One of the white characters, Sammy, raised in Aboriginal ways, is of "two minds ... carrying in me the deep roots of childhood spiritual experience, then educated as a grown man in the hard-edged logic of the New Age" (278–79). Sammy insists that there is "no distinct barrier" between these two ways (279), yet his description explicitly divides and opposes Indigeneity and whiteness: the former is experience, spirituality, childhood; the latter is education, logic, adulthood. In characters and descriptions such as these the stereotypical distinctions between white and non-white could hardly be clearer.

Yet racial barriers do break down in *Darkness*, collapsing the boundaries between cultures and genders and constructing a new world. Scientists have developed a machine that accesses the collective consciousness of humanity and reveals secrets and knowledge. The machine functions in the same way as a kurdaitcha's (Indigenous sorcerer) trances. The kurdaitcha's ability is "men's business" (234), and when Sammy transgresses this law and shares secret knowledge with a female character, Valda, he breaks "unnumbered years of tribal taboo" (288) and a koradji (medicine man) curses him with bone pointing. After the breaking of taboo, people plan to bring together many kurdaitchas who will train others — including whites and women — to access the collective mind in order to advance the new world. The novel ends with this utopian goal taking shape. Kostakis and the scientist Valda, both with Indigenous heritage, presumably embody the future of the new world that Indigenous people and women will co-govern.[9]

As in *On the Beach*, the prevailing attitude of the characters in Turner's novels is one of procrastination and baseless hope that problems might resolve themselves without any real action on their behalf. "The horrors to come meant little while I battled with the problems of the here and now. That's the human fashion. Tomorrow is always a long way off. Something will turn up, won't it? We'll muddle through. Won't we? Won't we? That's how the world became the way it is" (*Destiny* 321). Complacency is the real problem facing humanity:

> "Not in our time." That was Teddy, sure as ever.
> That phrase haunts all our lives. It has been the cry of the people and of their politicians as well as of scientists who calculated the imminence of disaster

and then sought reasons why it should not happen just yet. Refusal to believe is our surety that disaster cannot happen — at any rate, not today. And, every time, it does [*Drowning Towers* 24].

It is possible to avoid the dire predictions in his novels, Turner writes, but he apparently has little belief that governments will actually act to prevent future nightmare scenarios. "No country in the present world is likely to do this because no government can, by the nature of its provenance, plan beyond its own tenure. All governments busy themselves with preserving and continuing their own power. They do little else. There are no votes in projects twenty years in the future, let alone a hundred" (*Drowning* 317–18).

If there were any doubt as to Turner's intention with his novels, the Postscript to *Drowning Towers* confirms his self-appointed position as apocalyptic prophet, where he outlines potential problems facing the world and the costs of complacency. Turner denies any didactic intention, calling his work neither "prophetic" nor "a dire warning" (317), yet goes on to outline six key areas of concern that will have grave consequences if society ignores them. The first problem Turner lists is overpopulation, particularly in areas with "little arable land" (317). Australia, of course, is one of the least arable countries in the world. The implication is that the nation must therefore be careful with its population strategies and, by extension, its immigration policies. Other issues of concern include the potential lack of food in the future, unemployment due to increasing technologies that eliminate the need for human involvement, monetary system collapses, nuclear war, and the greenhouse effect. Turner says of the last that it may be "mild" or "a global disaster, striking with great suddenness" (318). By the time of the publication of *Down There in Darkness* in 1999, he reduced his list to four: "overpopulation, ineradicable pollution, rampant nationalism, and plain entrepreneurial greed — the four horsemen of the greenhouse apocalypse" (13). Echoing the genre's shift towards the culpability of humans rather than random acts of nature, Turner notes:

> We can be sure only that enormous changes will take place in the next two or three generations, all of them caused by ourselves, and that we will not be ready for them. How can we be? We *talk* of leaving a better world to our children but in fact do little more than rub along with day-to-day problems and hope that the longer-range catastrophes will never happen.
> Sooner or later some of them will.

> *Drowning Towers* is about the possible cost of complacency.
> Sleep well [*Drowning* 318].

There are dire consequences of complacency, of doing nothing, and Turner leaves no doubt that there will be consequences. Turner, at least, appears to believe that change is possible, albeit unlikely, in that his novels function as apocalyptic prophecies meant to provoke an active response. Like *On the Beach*, Turner's novels, while critical of government and political systems, also lay the blame for the ultimate catastrophe on human beings in general. Yet while *On the Beach* suggests that human indifference makes crisis inevitable, Turner repeatedly argues that if societies face problems rather than simply ignoring them, they can prevent or at least mitigate the effects of future catastrophes, however unlikely this might be in reality. Apocalyptic literature allows critique because it enables writers to imagine present systems of society coming to an end or illustrate how a new, revised world might be after a catastrophic event. There is, therefore, the potential for apocalypse to transform readers' perspectives, to warn readers as Turner does, although, as Wagar points out, "long experience suggests that no country will be deterred from waging total war in the future by literary doomsdays" (*Terminal* 128).

If the attitudes present in *On the Beach* and Turner's works seem like fearful relics of a post-war nuclear era, Dellamora reminds us that there is a "pervasive sense of unease in contemporary existence," writing that the "lack of confidence in the possibility of shaping history in accord with human desire(s) provides the bass line of culture — political, economic, and aesthetic" ("Preface" xi). More than a decade after Dellamora's remarks, a collective dread evident in literature and film has not abated. The immediate threat of nuclear war has perhaps diminished in the decades after World War II, yet terrorist activity and growing fears about global warming have continued to provoke recent images of apocalypse.[10]

Moreover, a group of Australian texts released in the twenty-first century confirms that there remains a recognizable strand of anxiety in Australian culture. Reality television programs emphasize "the dangers lurking on our doorsteps" (Bibby 4), such as *Border Security: Australia's Frontline*, and also *Surf Patrol*, or the fictional televisual drama *Sea Patrol*. It is the same anxiety about failing borders that sustains real-life debates about refugees, immigrants, and "boat people" attempting to reach Australia. For some commentators, the Australian government has at times employed a "politics of fear" which they link to the treatment of refugees, immigration, terrorism, and Indigenous land rights (see, for example, Gale, and Lawrence).[11] In 2006, meanwhile, Andrew McGahan's dystopian novel *Underground* was published, and it specifically references these anxieties. McGahan's work critiques contemporary politics that operate on fear, particularly the real-life American and Australian "war on terror" that leads, in his fictional work, to oppression and dystopia rather than security and freedom. In this many-layered novel, readers discover a suite of political conspiracies perpetrated by ruling governments to maintain their power by exploiting their citizens' fear of terrorism and Islamic groups. Australian society is in a state of emergency after television footage shows Islamic terrorists detonating a nuclear device in Canberra. Yet the protagonist learns that the televised footage of Canberra's ruins was a fake, and that the bomb was detonated only in the hills of Canberra rather than the city. This fake/real attack turns out to be an elaborate ruse suggested by American politicians and maintained by the Australian government for reasons of political gain.[12] McGahan's novel is perhaps not properly dystopian in the sense of taking place in a world very much worse than our own; his work too closely references our own society to read it as overly speculative. Yet the novel's conclusion warns readers that if Australians allow their leaders to exploit societal anxieties and govern by fear, all will be lost: "If— in this blind pursuit of security above all else — we poison our own society ... we will be more culpable than even the Romans" and such an experience would lead to a "Black" age (294). In its interrogation of fearfulness and security concerns, McGahan's novel confirms that there does indeed remain a cultural anxiety over Australia's security and its fragile shield of distance, and also implies that such fearful attitudes might lead not only to the loss of freedom but also to the loss of compassionate and fair-minded humanity.

There is a scene in *On the Beach* when Peter struggles with the concept of the end of the world: "I suppose I haven't got any imagination," said Peter thoughtfully. "It's — it's the end of the world. I've never had to imagine anything like that before" (79). The reality is that the literary imagination is always seeing the end of the world, and often in Australia. The case studies of this chapter demonstrate a continuing tradition that links Australia with apocalypse. The apocalyptic discourse of these novels suggests that hopes of a new world, a safe and abundant place in the south land, are unduly complacent and demonstrably false. They reveal that a utopian belief in Australia's position at the edge of the world and the protection isolation offers is dangerous and misplaced, for the country cannot escape the disasters occurring in the rest of the world, ultimately disproving the hopes for a new world.

The works referred to in this chapter show that apocalypse may be mobilized for a diverse range of agendas. Whether warning of global war, political and social complacency, environmental mismanagement, or the vulnerability of Australia's shield of distance against the world, these texts use apocalypse to reveal the future crises that will arise if ordinary people delay the necessary action until "tomorrow," not believing that threats are serious or will affect them. In these particular novels, apocalyptic destruction and disasters do not usually produce a better world but instead usher in either a new dystopia or the literal end of the world with no hope of a better one to come.

• THREE •

An Apocalyptic Landscape
The Mad Max *Films*

> This Pox-Eclipse happened and that's — it's all finished, just isn't there anymore.... [The desert is] worse than nothing. The first place you'll find is a sleaze pit called Bartertown. Now if the earth doesn't swallow you up first, that place sure as hell will.
> Max (Mel Gibson), from *Mad Max: Beyond Thunderdome*

If the apocalyptic discourse of post–World War II texts undermined belief in Australia's utopian isolation, there was another group of Australian science fiction works that suggested the threat to paradise comes not from outside but from within. These fictions adopt the early apocalyptic map that positioned Australia as the Antipodes, a strange environment, and reproduce and adapt a secularized Biblical attitude to land that reads the desert interior in particular as a menacing place of exile outside the utopian new world.

In this chapter I explore the three *Mad Max* films to consider their contribution to the apocalyptic tradition. In these texts, the outback is "the nothing," a threatening place that is hostile to humans. The trilogy reveals future disaster and appears to envisage a better new world, but then subverts apocalyptic hope by suggesting the new world is a false ideal because it only exists far from the Australian landscape and even then only in ruined, decayed form. The repeated dismissals of hope and the negative image of the Australian landscape undercut any security of feeling at "home," presenting instead a picture of exile and punishment in the desert.

Apocalypse and the Australian Landscape

We can see the rhetoric about the dangers of the Australian landscape in many places. One of the most popular ways of depicting Australia is to focus on its unique landscape in negative terms. Films, travel literature, and media reports have perpetuated the mystique of the dangerous Australian experience for humans. For instance, the first two *Crocodile Dundee* films emphasize (and celebrate) the harsh environment of the outback, and Bill Bryson's *Down Under* travel narrative focuses on the dangers of Australian wildlife and wilderness, explaining that Australia is a country with "more things that will kill you than anywhere else" (6). Although these dangers inspire pride and celebration as a point of difference for the Australian identity (and provoke adventurers to test themselves against such a land), they also enhance the apocalyptic tradition in the country. News reports contain lengthy coverage of people who vanish in the desert, such as the baby Azaria Chamberlain and British traveler Peter Falconio, or who disappear at sea, such as former Prime Minister Harold Holt, while swimming, and the Lonergans, an American couple who went missing while scuba diving in Queensland.[1] When adventurer Steve Irwin died from a stingray's barb, the then Prime Minister John Howard commented that his death was "quintessentially Australian" ("Tape" n.p.), an assertion leaving readers to determine for themselves whether or not this means dying while engaged in a much-loved career or becoming prey to Australia's dangerous environment.

Apocalyptic fiction inevitably reflects the rhetoric about the Australian landscape. Both local and international speculative authors and filmmakers utilize Australian landscapes — particularly the desert — to represent alien, hostile environments that threaten or even attack its human inhabitants. As with *Mad Max*, the audience might identify the desert settings of post-apocalyptic narratives as Australian (*Tank Girl*, *Thunderstone*, *The Time Guardian*) or the outback locations might simply be representative of a generic future rather than a specific place (*Salute of the Jugger*, *Pitch Black*, *Farscape*), but it is usually a place of trial and suffering for those who live or linger there.

Texts such as the *Mad Max* trilogy that represent the land as hostile have predecessors in novels such as Kenneth Cook's *Wake in Fright* and Joan Lindsay's *Picnic at Hanging Rock*, both adapted into films. Lindsay's

Three • An Apocalyptic Landscape

Picnic at Hanging Rock tells a story of the disappearance of several schoolgirls and a teacher while on an excursion to Hanging Rock, and Lindsay's writing juxtaposes civilized culture with a wild land. The girls attend Appleyard College, "an architectural anachronism in the Australian bush — a hopeless misfit in time and place. The clumsy two-storey mansion was one of those elaborate houses that sprang up all over Australia like exotic fungi" (8). The setting of Australia is not incidental but integral to Lindsay's scenario, because this is "Australia, where anything might happen. In England everything had been done before" (33). The headmistress, Mrs. Appleyard, reminds her pupils that the nearby Hanging Rock is "extremely dangerous" (15) before encouraging her students to write an essay on it, as if these cultured schoolgirls can impose form and meaning on the Australian landscape. After the girls and teacher vanish at the Rock, the essay project is abandoned. Lindsay portrays the landscape in grotesque, gothic terms. Hanging Rock is a menacing presence on an otherwise "empty yellow plain" (22), a "grey volcanic mass [that] rose up, slabbed and pinnacled like a fortress" (21); it "floated in splendid isolation on a sea of pale grass, in full sunlight its jagged peaks and pinnacles even more sinister" (86). The schoolgirls imagine the environment in gothic terms:

> The shadow of the Rock has grown darker and longer. They sit rooted to the ground and cannot move. The dreadful shape is a living monster lumbering towards them across the plain, scattering rocks and boulders. So near now, they can see the cracks and hollows where the lost girls lie rotting in a filthy cave. A junior, remembering how the Bible says the bodies of dead people are filled with crawling worms, is violently sick on the sawdust floor [150].

There is an ever-present contrast between the power of the hostile land and the helplessness of the civilized humans.

Mad Max exhibits the attitudes to nature that Cook's *Wake in Fright* also displays, where the land is the "Dead Heart." In the novel, schoolteacher John Grant travels to Sydney for his holiday and stops in a town, Bundanyabba, for an intended short stay on his way from his hated teaching post at Tiboonda. Tiboonda is "a variation of hell" (7) while Bundanyabba is a "larger variation of Tiboonda" (7) and Grant compares it to the utopian space of Sydney with its beaches and "graces" (6): "The schoolteacher knew that somewhere not far out in the shimmering haze was the State border, marked by a broken fence, and that farther out in the heat was the silent centre of Australia, the Dead Heart" (6). The Dead Heart proves an apt description for a place that becomes a nightmare. The desert is a "bleak and frightening land ... hot, dry and careless of itself and the people who professed to own it" (11), a "desolate territory" (9), full of "sadness" (139) and "loneliness" (14), descriptions that could equally fit the *Mad Max* films. Indeed, Grant's place in the landscape prefigures Max, for Cook describes him as "a lone figure, not worth a burst of machine-gun fire, he seemed doomed to wander the desolate terrain until he just dropped into oblivion" (44).

Simon Caterson has called the film version of *Wake in Fright* "arguably Australia's greatest feature film" (86):

> The film reveals that life in the centre of Australia differs only in the degree of hardship and loneliness from human existence elsewhere on the continent. With such emptiness at their geographical centre, it is understandable that Australians prefer on the whole to ignore it altogether and gaze from the coastline towards the far horizon and try to imagine themselves in London or New York, or anywhere. The tyranny of distance and the anxiety of isolation are as much a part of the Australian psyche as they ever were [87].

One could easily apply Caterson's assessment to any number of other Australian texts, including *Mad Max*. Leigh Blackmore argues that the landscape and social conditions allow Australians a "unique position from which to comment on the world at large" (viii). The landscape gives Australian horror filmmakers the opportunity to portray a variety of nightmarish situations. In his history of Australian horror films, Robert Hood suggests that the "grim picture of outback life" seen in the film version of *Wake in Fright* is indicative of a "civilisation in a state of moral collapse" (n.p.) and becomes the recurring theme in Australian horror films, whether small-town menace or more urban terror.[2] Brian McFarlane has written that *Wake in Fright* gives an "unusually harsh picture of outback Australian life, offering the severest critique of any Australian film of the bush-nurtured ideal of mateship" ("Literary" 91). Distributors released the film adaptation of *Wake in Fright* under the title *Outback* in the U.S., explicitly aligning the landscape with horror.

There are many other texts that focus on the Australian landscape. For instance, Peter Brennan's novel *Razorback*, which was also made into a film, depicts a horrifying land in which a giant, vicious boar and depraved people attack American conservationists in the outback. Brennan makes much of the bleak landscape, with its "relentless, endless flatness" (99), its "flat and cracked" land (7). In the films *Rogue* and *Black Water*, the land is home to monstrous crocodiles. Small towns offer no escape in Australian horror films, even in dark comedies: car accidents become sinister (*The Cars That Ate Paris*) or meteorite showers and zombies bring "the beginning of the end ... [of] the world, the universe, everything" (*Undead*). The films *Wolf Creek, Gone, Prey*, and *Road Train* (*Road Kill* in its U.S. release) are thrillers about travelers terrorized in the outback, a lonely location where no help is available. *Wolf Creek*'s director, Greg McLean, has spoken about the influence of the film *Picnic at Hanging Rock* and his own intention to present the landscape in *Wolf Creek* as initially "picture postcard" then changing to a "cold, emotionless, natural world that doesn't care if you are dying" (18). He describes this transformation as a shift from characters watching the landscape to the land "observing us" (18). McLean has said that "Culturally, our relationship to the landscape, since the time we were dumped here, has always been one of battle and fear. We're constantly struggling to cut it down or change it, but we can't because it remains bigger than we are" (19).[3] The director of *Gone* describes the outback in stark terms as "so lonely and so brutal and unknowable.... It has such an otherworldly feel, it's so timeless and yet it does feel ominous at the same time" (qtd. in Sue Williams 18). *Gone*'s original title was *Middle of Nowhere*; *Road Train*'s trailer depicts expanses of the Australian desert with the words: "Across the vastness of the outback there roams a beast possessed by evil, fuelled by terror, hunting for prey." Another Australian horror film set in the desert, *Prey*, concerns six vacationing people who are terrorized in the outback, with dialogue that directly references fears of being lost in the desert: "People don't just vanish"/ "In the desert they do." Meanwhile, an Australian horror film from 1978, *Long Weekend*, depicted strange, menacing events in nature for a vacationing couple. *Long Weekend* was remade in 2008 with an American title release of *Nature's Grave*. Its tagline was "Mother nature has a dark side" (Australian release) and "Don't mess with Mother Nature" (U.S.). *Prey*, meanwhile, was re-titled *The Outback* in its U.S. release (similar to *Wake in Fright*'s U.S. title of *Outback*). There seems, therefore, to be a consistent approach to marketing Australian horror films in the U.S. to conflate horror and the outback or bush. Many films are promoted as based on real events (*Black Water, Prey, Rogue, Wolf Creek*). That tourists are usually the victims in such outback nightmares raises certain questions about who belongs in this vast landscape. In many of these films at least, the answer is that white tourists certainly do not. The outback becomes a repository for any number of natural and supernatural hostile forces. There are many literary and cinematic texts, then, which construct the Australian landscape as a character in its own right and a danger to the human world, and this chapter explores the *Mad Max* films in the context of this tradition.

The Mad Max *Films (1979–1985)*

Along with Nevil Shute's *On the Beach*, the *Mad Max* films are among the most well-known Australian apocalyptic texts internationally. The trilogy is set in the outback and offers a classic vision of a lawless future Australia, where traveling gangs terrorize and attack families and communities. Society is in chaos after apocalyptic oil wars, and law enforcement agencies are unable to stop the degeneration. The flat and empty landscape confronts viewers and offers characters no respite or escape from the violence of the villains, whose power reaches from town to outback via the roads. The land becomes another enemy, enclosing those who seek it as refuge or attempt to leave it, offering only punishment for its inhabitants. Characters often raise the question of the future, with the groups wanting a better existence traveling away from the dead heart toward the coastal cities in order to find a new world. However, the films often show that the ideals of these groups and their hopes of new life away from the interior are false, and the antihero, Max, remains in the punishing reality of the outback.

The *Mad Max* films are within a tradition of speculative fiction that constructs Australian landscape in apocalyptic terms while revealing a dystopian future by extrapolating current problems in society. The trilogy's narrative themes and depiction of landscape also exhibit influences of Biblical attitudes to land and society, attitudes that have in turn influenced views of Australia as an apocalyptic space. At times darkly comedic, at other times sober, the trilogy adopts the features of the apocalyptic paradigm — destruction, the promise of a new world, the language and imagery of Biblical discourse — but subverts each aspect, ultimately presenting an Australia that is as far from the apocalyptic ideal as possible.

Mad Max began as a small, independently financed film of relatively unknown director George Miller and producer Byron Kennedy, and starred the little-known Mel Gibson. Made for less than $400,000, Miller felt "dissatisfied" with it and "constrained by my inexperience and our small budget ... I honestly felt it was unreleasable" ("Directing" 286). Upon release, however, the film earned over $100 million worldwide. Despite its success, American audiences were less receptive of *Mad Max*, and its theater run was short and critical reception minimal. The dubbing of the Australian actors' voices with American ones may explain this; U.S. audiences were only able to view the original version with dubbed dialogue. Miller and Kennedy released a sequel, *Mad Max 2: The Road Warrior*, in 1981, and this second film proved enormously popular in the U.S. and elsewhere. After Kennedy's death, Miller made the third film, *Mad Max: Beyond Thunderdome*, with George Ogilvie and this second sequel was similarly successful.[4]

In the decades since its release, *Mad Max* has provoked critical responses ranging from outrage at its violence to favorable in-depth analyses of its cinematic and thematic merits. At the time of its release, film critics were often hostile. *The Bulletin*'s Phillip Adams, in particular, denounced the film for having "all the moral uplift of *Mein Kampf*" (38), warning that it "must surely promote violence" (41) because it would be "a special favorite of rapists, sadists, child-murderers" (38).[5] Tom O'Regan recalls thinking the film "evil" at his first viewing (126); while Meaghan Morris wrote that her reaction to the film's horrific scenes of the pursuit of Max's wife Jess prompted her to "flee the cinema" ("White Panic" n.p.). Since the initial reaction, however, *Mad Max* and its sequels have secured a more respectable standing in the critical establishment, although there is little consensus on their individual merits. For instance, while some critics have expressed outrage, Jon Stratton argues that the films are conservative (56).

Many critics have read the films as generic or universal rather than Australian. Sandra Hall was concerned that *Mad Max* did not show the "particularity of Australian culture and experience" (n.p.) and Adams agreed, arguing that the only reason *Mad Max* would not incite violence in Australia was because it is "unequivocally an off-shore American movie" (41). Readings of the films have often focused on their construction of masculinity and sexuality (Biber; Johinke; Sharrett) and heroism (M. Broderick; Barbour). Such critiques often locate the films as offering universal rather than local perspectives and themes, although Theodore F. Sheckels's essay on heroism considers whether or not the films display specifically

Australian features (36). Mick Broderick in particular has read the films in terms of a generalized religious and mythological apocalyptic background, in light of Joseph Campbell's schema of universal archetypes of heroism in *The Hero with a Thousand Faces* ("Heroic" 257). Miller himself has encouraged mythological readings of the films in many of his interviews, claiming that *Mad Max* has "universal" appeal because of its similarities to other countries' myths, such as Viking warriors or Japanese Samurai ("Apocalypse" 39–40), without anything "specifically Australian" ("Directing" 280).

In contrast to this, some commentators have identified the films as embodying uniquely Australian themes and concerns, including Australian gothic (Dermody and Jacka; O'Regan) and landscape (Falconer; Stratton; R. Gibson). Others dispute this: Roslynn D. Haynes, who discusses the Australian desert at length in her book *Seeking the Centre*, suggests that one cannot take the films seriously in their depiction of landscape, for "the *Mad Max* trilogy spoofs the obsessive, mythopoeic focus on the land throughout Australian literature and film, and the concurrent implication that the land determines narrative, character, ethos, national identity—everything" (194). Adrian Martin similarly rejects landscape readings of the film (68), emphasizing instead a focus on its visual action narrative (20–21). Miller's own assertion that the first film was "pure and simply a piece of visual rock and roll" ("Apocalypse" 39) partly supports Martin's view. Miller, however, has since become more interested in mythic readings and claims this as the reason that he and Kennedy made the second film ("Directing" 286). In my reading, however, the landscape of *Mad Max* has particular interest because of its representation in the films and its resonance with attitudes to land in other Australian apocalyptic texts.

Reactions to the third film show the spectrum of varying opinions. Ross Gibson considers it to have "grandeur" ("Yondering" 26) and American film critic Roger Ebert hails it as the finest of the trilogy, "one of the best films of 1985" and "a movie of great visionary wonders" (n.p.). Martin, on the other hand, calls it a "misstep" (73), accusing it of "pop zaniness" with an imported "rock culture [that] deranges the film" (71). The negative view of *Thunderdome* has tended to predominate, with commentators dismissing it as over-stylized (S. Hall), "turgid" (Kitson 200), and "vastly inferior" (Dillon 33). Yet even as critical reception and stylistic differences separate the films, taken as a whole they are useful to discuss in terms of their ideological and thematic content. Read apocalyptically, the trilogy's construction of nation and land represents another important facet of Australian apocalypse.

The *Mad Max* films preserve the literal meaning of apocalypse in that they function as revelation. As futuristic science fiction, the films operate as speculative tales that both reveal and warn of a possible future extrapolated from contemporary events. The first film opens with a road strewn with debris and the subtitles "A few years from now." It depicts a dystopian society in which law enforcement is crumbling while violent motorbike gangs terrorize people and battle with police on the roads. The voiceover that opens the second film narrates the world situation that led to the current society:

> Another time when the world was powered by the black fuel and the deserts sprouted great cities of pipe and steel. Gone now, swept away for reasons long forgotten, two mighty warrior tribes went to war and touched off a blaze which engulfed them all. Without fuel they were nothing. They built a house of straw. The thundering machines spluttered and stopped. Their leaders talked and talked and talked. But nothing could stem the avalanche. Their world crumbled. Cities exploded. A whirlwind of looting. A firestorm of fear. Men began to feed on men.

The voiceover accompanies black and white newsreel footage of traditional means of warfare such as troops streaming off boats and battleships typical of World War II. *Thunderdome* further elaborates on the back story, this time via character dialogue, and it becomes clearer that there was an event of catastrophic proportions that changed the world. Bartertown ruler Aunty refers to the historical background as "the day after" and children's leader Savannah recounts her tribe's version of the past: "I sees the end what were the start. It's Pox Eclipse full of pain. And out of it were birthed crackling dust and fearsome time. It were full on winter and Mr. Dead chasing 'em all."

The "day after" reference is suggestive of religious apocalyptic discourse, and in interview Miller has framed *Mad Max* in prophetic, extrapolative terms. When asked about the inspiration for the first two films, Miller denies a nuclear setting[6] and instead points to real events:

> I think that the films are somewhat allegorical in nature. The function of a storyteller should be to reveal truths about human nature through the depiction of people and their problems in a particular place and time.... I think both films have value in that they help us explore the darker, more unthinkable

side of ourselves. They serve as warning fables.... What triggered off the *Mad Max* stories was in fact the petrol rationing we had in Australia in the late Seventies.... I was really stunned by how readily the normal fabric of society can start to disintegrate when you remove something that is as essential as gas. Australia is not a violent society, at least not overtly violent, but it took only a week or so for this severe rationing to have people trying to jump queues, resorting to violence, and going at each other with guns — just to get enough gas to go to work that week. So when we started thinking of our back story to *Mad Max*, we simply postulated the kind of events that would result from removing one of the fossil fuels from the Earth ["Directing" 281].[7]

That Miller intends the films to "reveal truths" is clearly one function of apocalyptic discourse. The films are intentionally extrapolative and they speak against a certain kind of future possible from the real world. Miller estimates that the "few years from now" is roughly fifteen years from 1984 ("Directing" 280) and this places it in the late 1990s, close enough to the millennium to resonate with fin-de-siècle fears. Indeed, the oil wars have created a dire world in *Mad Max*. Fuel is the ultimate prize, and those who have access to it have freedom and power; those who do not either perish or struggle for it: "Only those mobile enough to scavenge, brutal enough to pillage, would survive. The gangs took over the highways, ready to wage war for a tank of juice" (*Warrior*). Gangs, communities and individuals fight over fuel, siphoning it from vehicle wrecks and guarding what they have with violence and ruthlessness. In the first two films, the Main Force Patrol police the highways against violent gangs and their leaders Toecutter (*Mad Max*) and the Humungus (*Warrior*), who scavenge crash sites and terrorize people. When Toecutter's gang murders Max's wife and child, Max wanders the desert alone, as if in punishment.

These films reject common science fiction depictions of a future world that is filled with advanced technologies and interstellar travel. Instead, they show an Australia that is hostile, unwelcoming and largely empty — an image that can represent the present or past as much as the future. The first film signposts this discrepancy when Max takes his family on a holiday after his resignation from the police force. As the family station wagon crosses the flat yellow landscape, the camera passes the painted panel on the wagon. The panel reveals a typical imagined future: the 1970s design with its glamorous blue and white moonscape environment, shooting stars over snowcapped mountains and a landing spaceship. This futuristic image of space travel and interplanetary wars is an ironic contrast to and comment on the "real" future world of *Mad Max* with its flat dry landscape of endless roads and relatively prosaic cars. Jameson points out that utopian dreams of a technological future are outdated anyway: "we no longer entertain such visions of wonder-working, properly 'science-fictional' futures of technological automation. These visions are themselves now historical and dated — streamlined cities of the future on peeling murals — while our lived experience of our greatest metropolises is one of urban decay and blight" (*Archaeologies* 286). The *Mad Max* films translate the "urban decay and blight" into the desert. These landscapes are not the usual visions of the science fiction futures, and the films undercut optimistic ways of viewing society's progress. Many filmmakers set their post-apocalyptic nightmares in the city and depict the urban world at its worst. One can easily transfer such dystopias from one city to another across the world. In the *Mad Max* trilogy, however, the audience rarely sees the city, for it belongs to the distant pre-disaster past. Urban skylines appear just twice: once in the early parts of the first film, where it is a gray and indistinct skyscraper-lined horizon in the far distance; and again in the closing of the third film, where the Sydney skyline is in ruins and buried under dust.

Instead, these films narrate a future Australia where the outback is the setting for apocalypse — in fact, the outback, the land, is apocalypse. Wagar writes that secularism comprises three attitudes to the natural world: nature is transcendent and to be worshipped; nature belongs to humans and is for their benefit — both of which constitute largely benign views of nature — or the third view, where nature is "indifferent to human aspiration, and wholly absorbed in her own mindless processes, which now and then casually lay waste to all that reason or goodness can fashion" (*Terminal* 86–87). This "casual" destruction is random. However, Australian fictions provide a fourth category to Wagar's attitudes, for they show a world where nature is hostile towards its inhabitants. In his discussion of the *Mad Max* films, Jon Stratton references Thomas Hobbes's theories on the State of Nature and the State of War where conflict is rampant and uncontained, and contrasts this to the State of Law, where systems of authority are in place: "It is this image which post-apocalypse films ... activate and utilise as their fundamentally dystopian social organising principle" (39). Hughes similarly links Hobbes and Australia in his work on Australia's history:

> The late eighteenth century abounded in schemes of social goodness thrown off by its burgeoning sense of revolution. But here, the process was to be

reversed: not Utopia, but Dystopia; not Rousseau's natural man moving in moral grace amid free social contracts, but man coerced, exiled, deracinated, in chains. Other parts of the Pacific, especially Tahiti, might seem to confirm Rousseau. But the intellectual patrons of Australia, in its first colonial years, were Hobbes and Sade [1].

Stratton points out that in *Mad Max* "the location of the city as the repository of the values of civilisation enables the Australian natural environment to be articulated as alien and destructive to civilisation" (41), and he calls this view a "suburban, European, perception which informs the articulation of the Australian environment as dry and equates that dryness with a moral drought" (46).

The negative constructions of Australian landscapes have their origins earlier than Hobbes's theories, however, for it is possible to see similar ideas in Biblical understandings of land. Biblical descriptions influence the association of the desert with a place of punishment, because the promised land prefigures the apocalyptic new world promised in Revelation and Isaiah. This promised place contrasts with the wilderness that was often a site of punishment and conflict, where physical location mirrors moral situation. This is an enduring theme throughout the Bible. Eden was an abundant garden; outside the garden, Adam lived in a place of "painful toil" and "thorns and thistles" (Genesis 3:17–18). The blessed and faithful people of God inhabit green lands of plenty — the Canaanite promised land of abundance, a "good and spacious land, a land flowing with milk and honey" (Exodus 3:8). God favors the promised place with water and produce and abundant life, "a land of mountains and valleys that drinks rain from heaven" (Deuteronomy 11:11). This land is vastly different to the desert, which is a cursed place: "the least of nations — [is] a wilderness, a dry land, a desert" (Jeremiah 50:12), it is a "barren wilderness ... a land of deserts and rifts, a land of drought and darkness, a land where no one travels and no one lives" (Jeremiah 2:6). The desert, then, in this discourse is an unfruitful place — even the end of all life — and a wasteland where nothing can live.

Secular thought about land often unconsciously imports these depictions, imagining verdant scenery as fruitful and fortunate and dry deserts as cursed places of death and exile, far from "home" and the promise of better lands. In Australia, a country of mostly desert environments, the similarities are stark. People often refer to the center of Australia — its "heart" — as the "red centre" or the "red heart," and the negative version of this has been the "dead centre" and the "dead heart," the "never-never" and "nothingness," a cursed place of punishment while hope for the future is away from the interior. There are not only religious associations with this depiction of the interior of Australia as a wasteland, but descriptions of Australia as "terra nullius" that signify a land of nothing also inform such images,[8] while Haynes points out that the Australian desert has also been called the "hideous blank" (36). There is a feeling of vacancy and depravity associated with the dead heart, while the cities on the edges of the continent represent vitality and life. A competing idea constructs the interior as a spiritual place, which Chapter Five discusses.

The films adopt an apocalyptic paradigm and Biblical language and imagery but then subvert these aspects, sometimes comedically, in order to suggest that the positive sense of apocalypse, the new world, does not apply in this future Australia. Instead, this is a hellish vision, an apocalypse without the promise of heaven. In the films, the town called Wee Jerusalem is far from a holy city of the chosen people and closer to a town of horror and terror (*Mad Max*). Graffiti on a truck warns the audience that not the meek but "the vermin have inherited the earth" (*Warrior*). The gang leader Nightrider derives his speeches from Biblical language, but distorts them into a road creed: "I am the Nightrider, I am the chosen one. The mighty hand of vengeance sent down to strike the unroadworthy" (*Mad Max*). In the second film, the leader of the gang is "The Lord Humungus" and his "dogs of war" accompany him and carry out his commands in the wasteland called the Valley of Death: "The Humungus will not be defied.... There has been too much violence, too much pain. None here are without sin" (*Warrior*). The Bible calls for people to turn to God to escape judgment in the apocalyptic final days; in the films the last days have already occurred and the judgment has taken place, leaving only chaos and hopelessness.

Mick Broderick has pointed out that the reference to the Humungus as the Ayatollah — an Islamic name — reinforces "the cultural amorality and 'otherness' of the marauders, since the Ayatollah epithet equates Islam as the terrible historical and contemporary foe of Western Judeo-Christian (significantly, petro-chemically dependent) capitalism" ("Heroic" 263). Broderick views Max as messianic ("Heroic" 259) because the apocalyptic discourse of the films invokes savior figure ideas by association. This is indisputable, yet the parallels are limited. Max does (unwillingly) facilitate the escape of the children and Northern Tribes to better lands, but he does not guide them nor lead by example, and his aid is limited and temporary and certainly local rather than universal. Although the children's tribe in the third film attempts to read Max as a savior figure, he bluntly disabuses them of this notion: "That ain't me. You got the wrong guy." These films construct the Australian "heart" as a place of irreligion and false gods with inverted religious symbols, where the land is a punishing force for those who live on it.

The *Mad Max* films reinforce their subversion of the apocalyptic paradigm by locating the future world in the wilderness, traditionally a place of punishment, while revealing fruitful coastal lands to be a false hope. Whether city or rural, outback or water, small town or desert, the land is always bleak and unpromising in the *Mad Max* films. The Australian nightmare in these films bypasses urban decay for rural horror, with an outback setting that is unique to the country. The desert wilderness of the outback has particular resonance in Australian fictions. Paul Williams suggests that one can understand the use of the desert in nuclear apocalyptic tales as "an expression of two converse impulses: the terrifying contemplation of the empty space of the world after nuclear war, and the exhilaration that this blank canvas is the stage for feats of adventure and heroism" (301). Exhilaration there is, yet also horror, for the films appear to engage in a particular Australian discourse that reveals paradise to be false, where the empty spaces are brutal.

Miller sets his films almost exclusively in rural surroundings, and it is a recognizable Australia with its settings of outback, desert, and small town. Popular culture has often constructed inland rural and outback locations as places of refuge and spiritual regeneration, but the films reject this notion, turning rural retreats into horrifying places. Brian McFarlane calls this a "duality — this awareness of menace as well as spectacular beauty" in which those unfamiliar with Australian landscapes, such as Europeans, can find the endless horizon "menacing in its dreary, monotonous emptiness" (*Australian Cinema* 70). McFarlane offers the landscape of *Wake in Fright* as an example, but one can equally apply his point to the *Mad Max* films. Characters find little comfort in the landscapes depicted in any of the films, no matter what the beauty. Morris calls *Mad Max* unprecedented because of its "convincing sense of spaces in which *anything might happen*" ("Fate" n.p.). She writes that there is a sense of "unpredictability" —

that is, not normal, not expected ("Fate" n.p.). Morris's use of "spaces" also suggests the concept of tabula rasa. The *Mad Max* films are futuristic tales and it might be expected that Miller can portray "anything" on what is, after all, a blank slate, but this is certainly a dystopian future.

Miller shot the films in Broken Hill, Coober Pedy, and outside Melbourne, and the majority of the featured landscape is flat and uninspiring, with fields or the desert stretching out to the horizon. A *Thunderdome* behind-the-scenes article published in 1985 suggested that the film contained universal archetypes "amid flat, unsignifying Australian expanses" (Loder 42) that allow the action to readily transfer between countries and cultures with little effect on meaning. Yet for an article claiming the universality of the location, the text is oddly intent on establishing the uniqueness of the Australian environment that makes it an ideal location for apocalypse. Even as the journalist insists that the setting is generic, he begins with several paragraphs detailing the extreme, harsh realities of that very land with its "lunar scrublands" and "broiling sun" (Loder 42):

> According to a sweat-dappled cook ... the actual temperature — *out there*, that is, under the brain-sizzling sun of South Australia — has got to be a good 125.... It is late November — summer in Australia — and the heat out here, 400 miles north of Adelaide and the nearest balmy coastline, is homicidal. So far today eight crew members have dropped from sunstroke and dehydration, and last night another camel died, joining two previously deceased beasts [40, 42]

He later discusses Coober Pedy, where Miller filmed much of *Thunderdome*, as a place where "after a while they [its inhabitants] may start acting rather strangely" (44). He quotes the location manager for *Thunderdome*, who recounts the story of a miner's failed attempt to kill his girlfriend: "'Coober Pedy,' says Mannix, 'is the perfect place for a Mad Max movie'" (44). Such commentary suggests that this landscape is not, after all, a generic, unsignifying space able to stand in for other places but instead is particular to Australia.

The representation of the Australian landscape as flat and empty changes somewhat in parts of the third film, when brilliant colors showcase a more obvious beauty in the landscape. The cinematography contrasts Max's flowing black robes against yellow sand dunes and pale blue horizons with night shots of midnight blue skies and white sand. A green and brown chasm called the "Crack in the Earth," a canyon of emerald rivers and chocolate walls where the lost children live, interrupts the endless yellow sand dunes. The colors, however, become chilling in the last scenes of *Thunderdome*, when spectacular red dusty cliffs turn out to be the empty bowl of Sydney Harbour, and the reddened Harbour Bridge is shown with an enormous gash in its middle, leaving only crumbling edges stretching out to nothingness. The children journey through the decaying crimson ruins of the cityscape to find shelter in the shell of a factory under a dark blue sky. It is a beautiful and chilling contrast to the earlier images of Sydney the children had admired. In the films, the contrasts and silhouettes provoke both admiration of and unease about the landscape: the camera silhouettes Max on the road or in the desert, and he becomes the dominant feature of the landscape because he is the last left standing after a road battle. The third film merely moves him from the endless roads to sand dunes that stretch out forever, a lone figure in the wilderness.

The *Mad Max* films remain among the most famous examples of Australian apocalypse. The desert is the setting for a post-apocalyptic wasteland that seems devoid of hope. Max (Mel Gibson). *Mad Max: Beyond Thunderdome*. Dir. George Miller and George Ogilvie. Warner Bros., 1985.

Max's exile in the outback reinforces a popular association of desert and judgment. The idea of Australia as a place of punishment reflects the origins of British Australia as a penal colony, where England might forget the nation's criminal inhabitants; prison films that directors have shot or set in Australia continue this association, even if indirectly (for example, *Escape from Absalom, Fortress, Ghosts ... of the Civil Dead, Turkey Shoot*). The depiction of the Australian landscape as harsh therefore aligns with the location of criminality and lawlessness; in a secular sense, the harsh continent was a deserved place for criminals. For instance, *Thunderdome* invokes penal colony associations when characters refer to the desert as the Gulag. When Max refuses to kill another character, Blaster, he must spin Aunty's "Wheel" to determine his punishment; when he spins "Gulag," Aunty's men tie him to a horse and leave him in the desert to die. The Gulag was the name for the Russian prison labor camps, and using the word for Max's punishment in the desert is apt in the schema of the films' construction of landscape, with links also to the early designation of Australia as a penal colony. Robert Hughes, for instance, has elsewhere suggested that the historical Gulag was a later version of the penal colony Australia (2). The construction of land and morality in the *Mad Max* films is why the Bartertown inhabitants, unlike the two tribes, can continue living in the outback: despite Aunty's rhetoric, the film clearly constructs them as amoral. Their way of life corresponds to the scavenging lifestyle that the landscape makes necessary. The Australian space encourages the very lifestyle that society disdains: violence and fighting for survival. It is not a land of plenty but of little.

In *South of the West*, Ross Gibson argues that the films' use of "the old myths of outback purgatory" is ironic rather than serious, for the trilogy treats the land with a "comic book aesthetic" (77) and constructs the land as a "respectable" force, "something to be learned from" rather than "an obstacle to be subdued" (17). Yet even as we can see dark comedy and lighthearted exuberance in parts of the trilogy, it seems an oversight to dismiss the importance of landscape entirely in the films as others have done. The *Mad Max* films do demonstrate ongoing interest in the physical setting. For instance, characters in *Thunderdome* call the interior of Australia "the nothing" and those who venture out into it are unlikely to survive, "swallowed by the sand" instead. The outback becomes a vacuum for its inhabitants who risk their lives on the endless sand dunes, for it devours its victims — horses, children — in quicksand, if the saturating heat and sandstorms have not destroyed them first. There is nothing here for the future of society in *Mad Max*, and people can only find hope elsewhere, as far from the dead heart as possible. Both communities in *Warrior* and *Thunderdome* want to escape this nothingness, to leave the outback for the outer edges of the continent to find the promised land. The Northern Tribe community in *Warrior* lives in a desert fortress of an oil refinery and is under siege from the Humungus, with little chance of escape. Their plan is to travel north to the idyllic beaches of Queensland's Sunshine Coast, as seen on a postcard. The children's tribe is also in a desert prison, because the harsh and dangerous outback region effectively limits them to their small oasis, and their future depends on their leaving the desert for the east coast, to Sydney. A Northern Tribe member unfolds a postcard concertina of familiar images: yellow beaches, blue skies, turquoise waters, girls in bikinis. The postcard reads Sunshine Coast and the man outlines its attractions as "plenty of sunshine, fresh water and nothing to do but breed," while the children view old pictures of the beautiful Sydney skyline and dream of living there. These two tribes who represent the future can begin their reconstruction of society only after leaving the desert wilderness for more plentiful, fruitful lands on the coast. Much of this bears very close similarities to Old Testament accounts of the Israelites' time in the desert wilderness until God judged them fit to occupy the promised land.

The trilogy therefore appears to be espousing an apocalyptic discourse that promises the hope of paradise. Yet each time the films evoke these promises, they undercut them. For instance, in *Thunderdome*, the Bartertown sign insists that the outpost is actually fulfilling an apocalyptic ideal: "Helping Build a Better Tomorrow!" and the leader of Bartertown, Aunty, outlines her future ideals to Max as she shows him the town she has built: "All this I built.... Where there was desert, now there's a town. Where there was robbery there's trade. Where there was despair, now there's hope. It's civilization and I'll do anything to protect it. Today it's necessary to kill a man." Aunty's ideals of trade and "civilization" take place within a violent regime, and her approach contrasts with the children's desire to find Tomorrow-morrow Land, which is the city Sydney.

The communities' desire to escape the barren landscape of the interior — characters call it a "wasteland" — in order to start anew appears to indicate a better world is possible after destruction. These examples suggest that the films are operating within an apocalyptic framework that pictures the fruitful land as the future, but the *Mad Max* films ultimately reject the promise of a new world by suggesting that the only reality is the desert wilderness while the coastal perfection is a false illusion. Characters talk of going to the Tropics to recover, and Max takes his family on a road trip away from the horrors of his job, but no respite is offered anywhere (*Mad Max*). Max tells the children "there's no Tomorrow land," and their journey reveals their hope to be a false dream with the paradise vision of Sydney reduced to dusty ruins (*Thunderdome*). The characters dream of the ideal, but it remains inaccessible. The films never show the idylls that characters dream about; instead, the focus is on the wilderness. There is a sense that these characters cannot escape the despair and flatness that marks so much of this world; the horror has permeated city, outback, beach and town, and any dreams of hope elsewhere are false.

In the hostile environment of the outback, the "nothing," it is Max and Aunty who are most at home. Arguably the characters with the least heroic qualities (Aunty is a villain; Max has abandoned heroism), these characters are both called "nothing" as well. Aunty asks Max: "Do you know who I was? Nobody. Except on the day after, I was still alive. This nobody had a chance to be somebody" (*Thunderdome*). Morris has pointed out the distinction between the names Aunty Entity (something) and Savannah Nix (nothing), arguing that it represents their essential opposition: "Nix is to Entity as white is to black, innocence to sophistication, idealism to pragmatism, memory to forgetfulness" ("White Panic" n.p.). Morris argues that Aunty Entity represents the "black ruler in the Outback, 'in the place' of the Aboriginal women" ("White Panic" n.p.). Although this may seem to read too much into the names, Morris's analysis is worth closer attention, for the names and roles of Aunty and Savannah offer a rich contrast.

The oppositions are there between Aunty and Savannah, yet there are several issues that confuse clear distinctions, with implications for Aboriginality and the Australian space. "Aunty"— played by the American Tina Turner — is a traditional designation for an Australian Indigenous woman, a wise, older woman. However, Aunty's role as Bartertown's leader places her in the heart of commercial enterprise, traditionally seen as white space. Savannah, meanwhile, is white, but she is the leader of the children's tribe and guardian of the oral tradition, which places her closer to an idea of

Aboriginality than Aunty's character, removing Aunty from that position. Furthermore, characters always refer to her as Aunty never as Entity; only the credits list her as Aunty Entity. The potential for Aunty to infer Anti-/Anti-Entity = negative/nothing is thus clear.[9] Aunty's designations as either "Nobody," Anti, or Anti-Entity reveal her lack of real identity, particularly given her proximity to the desert, "the nothing." Robert Dixon writes that the desert was a site of production for the new nation's identity (63), but as a "nameless blank" the interior reflected fears that the Australian identity might also be nothing compared to its English heritage (72). Dixon argues that this fear is present in the early lost race romance genre, which reflects "an anxiety that English identity will be lost in Australia; that the unformed identity of White Australia will be absorbed by the hostile land and its savage inhabitants" (66). In the *Mad Max* films, the desert is a nothing and those who live there also have no real identity.

Importantly, characters call Savannah by her first name, never Savannah Nix or Nix. Again, it is only in the credits that her name is given as Savannah Nix. The two characters are indeed opposites, but it seems that a reverse reading of Morris's binary oppositions may perhaps be even more intriguing. Savannah is the leader of the future hope in the ruins of Sydney; the films allow her to be "somebody"—but only outside the desert. The name Savannah itself reinforces this, for it describes a plain with grass and trees, particularly in tropical regions (savanna/savannah), contrasting with the dry desert of Aunty's home. While one might assume the name Savannah Nix signifies "no savanna," the apparent allusion to Savannah in terms of fruitfulness is reinforced in the closing scenes of the third film that show her holding a baby.[10]

The people, then, who belong in this harsh land are those who are "nothing" while the "fruitful" belong elsewhere, in the more abundant promised land. It is not only Aunty who is "nobody" but also Max: "Ain't we a pair, raggedy man." The trilogy increasingly diminishes Max's identity. In the first film, the camera in the opening scenes painstakingly establishes Max as a unique, dominant figure, interspersing shots of his boots, his hands, and so on, before finally showing his face. Yet in *Warrior*, Pappagallo calls him "nothing," someone who is "out there with the garbage," and by *Thunderdome* Max has become "the man with no name." The children claim that he is the "somebody" they have been waiting for, but Max says "That ain't me." When another character, Pig Killer, asks him, "What are you laying for?" Max answers, "Nothing." To Pig Killer's "Who are you?" Max's response is brief: "Nobody."

The exodus of Savannah (somebody) to the outskirts of Australia (Tomorrow land) while Aunty and Max (nobody) remain in the desert (the nothing) is appropriate. The constant negations of heroism, hope, utopia and future in the films consistently undercut the apocalyptic desire for a better place. Marlene Goldman writes that Canadian authors of apocalypse reject the notion of home, preferring the empty space of "placelessness" to the confining boundaries of place: "Indeed, rather than accept the myth of apocalypse, its distinction between the elect and the non-elect, and its promise of the New Jerusalem, which, translated into secular terms, often entails embracing exclusionary and violent forms of nationalism, many ex-centric Canadian authors champion, instead, what might best be described as placelessness and drifting" (165). Goldman refers to a Canadian short story where a character "chooses namelessness, placelessness, and drifting over stasis and identity" (166), but we can read her comments in terms of other postcolonial nations. In a similar way, the repeated notions of "nothingness" and void may suggest a feature of Australian apocalyptic discourse where texts simply reject debates over nation and identity in favor of non-identity.

Fittingly for a "nobody," Max is virtually mute, rarely saying anything throughout the three films. Max's extremely minimal dialogue is in contrast to the speeches and incessant monologues from the leaders of each of the tribes. Pappagallo, Aunty, Savannah and the gang leaders all deliver speeches, each presenting a different vision of the future. Pappagallo — whose name is Italian for "parrot," as Dermody and Jacka note (177) — talks about rebuilding the future, Aunty promotes commercial enterprise, the gang leaders preach domination, and Savannah repeats oral histories. Language, then, is highly significant in that characters use it to articulate their plans for the post-apocalyptic future. Importantly, Max's silence represents his own repeated rejections of future hope. Other characters mock the leaders who talk, and by implication their utopian ideals for the new world as well: Pappagallo's speeches are "Words! Just words!" while the two groups who initiated the original oil wars simply "talked — and talked — and talked" with no result whatsoever (*Warrior*). The implication is that future ideals — apocalyptic hopes — are mere words, not grounded in reality, and cannot be taken seriously.

The connections between tabula rasa, the desert as "the nothing" and those who live in it as "nobody" are significant, critiquing the apocalyptic ideal of a home that is secure and fruitful and implying home is elsewhere. There is an apparent nostalgia in the films for European civilization, and this suggests discomfort with the notion that Australia is "home." For many British settlers and subsequent generations, England remained Home; there was a sense that Australia could never be their true place of belonging. Jameson has suggested that cinematic re-creation of past styles and imagery can provoke a nostalgia in the viewer for the (film's representation of the) past, even if that representation of history is far from reality (*Postmodernism*). The *Mad Max* trilogy's use of medievalism and language demonstrates nostalgia for the European traditions that exist outside Australia. Neo-medieval weapons and instruments of torture are common in the films and Miller has acknowledged that the films are "more medieval than futuristic" ("Directing" 281). The juxtaposition of medievalism with outback Australia suggests a desire for a past that the country did not have, importing an "alien" society into a landscape as unlike the stereotypes of medievalism as possible.

In the third film, the children's exodus from the desert to the outskirts of Australia is an expression of the discomfort felt in this alien landscape and the desire to leave "the nothing" to find a place where they belong. The children want to go "home" and the final scenes of *Thunderdome* particularly emphasize this theme when the children dutifully repeat a gramophone French lesson that includes the phrase *Je vais chez moi*—"I am going home." This is in contrast to the children's heavily stylized speech patterns: "Some had got the luck and it leads them here. One look and they's got the hots for it. They word it 'Planet Earth'" (*Thunderdome*). The children, who presumably represent and embody the future of this fictional Australia, appear to abandon their peculiar speech for the civilized French language on their way out of the desert to their new "home."

The most incongruous aspect of this sense of displacement is *Thunderdome*'s apparent positioning of the children as indigenous to Australia. Delia Falconer suggests that the children are "marked as 'indigenous' by a pastiche of 'native' dress styles and rituals" (39). As Adrian Martin points out, this "evokes a cultural commentator's worst nightmare of white Aboriginality" (70). This may overstate the conscious use of Indigeneity — the stereotypes may simply be from any "lost civilization" narrative, and are similar to the lost boys of *Hook* and *Peter Pan*, for example — but the evidence is there. Any nostalgia on the part of the "Indigenous" children for a European language or home therefore seems a strange choice for the filmmakers, yet it is apparent in the children's desire to escape their desert wilderness for the city, and the French speaking lessons they repeat on the way there. That the "Indigenous" tribe of children leave their home for the culture and technologies of the city while learning a new language on the way may suggest that European influences are erasing and replacing the children's Indigeneity, if it can be called that. Yet the film shows the tribe maintaining its oral tradition, and Savannah's voiceover at the conclusion of *Thunderdome* retains the tribal children's language patterns.

There is only a negligible Indigenous presence in the films, the group most at "home" in Australia.[11] The use of "tribe" to describe the various groups of people in the films invokes Indigenous associations, but all the tribes are far from Aboriginality. The narrator of *Road Warrior* talks of the "two mighty warrior tribes" who initiated the apocalyptic destruction against a montage of European and Western war footage scenes. The Great Northern Tribe members are all white people who wear white clothes. The children's tribe members call themselves "The Waiting Ones" and are listed in the credits as The Tribe Who Left and The Tribe Who Stayed. Again, this "tribe" is all white.

Paul Williams questions readings of *Thunderdome* that view the film as racist, arguing that there is an imperial narrative in the film that reworks traditional constructions, "undermining the claims of colonization, imperialism, and the civilizing mission" (307), because Aunty, a black female, defies "European colonial projects" by creating a civilization (304):

> Max, white and male, leads an uprising of indigenous and working-class peoples against Aunty Entity, the success of which leaves some ambiguity surrounding the film's depiction of the imperial narrative. Audiences cheering the victory of those whose race and gender fits the ideological project of the European empires are also celebrating the collapse of the ideals of civilization and colonial urbanization [312].

Yet Indigenous representations do appear to be stereotypical. The second film perhaps intends the Feral Kid to represent Indigeneity, although Williams at least considers his "racial identity" to be ambiguous, albeit "racially Other" (310–11). Stratton calls the Feral Kid "the focal point of the film's mythic resolution," bridging the differences between "the white, alien, and the Aboriginal, natural harmony" (51). Because the Feral Kid wears animal skins and is able to use his environment for attack and defense, Stratton suggests that he participates in "a modern discourse of Aborigines which places them as being at one with nature" (49); the Kid unites the natural world with the mining one of the Tribe in several ways, by using a boomerang made of metal (50), and by becoming the eventual (Indigenous) leader of the Northern Tribe (51). Stratton's argument brings up two issues. *Warrior* depicts the Feral Kid as akin to his natural environment, but he is also ignorant of the world outside his own environs. These are two common stereotypical conceptions of Indigenous culture: naïveté about the (white) world and unity with nature. Both are present in the films. The stereotypes reappear in the third film, where the tribal children's ignorance of the world and their daily ritualistic "Tells" are contrasted to Max's worldly knowledge, and their outside habitat positions them as presumably close to nature. Despite this, the children are not attuned to the elements — though they ought to be, having lived outside all their lives — instead, it is again Max whose greater knowledge protects and guides them through the dangerous land. Max is, of course, white.

Even while the *Mad Max* films reject apocalyptic ideals of a new world and a secure, fruitful "home" there appear to be attempts to portray the interior as a place of redemption that may eventually lead to the promised land. *Warrior*'s introduction describes Max as "a man who wandered out into the wasteland. And it was here in this blighted place that he learned to live again." Yet characters do not find hope for the future in the outback and desert; in spite of the occasional comedic elements, it is largely a place of despair. Max does not learn to "live again"; his brief moments of humanity, seen mostly in *Thunderdome* in his refusal to kill Blaster and his aid of the children, do not restore him or reintroduce him to society. Instead, he remains on the outside. Gibson suggests that Max's character has made progress and adapted to the Australian environment: "He is learning, and adapting ... he has given up trying to police the continent, trying to coerce it to his law.... Now Max is simply moving with the continent, reading it a little more cannily, growing from it" ("Yondering" 32). Gibson also argues that Max is becoming interested in life again, evidenced in his asking Pig Killer as they leave Bartertown, "What's the plan?" ("Yondering" 32).

The film's conclusion might offer hope for the future for the children, but Max remains outside their utopian hope, doomed to walk an inhospitable land. It is the new generation who must lead the way forward, and find their place in the world, although it is clearly as far from the reality of the Australian outback as possible. Whatever Max's involvement with any community in the films, it is short-lived. Max continues to exist disconnected. Significantly, Max chooses to remain a wanderer in the desert while others abandon it for the future society. He does not return to the continent edges, remaining inland and alone, last seen journeying further into the dead heart, and the three films end by abandoning Max in the desert to his self-imposed exile.

The trilogy's conclusion in this way thus engages in the apocalyptic discourse that positions Australia and the outback landscapes in particular as places of punishment, lawlessness and exile, while hope and civilization are always elsewhere. The films articulate and then subvert apocalyptic desires for a new world, suggesting that if there is one, it is away from the Australian landscape, and negating even that hope by showing that those other places also offer only disillusion. The representation of the outback as "the nothing," a "wasteland," and "blighted place" reflects the theme that the desert wilderness is a place of punishment that will always be outside the fruitful land promised to the faithful.

These ideas are not unique to *Mad Max*, however, for uncertainties over national identity, "belonging" and Indigeneity recur regularly in Australian fictions. In the next chapter, I explore how children's literature from the last few decades appropriates these very ideas in order to re-formulate and re-state an apocalyptic discourse about Australia.

• Four •

Children of the Apocalypse
Australian Children's Literature

> For some years now the city had been tossing up this small tide of human flotsam, wide-eyed youngsters who roamed the hills for a while, sick with fever, some doomed to die ... their numbers were perilously small.
> Lee Harding, *Waiting for the End of the World* 31–32

One might not expect that apocalypse would be a popular theme in children's fiction, yet a glance at Australian adolescent literature and television reveals a considerable proportion of dystopian and apocalyptic works. Adolescent apocalyptic novels position the child in danger where young heroes are away from their families, often forming "lost tribes" with other children who are hiding in bushland and fighting for survival after a disaster, much like the children's tribe in *Mad Max: Beyond Thunderdome*. This chapter explores apocalypse in children's literature with reference to literary attitudes to children, nature and dystopia. Examinations of works by Lee Harding, Victor Kelleher, and John Marsden then focus on how these writers adapt apocalyptic themes for a juvenile audience. Their novels display tyranny, large-scale catastrophe, invasion, and children in danger, and their apocalyptic settings reveal anxieties about isolation, invasion, Indigenous land rights and colonization.

Children and Nature

Romantic ideas about childhood construct children as "innocent and pure, close to nature" (Hintz and Ostry 6). Noga Applebaum notes that "the persistent bias towards nature and against technology in Young SF sheds light on the extent to which the myth of the innocent child still influences adult ideas on childhood" (19).[1] While this chapter explores how Australian texts frequently reject such Romantic ideals, it is worth noting that some Australian children's fictions do celebrate nature as opposed to the dangers of the city. For example, in Joan Phipson's 1978 novel *Keep Calm*, widespread strikes over a proposed nuclear reactor leave Sydney "vulnerable" (61), a "waking nightmare" (60), a menacing place where beneath the façade of order lies ready chaos — "it's nothing but an eggshell we're living on" (166). Nature, in contrast, is solid and dependable, and represents a haven for those who can escape the city: "sky, trees, earth beneath the feet. Space. Things to rely on" (76). Indeed, nature overpowers the city when animals and birds take over the empty city buildings, as if the wildness of nature ultimately outlives and overcomes civilization and all its markers (skyscrapers, architectural landmarks). When humans leave, Sydney has a "new population of animals and birds" (142), and city parks, which surely represent enforced human control and European designs on a wild environment, will become chaotic again:

> Nothing had altered in the park.... Except that the gardeners were gone, too, and slowly, ineluctably, the grass was growing longer and weeds were springing up unchecked ... with no one to guide it, to restrain its exuberance, the grass would soon grow long and rank, the roses would be smothered, and in time, as birds and the wind dropped seeds, gum trees would grow again. Trees from other lands, lacking water, would die and the gum trees would take over. The park would become what it had been before — coastal scrub [118].

Here nature is recognized as a dominant force, and the Australian ecosystem in particular can re-assert itself against an imposed European order.

For other authors, the Australian natural environment is both to be feared and admired. Lucy Christopher's *Stolen*, published in 2009, uses the Australian outback as an alternatively menacing and restorative space that imprisons its teenaged protagonist, who is kidnapped and held captive in the interior, effectively lost to those who seek her.[2] The British teenaged protagonist, Gemma, is kidnapped by an Australian boy, Ty, who holds her captive in a remote location in the Australian outback. Christopher's work conflates Ty and outback, so that Gemma's attitude to both man and landscape undergoes a shift from hatred of a hostile, inexplicable entity to a more nuanced understanding and appreciation of a beautiful, powerful force. Again, we see a dual vision of a menacing beauty, a dangerous attraction. Gemma's growing appreciation for the landscape is far less problematic than her love/hate relationship with her kidnapper, which becomes the focal point of the text. This duality is neatly summed up near the end of the novel in words that also recall the common theme of vanishing in the desert: "It's a place for disappearing, you'd said, a place for getting lost ... and for getting found" (298).

Still other authors interrogate the Romantic idea of a special kinship between children and nature and instead represent the landscape as a hostile place rather than home for children. Maureen Nimon and John Foster suggest that in early Australian adolescent fiction "the land itself was frequently the antagonist" (45). This perhaps reflects and refines the myth of the hostile Australian landscape, discussed in Chapter Three, where children in particular are the victims of a harsh environment. Australian culture is replete with tales of lost children in the outback or the bush, from the schoolgirls who vanish in *Picnic at Hanging Rock* to the widely reported real-life case of the baby Azaria Chamberlain, apparently the victim of dingoes in the desert. Peter Pierce's work in particular explores the idea of Australia as "the place where the innocent young are most especially in jeopardy" (xi).[3] For Pierce, the recurring image of lost children is particular to Australia and a source of anxiety for society. He suggests that the endurance of the missing child tradition reveals an acute Australian fear: the unease of European settlers about having to "settle in a place where they might never be at peace" (xii). Robert Holden has also described the Australian imagination as rife with anxiety over children: "The folklore was thus engendered by fear for the safety of the settlers' children and uncertainty as to their relationship with an alien, unforgiving land — one which seemed to demand and then extract sacrifice" (61). The idea of missing children is especially haunting because culturally children represent the future, and if they are in constant danger or even vanish then the outlook for the nation is bleak. This is particularly true in colonized nations such as Australia that the European imagination views as "young" because of their lack of white history and subsequent emphasis on the future. Gerry Turcotte argues that "for some [critics], since Australia had no history to speak of, one needed to celebrate its future potential" ("Australian Gothic" 11). Pierce's point about the anxiety over disappearing children in Australia is therefore even more significant. In this way, then, Australian texts counteract traditional depictions of children. Nature is often a dangerous place for humans rather than a safe refuge, particularly for children, who are not quite at home there.

Dystopia and Children's Literature

Dystopia is a common choice for children's writers internationally, with just some of the more recent examples including Suzanne Collins's *The Hunger Games*, Jeanne DuPrau's *The City of Ember*, and Patrick Ness's *The Knife of Never Letting Go*, and their sequels.[4] Elizabeth Braithwaite notes that many dystopias for children emerged during the Cold War and focused on nuclear fears, while contemporary examples imagine different scenarios such as environmental disasters (50). In an essay surveying contemporary young adult disaster literature, Patty Campbell suggests that the end of the world is a fitting metaphor for adolescence with its end of childhood and changing boundaries (634). This is a point taken up by Carrie Hintz and Elaine Ostry, who note that while utopia characterizes children's literature, young adult fiction uses dystopia because it is "a powerful metaphor for adolescence" (9). Heather Scutter argues that dystopia is "especially suited to an adolescent audience because it meshes so well with hostility to the perceived adult version of the world. It is often full of disgust at the way things are, and charged with an overweening idealism as to the way things might be" ("Billabong" 30). This idealism means that dystopian children's literature will often have a political agenda as they "predict the overthrow of our way of life through socioeconomic breakdown" (Esmonde 212).

Dystopian settings or elements occur in many works of children's writers in Australia.[5] John Stephens (126) and Heather Scutter (*Displaced* 35) have each noted that there is a very high number of dystopian, apocalyptic works for children in Australia (126),[6] while Maurice Saxby attributes the rise of dystopias to the bleak spirit of the 1980s, a time that Scutter has called the "Decade of Dystopia" ("Billabong" 30). Scutter argues that dystopian speculative fiction "seems almost to have died out in the 1990s" to be replaced by post-disaster realist novels (*Displaced* 33). In contrast, however, Bradford, Mallan and Stephens label the 1990s as a time of a "dystopian turn" in Australian children's literature (359), when authors began to "'write back' against the colonial ethos" (350). Indeed, colonialism is addressed in each of the novels discussed later.

Australian authors choose a variety of settings for their dystopias. Some writers draw from science fiction, such as Paul Collins's *The Earthborn Wars* series; others utilize cyber elements, as in Gillian Rubinstein's *Space Demons*, *Skymaze*, and *Shinkei*; and some use fantasy elements, including Richard Harland's *Heaven and Earth* trilogy and Patricia Wrightson's *The Ice Is Coming*. Such works have different themes ranging from alienation (Lee Harding's *Displaced Person*), nuclear issues (Phipson's *Keep Calm*, Rubinstein's *Beyond the Labyrinth*), war and violence (Peter McFarlane's *The Enemy You Killed*), and totalitarian regimes (Penny Hall's *The Paperchaser* and *The Catalyst*). Yet despite their differences, these novels typically feature the adolescent characters confronting corrupt adult governments or systems in order to bring about a more positive world, and they must learn to question what they are told (Jill Dobson's *The Inheritors*).

Many of these novels are didactic. Children often travel through time to a future world and witness a post-apocalyptic future, as in Caroline Macdonald's *The Eye Witness* and Harding's *The Web of Time* or television programs such as *Thunderstone*, *Quest Beyond Time*, and *The Girl from Tomorrow: Tomorrow's End*. The experience changes the protagonists and they return to their time and vow to play their part in building a better society. The popularity of the time travel motif may suggest authorial reluctance to permanently situate their child protagonists in a bad society; time travelers have an escape clause. While some of these texts depict the post-apocalyptic society as utopian or preferable to the world of the time-traveling protagonist (for example, *Thunderstone* and *Quest Beyond Time*), usually the future society is far worse (*The Eye Witness*, *The Web of Time*).

While there are many apocalyptic Australian children's fictions, not all are relevant for the purposes of this book. Several authors use the apocalyptic mode, such as Isobelle Carmody's *Scatterlings* and *The Obernewtyn Chronicles*, Patricia Bernard's *The Outcast Trilogy*, Macdonald's *The Lake at the End of the World*, and Kelleher's *The Makers* and *Parkland*, but they do not use a specifically Australian setting, so their novels do not meet the parameters for case studies outlined in this book. The case studies here include Harding's *Waiting for the End of the World*, Kelleher's *Taronga* and *Red Heart*, and Marsden's *Tomorrow, When the War Began* series. The authors of these novels portray dystopian settings and use apocalyptic imagery and religious references to describe a future Australia. Each author uses a recognizably Australian location, and these works reveal a perspective of Australia where the nation is vulnerable to outside attack as well as to hostile forces within, although the authors adopt different stances on these issues.

There are several points to make here that recur across all case studies, and they relate to the adventure romance and uncanny. These apocalyptic novels interrogate notions of colonization, belonging, and identity. In many ways, they display — and either reinforce or reject — particular colonial motifs. Chapter One discussed Robert Dixon's analysis of nineteenth-century adventure texts, and one can trace the themes in these adolescent novels back to that genre. Dixon argues that the adventure story, in its various incarnations of the invasion narrative or the lost race tale, revealed anxieties about national identity and gender. By World War I, the adventure story appeared to have lost its potency as society questioned the morality of imperialism and its unequal trade relationships, resulting in the possibility of the genre's "collapse" due to a "profound malaise in imperialism" (179). Dixon suggests that adventure stories have resilience, and that to predict the genre's end "seriously under-estimates the capacity of adventure and masculinity — and indeed imperialism — to renew themselves in the twentieth century" (190). He notes, too, that a major factor in the way the genre revitalizes itself is through violence (190). This is a key point here because of the way the writers of these children's novels often link violence with colonization. The anxieties about invasion and white identity that Dixon describes have emerged a century later into much of the apocalyptic speculative fiction for children.

The novels discussed here are also preoccupied with questions of legitimacy. Each text interrogates the notions of home and belonging in a post-apocalyptic Australian setting, particularly in the context of imperialism and Indigeneity. Here we can refer back to the intersections between postcolonial concerns, the gothic and the uncanny, as described in Chapter One. Turcotte argues the uncanny corresponds to postcolonial issues because of its "emblematic articulation" of "fears about settlement, dispossession, miscegenation, and contamination ... the uncanny is frequently produced as and by a crisis of (il)legitimacy — engendering stories which agonize over the right of belonging to an invaded space" ("Fearful Calligraphy" 124–25).

In these case studies from children's literature, feelings of alienation and displacement haunt the protagonists because recognizing an Indigenous presence diminishes their sense of belonging in Australia. The novels negotiate these issues in different ways by either expressing ambivalence to white inhabitation or asserting the characters' right to be there. The preoccupation with these dilemmas in these texts suggests that questions of national identity simmer in even the nation's literature for children.

Lee Harding: Waiting for the End of the World *(1983)*

In *Waiting for the End of the World,* Harding adopts the apocalyptic framework of future disaster and suggests that catastrophe potentially clears the way for a better world. Harding's work engages with Indigenous issues by insisting that white inhabitants are outsiders who have wrongfully colonized Australia. Yet his use of British ghosts complicates this anti-colonial discourse by suggesting that white people do in fact legitimately belong in Australia.

In *Waiting,* oppressive and violent authorities control citizens in a fortified city in a future Australian setting. Wars before a period called the Darkness have left a "world faced with economic ruin" (22) where children dream of a coming "holocaust" (165) and the "long dark" (136). It is a world where "kids don't count for much any more" (28). The rulers feed citizens information and censored versions of history via "the video." Nimon and Foster suggest that recent Australian adolescent literature shows "a greater willingness to admit to ambiguity, complexity and uncertainty in regard to determining notions of truth and justice" (52); they also note that some overseas publishers have rejected Australian texts for children because of their apparently subversive attitude towards authority (41). Like many other adolescent novels, Harding's work suggests that those in authority cannot be trusted: "The government only makes available to us those portions of the past that have been rewritten and approved. History is now more a lie than was ever imagined in the past" (176). As one character claims:

> They've been getting away with it for years. Imagine! pumping the water full of all kinds of drugs — drugs to make you calm when you're not, drugs to

make you feel well when you'd rather feel rotten ... they also dose the water with contraceptives, to make sure the population remains stable. Don't look so surprised! How else do you think they keep everything under control? By keeping people drugged, *that's* how. Things must have been in a bad way last century, if we're to believe what the video tells us. But people in the city, they're not bothered by the problems that plagued our ancestors. No disputes, no unrest, no protests and no terrorism — well, hardly any. That depends on how much you believe out of what they feed us... [27–28].

Scutter notes that "adults are expressly regarded as the cause of the catastrophe" in children's literature (*Displaced* 33), a theme that is common in each of the novels discussed in this chapter. Kay Sambell suggests that children's dystopias "force readers to think carefully about where supposed 'ideals' may really lead, underlining the point that these hugely undesirable societies can and will come about, unless we learn to question the authority of those in power" (248). Hintz and Ostry have argued that such novels are therefore "subversive" because of their critique of adults and society (8). Ann McGuire points out that dystopian adolescent fiction allows "young readers to 'see' some of the inadequacies of their own culture" (5), a remark that suggests the affinity of this literature with apocalypse, given the common interest in revealing new perspectives and critiquing social problems. Yet most apocalyptic texts are more interested in the dystopia than imagining a utopia; as Patricia Kennon argues, young adult dystopias actually show a "deep ambivalence" about the possibilities for change (40).

Waiting is certainly ambivalent about the likely success of making positive changes in society, suggesting that escape rather than revolution is the solution to oppression. The protagonist Manfred leaves the city when his father dies, joins a group of outcasts led by adults Fergus and Sally, and the group scatters after Patrol officers attack and burn their safe house. The only course of action in the novel is escape. Yet the novel ends with the implication of utopia as Manfred and his companions journey further inland to Killara in a bid for freedom in a new world away from the city. While others claim Killara is a lie (192), Fergus describes it as a refuge, a paradise secure from outside threat, in language that evokes the allure of the promised land:

> Up there, somewhere, was a valley such as one usually dreams about. Well sheltered, as I remember. In some ways, a natural fortress. And the people who lived there, they weren't disagreeable and desperate.... No, they lived at peace with their surroundings and in harmony with the seasons. In those

days, there was no need for them to fear the Patrol. I fancy it would be the same today [177].

Waiting asserts the fulfillment of the apocalyptic paradigm: the hope of restoration follows destruction. Indeed, Harding suggests that apocalyptic destruction can be a positive event: "fire was not only a destroyer ... the fire, that was so essential for the survival of the golden wattle, would also encourage another kind of germination in the soul of human kind" (205).

Harding's novel is of particular interest because of its ongoing preoccupation with the notion of England as home, a theme that displays underlying ambivalence to white existence in Australia. Nimon and Foster note that culturally there exists "a tension between the home at hand and the home far distant [England] which non–Aboriginal Australians mentally inhabit" (29). In *Waiting*, England is "home" for Manfred, who hides from reality and prefers to immerse himself in British folklore and legends. Braithwaite argues that "home" is often a concern in adolescent texts, noting that "in post-disaster fiction the original home has almost invariably been destroyed or irrevocably altered" (52). In each of the novels discussed in this chapter the notions of "home" and belonging are significant themes, where the protagonists are uneasy because they feel alienated. For instance, in the conclusion of Harding's novel, as well as Kelleher's *Taronga*, the main characters travel away from their homes as if to begin a new life elsewhere. Yet these texts discussed have a particular significance because of the way they all contextualize the search for home in terms of colonialism and imperialism. Harding's work frames this issue in a colonial context; the characters are not at home because they are white colonists who inhabit a land that actually belongs to the Indigenous people. One of the characters in *Waiting* refers to Aboriginal groups as "the First People"; they are "the race that inhabited this land in olden times, before our ancestors took it from them" (177). These "ancestors" are white people, and Fergus tells Manfred that "we do not rightly *belong* to this land. Our ancestors stole it from a much older race. *Our* roots lie elsewhere, on the far side of the world" (98). These references, then, give a negative picture of the European colonization of Australia, for the white people "stole" the land and therefore cannot "belong" there.

While there is clearly an argument that interrogates and rejects the legitimacy of colonization in *Waiting*, Harding's use of ghosts in the novel confuses the issue by denying white guilt. British apparitions haunt Manfred and their presence has a significant impact on his sense of belonging. Harding's novel is not a ghost story, yet the significance of the specters within the narrative does provoke questions about colonization and the issue of belonging. Critics have argued that Australian ghost stories often intersect with postcolonial themes.[7] For instance, Ken Gelder and Jane M. Jacobs suggest that "ghost stories are traditionally about possession.... But the postcolonial ghost story speaks not so much about possession as (dis)possession, coming as it does *after* the fact of settlement. It deals with post-occupational matters" (32). David Crouch argues that "the non-indigenous desire to belong to a stolen land, gives the Australian ghost story a peculiar resonance.... In this country the presence of ghosts can be read as traces of historical traumas, fears which are often exposed in expressions of apprehensive (un)settlement" (94).

Yet Crouch also points out that ghost stories can actually justify colonization rather than interrogate it: "But should the presence of ghosts always be a dark reminder of colonisation and uneasy settlement? Possibly these ghosts are attempts to legitimate colonisation and white settlement; discursively populating the place with spectres could be a way of securing the country within white mythology" (96). He notes that the ghost story may function by "silencing an indigenous presence" and validating white colonization (102). Gelder similarly relates ghosts to colonial issues:

> To see a ghost in nineteenth-century Australia is to make a new country appear older than it is—without depending on the Old World. This may be unsettling in one sense; in another sense, however, it can work to *legitimate* settlement. A ghost on your property can make that property significant—and valuable. It can connect you to a past without necessarily involving you in ... "the guilt industry." In fact, a number of these stories operate by laying guilt and ghost to rest simultaneously [xiv–xv].

In Harding's modern text, his ghosts are from the Old World and their presence suggests that contemporary white inhabitation of Australia does indeed depend on a continued connection with England. The English apparitions directly work against a sense of guilt over white occupation of Australia, for if ancient British ghosts appear in the Antipodean landscape their presence asserts the justification of contemporary white inhabitation of the land.

Turcotte writes that the figure of the ghost is a "tattoo that lives on, within, and beyond the skin. It marks, it covers over; it transforms through its inscription" ("Ghosts" 109). In *Waiting*, the British people and landscape cover and transform the land around them when they appear to Manfred. He has visions of an ancient, ghostly army of Arthurian knights that accompanies him as he learns archery. The presence of the specters changes the Australian landscape around him: "On these occasions the forest would undergo subtle transformations. Bracken and tree ferns would recede and slowly disappear, elegant eucalypts and towering pines would merge and give way to birch and elm and oak, and the soft swell of an English meadow would replace the familiar clearing" (74). When the vision ends and Manfred returns to his real surrounds, the prosaic "smell of eucalypts and pine" replaces the romanticized "sweet scent of an English meadow," and this occurs with an "unsettling jolt," an "aching sense of loss and confusion" (75). Harding describes the change in terms that make it clear it is uncomfortable and disquieting to return to the reality of the Australian environment. In an important sense, then, these white phantoms of *Waiting* "mark" and "cover" the Indigenous history in Australia, appearing in a way that promotes instead their own right to be there.

Therefore, even as Harding's novel insists that white people do not belong in the land, there is also a competing discourse that asserts that English people rightfully belong in Australia because of a spiritual connection. For example, Harding describes Manfred's ghostly link with his ancient British past as an inheritance that gives him power and assurance: "The power of the yew had brought them this far. It would surely take them further" (206). The yew is symbolic of Manfred's English heritage, and its legacy gives him "new determination" and "confidence" because the "ancient world was intact inside him" (206). Indeed, Harding's novel speaks of "the ancient world reasserting itself *through* [Manfred]" (98), as if England is staking a claim on the land. This assurance replaces Manfred's earlier uncertainty over his identity and sense of belonging and home. The novel, then, simultaneously suggests that Manfred and his fellow white inhabitants do not belong in Australia while also implying that their British blood gives them a mystical right of presence.

Harding's novel is one example of Australian children's dystopias that grapple with questions about European colonization and inhabitation, Indigenous issues, and who "belongs" in Australia. In the following decades, writers such as Kelleher and Marsden would further elaborate on these themes and articulate similar anxieties about relations between white and Indigenous peoples. *Waiting* attempts to answer the question by suggesting that even if white people do not belong in Australia they somehow have a special right to be there. Other novels that address the same dilemmas, such as Kelleher's *Taronga* and *Red Heart*, find the problems harder to solve.

Victor Kelleher: Taronga *(1986) and* Red Heart *(2001)*

In Kelleher's *Taronga*, events take place two years after the Last Days when global wars decimated the world leaving few survivors, most of whom are children. In the novel, invaders and refugees compromise the security of Taronga Zoo — symbolic of Sydney, as well as Australia — and the people who have taken refuge within the Zoo defend themselves with force rather than share their resources. Kelleher's use of apocalypse exposes the violence that characterizes protectionist policies, but he offers no solution to this dilemma.

When the main character, a teenager called Ben, arrives in Sydney alone after gangs murder his parents, the wars have apparently left the city untouched. Yet the reality is darker:

> There was nothing timeless about it now, the illusion of permanence shattered by the prevailing air of ruin and decay. It was apparent in everything he saw: the steelwork of the bridge streaked with rust; tiles missing from the shell-shapes of the Opera House; the upper storeys of the skyscrapers almost windowless. The whole distant scene speaking to him of sadness and loss [94].

Attacks have turned Sydney icons into a succession of nightmarish images: "The burned-out skeleton of a ferry lay in the shallows and the wharf itself leaned at a crazy angle, some of its wooden piles burned through" (55). Ben discovers Taronga Zoo, an apparently safe haven where a group of survivors has congregated. He initially believes that Taronga is like the "Garden of Eden" (82) but it becomes apparent that "this isn't really paradise: it's more like what was left after they messed it up" (83). The Zoo has become the city's only refuge from dangerous gangs, yet corrupt and violent adults rule it and they abuse their power. Ben is told, "You're no freer than the animals. You just do as you're told, the same as them. Molly gives all the orders around here because she has the guns to back her up.

She's the one with the power. The kind of power that wrecked Sydney. And one of these days she's going to use it" (103).

Kelleher frames Taronga as a haven that outsiders try to invade and in this way the Zoo functions as a microcosm of Australia, facing the same problems of immigration and refugees. Taronga is the only place in Sydney where people can find food and protection, and as such its colonists guard it fiercely and violently against any outsiders who attempt to break in. Kelleher titles the third section of his novel as "The Answer" but offers no real solution to the problem of limited resources. Kennon suggests that adolescent dystopias do not always give solutions to social problems because "optimistic possibilities for emancipatory agency seem intertwined with pessimistic acknowledgement of the limitations for the transformation of society" (40). *Taronga* interrogates the violence inherent in protectionist policies, but cannot suggest any viable alternatives. For example, the children consider options other than their violent defense of the Zoo: "Molly could try helping some of those people … maybe even expand Taronga a bit. That's our only real hope: to make Taronga bigger and bigger, until everyone's inside. Keeping most of them out won't work" (106). Yet this idea fails. Instead, Ben and his friend Ellie defy the leaders by breaking open Taronga and allowing the animals to escape. This act contaminates the Zoo with the dangerous outside world and effectively ends it as a sanctuary for anybody. As a model for Australia, then, the Taronga experience suggests that humanitarian ideals of shared resources and open border policies cannot operate in reality.

In *Taronga*, the characters wonder why Australia's island location does not protect them from the disasters that overtake the rest of the world, a theme that evokes the "shield of distance" discussed in Chapter Two. During Last Days, "ships had stopped coming to Australia and no planes had landed for weeks. Everything was breaking down" (102). Isolated from the rest of the world, the characters struggle to comprehend the disaster that occurred:

> "What went wrong?" he asked. "They said it wasn't going to affect us. It was all up there, in the northern hemisphere. We were supposed to be the lucky ones, who'd escaped. That's what they said on the radio and telly. I heard them."

Opposite: Apocalyptic and dystopian themes are in many Australian children's novels. The cover of *Taronga* shows Sydney in ruins after the Last Days. *Taronga*, Victor Kelleher. Ringwood, Vic.: Puffin-Penguin, 1986.

> ...
> "I think it had something to do with being cut off. The way we are here in Taronga. Everything just went bad after that" [94].

Ben and Ellie escape to the bush, but the natural world is as dangerous as the brutal city. This construction of land and childhood challenges traditional beliefs of children as being close to nature. For instance, *Taronga* depicts the city as a desperate place, yet nature is also powerful and menacing:

> He tried telling himself that things would improve as he drew nearer to Sydney — that the outlying towns were so dangerous because of the influence of the bush. But it didn't take him long to realize his error. As he passed through one built-up area after another, the nightmare only grew worse. More and more frequently he was waylaid, wild figures leaping out of the scrub, rocks and sticks whistling past his head, howls of anger disrupting the stillness of the night [33–34].

The wild animals of Taronga Zoo have much in common with the "savage heart of the city" (174). Sydney can only fend off the wilderness for a while but eventually nature will triumph and bring devastation to civilization because of "the burgeoning wilderness which was rapidly reclaiming the once flourishing city" (192). The protagonists head west to wait until the city is safe for them to return to, but nature is not a refuge because the interior is "hard country to survive in" (195). As in *Waiting*, Kelleher's novel suggests that the characters do not belong and must find a home elsewhere. Scutter argues that conclusions such as this, where the protagonists abandon a "closed" world for a "version of the pastoral" in the wilderness, are "common to the point of cliché" and effectively backward-looking because they insist that one must return to the past in order to create a future world (*Displaced* 38).

Kelleher's novel exhibits an uncertainty about white existence in Australia and the effect of imperialism, themes he later develops in his novel *Red Heart*. In *Taronga*, Ben tells Ellie, an Indigenous character, that "this was your country ... your people have been here for thousands of years" (193). Ellie is the only one who will talk about the past, because "I'm Aboriginal. We don't forget about things that easy. We have our stories to remind us. My dad always reckoned that's why we've survived as a people. Because we remember so much, even the bad things" (84). Presumably these "bad things" refer not only to the fictional events of the Last Days disaster but also to the European settlement of Australia, yet nothing more is said. Indeed, when Ben and Ellie discuss if their decision to free the Zoo animals was wise, Ellie suggests that it was merely a "change" in Australia like white colonization rather than anything more serious: "'Well, there've been other changes in Australia before this. The Aboriginals brought the dingo here thousands of years ago — think of the difference that must have made. Then there was the coming of the Whites, with their own plants and animals'.... She indicated the general disorder ... 'there had to be some sort of beginning. And you can't have beginnings without change.'" (193)

Berger critiques a similar discourse in the American context, where rhetoric reframes Native Americans as simply one more group of migrants. He insists that this argument is a deceptively racist notion because it implies that "Native Americans now are immigrants just like the rest of us, and therefore could not possibly have been, or continue to be, victims of any injustice" (135). This is not unlike Ellie's reference to Aborigines and whites coming to Australia, where colonization is simply one more innocuous event over time. The fact that it is an Aboriginal character who articulates this dismissal of history and the negative impact of colonization is surprising, particularly given the novel's apparent critique of colonial and protectionist practices.

While Kelleher's exploration of colonial themes in *Taronga* ultimately offers an ambiguous message about colonization, his later novel *Red Heart* is emphatically critical of imperialism. As with *Taronga*, Kelleher uses apocalyptic motifs in *Red Heart* to symbolize the violence that is at the heart of power, but he develops the theme and frames this discourse in an imperialist setting. His language borrows heavily from Biblical ideals of paradise and new worlds and he reveals the promised land to be hell. Kelleher deliberately invokes and then challenges ideas of empire and colonialism in *Red Heart*. He places apocalyptic language alongside imperial discourse, a fusion that ultimately suggests a judgment against colonial practices, including in Australia.

The characters of *Red Heart* live in a future Australia after an event called Greenhouse has left the once drought-stricken continent facing massive flooding and disease. Following a "climate shift" (4), water covers half of Australia's territory and "since Greenhouse there're *only* bad years. Things will go on getting worse for people like you, not better" (5). In this new world, "the Company" is the "only real law" because it owns half the settled land in Australia and is beyond the authority of the nation's government (5). As such the Company ejects farmers at will, sending "henchman" and "heavies" (6) to intimidate people who miss payments. When the Company threatens his family, the teenaged protagonist Nat journeys into the literal "Promised Land" (32), the "land of milk and honey" (35), to seek his mysterious uncle Jack's financial assistance. He discovers that his uncle is a violent leader of a cult and he has achieved this position through "brute force" (132). Jack's cult practices cannibalism, and he quotes from the "Good Book" and is obsessed with establishing the "New Jerusalem ... the holy city of the future" at any cost (119). According to Jack, "the whole downriver world is finished, dear boy. It's a part of the old order, soon to be swept away in the deluge" (119). He attempts to groom Nat as his successor by telling him "the only way forward is to become like them. Ruthless. Uncaring. A force of nature" but Nat is appalled at this form of rule and rejects his uncle's ways emphatically: "I don't *ever* want to be like you. It's the last thing on earth I want" (120). Nat and his friends experience horror and brutality in Jack's Promised Land, and their only hope is to escape.

The novel, then, is redolent with apocalyptic imagery and Biblical language, and Kelleher combines this apocalyptic framework with a discourse that is deeply critical of imperial practices. Kelleher prefaces *Red Heart* with a quote from Joseph Conrad's *Heart of Darkness*: "The tranquil waterway leading to the uttermost ends of the earth flowed sombre under an overcast sky — seemed to lead into the heart of an immense darkness" (n.p.). Kelleher therefore immediately imbues his novel with the shadow of imperialism and its problems. Nat's uncle, called Jack Curtis, is the counterpart to Conrad's character Kurtz. Like Kurtz, Nat's uncle is "carving out an empire" (8) in the flooded landscape. Berger has written that in Conrad's *Heart of Darkness* "enlightenment is indistinguishable from barbarism. Moral distinctions themselves compose the surface that is shattered, and under that surface is a universal murderous chaos" (8). *Red Heart* works with these ideas to implicitly argue that colonialism necessarily entails violence and brutality. Bradford, Mallan and Stephens have also noted the novel's interest in imperialism and they point out that the map in the book incurs associations with colonial "acts of (re)naming [that] encode the territorialising of a new world, which elides the indigenous presence" (354).

Four • Children of the Apocalypse

Kelleher's *Red Heart* and *Taronga* appear to mirror each other in their concerns with limited resources, border protection and land possession, but in both novels there is no answer to the problem of violent colonization and occupation except escape. As in *Taronga*, safe havens in an apocalyptic Australian landscape are few, and Jack closes the Promised Land to outsiders: "This whole place, it's Jack's private kingdom, and he's sitting in the middle of it like he's king of the castle ... he decided to close the borders" (86). "Close the borders" is, of course, a phrase that immediately invokes the language — and fear — of immigration and refugees.

The descriptions of the Promised Land suggest a link between Jack's kingdom and the violent colonial experiences in other parts of the world such as Africa: "[Nat] imagined the drummers themselves: the strain written on their firelit faces; their naked bodies streaked with sweat and coloured pigments; their muscled arms beating out a message of grief and loss" (92). These descriptions of the tropical interior of Australia evoke literary associations with imperial narratives set in Africa. As Dixon points out, the cultural imagination has long read the Australian tropics as the Other: "tropical Australia is a liminal zone, a place that is recognisably different to the rest of the country because of its proximity to Asia. To enter the tropical jungle is to enter that dangerously unstable and unreadable zone in which the self bleeds into its others — effeminacy, indolence, the East — producing images of the hybrid, the second grotesque" (148). Jameson has also suggested that narrative constructions of the tropics can reveal anxieties about the threat of the Other:

> The preoccupation with heat, the fear of sweating as of some dissolution of our very being, would then be tantamount to an unconscious anxiety about tropical field-labor.... The nightmare of the tropics thus expresses a disguised terror at the inconceivable and unformulable threat posed by the masses of the Third World to our own prosperity and privilege [*Archaeologies* 269].

We can apply these ideas to read *Red Heart*'s tropics in terms of fears about Australian identity and its Asian neighbors, where the Otherness of the jungle inhabitants is frightening and dangerous. Yet this would miss the obvious links that Kelleher draws between Australia and other colonized nations, where Jack's kingdom represents both Africa and Australia. The colonizer Jack maintains his rule by a mix of violence and mysticism that threatens the stability of Nat's world. By describing the tropical setting in terms that are bound to link Australia with Africa and its brutal imperial history, *Red Heart* invites a reading of Australia as a place of similar exploitation. Kelleher, therefore, simultaneously positions the jungle, the African continent, and Australia all as colonized lands. His conflation of the fictional Promised Land with Africa and Australia insists that colonization is a violent practice that society must not tolerate.

Kelleher reinforces this attitude to colonization by depicting Indigenous people in the novel as the true inhabitants of Australia while white people do not belong. His narrative is similar to Harding's novel where white people are the invaders, the outsiders. Although others have suggested that *Red Heart* closes with "a tentative move towards a new beginning ... a renewed sense of belonging and identification for the protagonist and secondary characters" (Bradford, Mallan, and Stephens 353), this seems to be undercut in the novel. For instance, Nat's companion Clarrie calls herself "First Nation" and refers to Nat as "white boy." Nat is lost and out of place, saying, "I grew up by the Murray. These big rivers are what I know best, so I should be at home right here. But somehow..." (57). This confusion over belonging and identity contrasts with Clarrie, who laughs at the idea of feeling lost. "This is my country. How can you feel lost in your own home?" (57). Later their enemies capture Clarrie, but subsequently release her because "she's First Nation! She *belongs* here" (142). Sharyn Pearce has outlined key tropes in Australian fiction that include "displacement and dislocation, the reconciliation of personal and national identity, and the establishment of a sense of belonging" (239). Bradford, Mallan and Stephens discuss belonging in *Red Heart* in terms of the novel's promotion of a multi-racial utopian society and, alternatively, belonging in the context of relationships rather than place (355).

Yet place remains a crucial theme in Kelleher's *Red Heart* and *Taronga*. These works reinforce the associations between Indigeneity and belonging versus whiteness and dislocation, where being white means being out of place and away from home. Kelleher's juxtaposition of the concerns about imperialism in an apocalyptic context leaves the impression for the reader that apocalyptic disaster will always shadow and haunt imperialism and colonial practices. In *Taronga* and *Red Heart*, time will ultimately bring colonists to justice and judgment, particularly those who abuse their authority and exploit faithful followers in order to justify their imperial violence.

John Marsden: Tomorrow, When the War Began Series (1993–1999)

Of the texts examined here, Marsden's *Tomorrow* series is notable for the extent to which it particularly reflects the anxieties about land and nation that Dixon discusses. The seven novels in the series are: *Tomorrow, When the War Began*; *The Dead of the Night*; *The Third Day, The Frost*; *Darkness, Be My Friend*; *Burning for Revenge*; *The Night Is for Hunting*; and *The Other Side of Dawn*. A second series, *The Ellie Chronicles*, continues the story of the main characters now living in a post-invasion Australia and includes *While I Live*, *Incurable*, and *Circle of Flight*.[8] Marsden's novels speculate about a future Australia with a realist tone that purports to "tell things as they are" (Mayers 18); the covers of some editions proclaim that the novels are "frighteningly real" (*Tomorrow*).

In Marsden's novels, a teenager Ellie and her friends experience the "end of our world" after a foreign country invades Australia (*Burning* 238). In the first novel — published in France under the title *Apocalypse*— Ellie's group is camping in a hidden wilderness location called Hell when they discover that soldiers have captured their town, Wirrawee, during the invasion and imprisoned or killed most of the adults. The teenagers mount a guerilla campaign from their remote camp, and the novels describe them at one stage as "four riders galloping into an apocalypse" (*Darkness* 118).

While Marsden's *Tomorrow* and *Ellie* series reference God at various points, this is very much a secular apocalypse. Yet his invasion theme mirrors Biblical discourse in many ways. In the Bible, invasion occurs when Israel strays from its relationship with God, and consequently foreign neighboring powers such as Assyria and Babylonia invade and subdue the nation. In Isaiah there are prophecies of the invasions to come, yet Israel ignores the warnings and as a result suffers terribly for its indifference and complacency. In Marsden's secular version, invasion is a consequence and punishment for a nation that is heedless of all warning. Like a blind and deaf Israel ignoring the prophecies of Isaiah about forthcoming danger, the Australian government is shown to be lazy, weak, unprincipled, and deliberately blind to the danger awaiting them. In the opening of the first novel in the series, Ellie sees part of a television program in which someone criticizes Australia's foreign minister because the government has reduced its defense budget; the minister is a "wimp" and "the new Neville Chamberlain"

(*Tomorrow* 9). After the invasion, Australian politicians leave the country for the safety of the U.S., a departure that the characters portray as desertion: "our Great Leader, the Prime Minister ... jetted out of the country in a wild hurry when he realised the war was being lost" (*The Dead of the Night* 186). Unlike the tragedy of invasions in Biblical apocalypse, however, Marsden's secular invasion narrative has an ambivalent attitude towards the invasion, as if simultaneously presenting it as a terrible act while also suggesting it may have positive aspects because the invasion matures the teen protagonists and gives them freedom and space for adventures. Wendy Michaels notes that while in other adolescent fictions "the adolescent protagonists are supported," in the *Tomorrow* series "the adolescent has to do it alone" (56). When the teenaged group finds adult survivors in the second novel, they initially welcome the guidance and security they offer, but eventually reject the adult resistance fighters because they are inferior to themselves.

As in *Taronga* and *Red Heart*, Marsden's novels articulate concerns about immigration and refugees in relation to who belongs in Australia. The *Tomorrow* series shows that the nation's isolation makes it vulnerable to attack and distanced from allies. An unnamed nearby nation invades Australia (*Tomorrow* 168), presumably from Asia, after which most other countries abandon the nation, even ones that the Australian government might expect to come to its defense. The invading country gives its reason for attack as "reducing imbalances within the region" (*Tomorrow* 168). When Ellie's group asks why a nation has invaded them, one of the characters wonders if the problem is due to the lack of resources between the different groups:

> We've got all this land and all these resources, and yet there's countries a crow's spit away that have people packed in like battery hens. You can't blame them for resenting it, and we haven't done much to reduce any imbalances, just sat on our fat backsides, enjoyed our money and felt smug ... if you'd lived your whole life in a slum, starving, unemployed, always ill, and you saw the people across the road sunbaking and eating ice cream every day, then after a while you'd convince yourself that taking their wealth and sharing it around your neighbours isn't such a terrible thing to do [*Tomorrow* 170–71].

Ellie suggests that the solution is not "turning the place into a fortress" to protect land and resources — as Molly and Jack attempt to do in *Taronga* and *Red Heart*— but instead to "help other countries get better incomes, so that they don't feel any great urge to rush in here" (*The Third Day* 31). Marsden populates his narrative with characters of white Australian, Greek, and Thai-Vietnamese heritage, and also includes passing criticism of the Australian government's hostile treatment of refugees before the invasion (*Circle of Flight* 85). While these discussions between the characters articulate genuine concern about other nations, ultimately Ellie and her friends reject a compromise or any other solution except to resist invasion and effectively treat Australia precisely as a fortress. Like the Zoo in *Taronga*, Australians will fight for this land in Marsden's novels and, unlike the child heroes in *Taronga* who want to share the land and decide to leave when this is not possible, Ellie's group want Australia to remain guarded against intruders: "Let no stranger intrude here, no invader trespass. This was ours, and this we would defend" (*The Dead of the Night* 63). One of the group echoes many an opponent of immigration when they say: "I hate them. What are they doing here? Why can't they just go back where they came from?" (*The Dead of the Night* 215).

Marsden has said that his writing is not specifically about Australian concerns but has universal applications. "I'm not into writing Australian books. In fact, I don't even use the word 'Australia' in the books. I try and avoid it because I'm not a fan of that kind of flag-waving, 'Waltzing Matilda'-singing, jingoistic patriotism that seems to have infested so many countries … I try to write about universal situations" ("John Marsden" n.p.). Yet Adrian Caesar has suggested that Marsden's novels reflect specifically Australian fears, namely an ongoing "paranoia" about Asian invasion (46). Caesar argues that such writing "encourages the fear and loathing upon which racism breeds" even if this was not Marsden's intention (49), which certainly seems unlikely. For Catriona Ross, "Marsden may evade charges of overt racism by never specifying [the] Asian threat, but it is a very thin veneer of cultural egalitarianism that coats his narrative" (96). Ross claims that the series is "deeply problematic for reinvigorating old discourses of racial anxiety for young readers" (87). Scutter similarly argues that Marsden's series "sets up a vast undifferentiated 'other,' against which the group of teenagers is pitted. There is nothing new here from the old narratives of empire: this is a brutal colonising book whose replay of stale adventure quests also enacts old codes of cultural centre and difference" (*Displaced* 184).

Indeed, a review of Dixon's discussion of nineteenth-century adventure stories offers striking parallels between Marsden's work and that genre.

In *Writing the Colonial Adventure*, Dixon attributes the popularity of the invasion trope in the late nineteenth century in part to the decline of the British Empire against the growing strengths of other countries:

> The literature of imagined invasion reflects the mood of accumulating crisis that characterises the Edwardian period ... a mood of anxiety ran through public debate. Britain, "the heart of the empire," was in decline; her moral and spiritual life were deteriorating. Commentators pointed to a lack of patriotism, even a lack of physical vigour in the working classes. They warned that an excessive "love of luxury" had produced a state of mind opposed to any idea of self-sacrifice.... Beyond these was the nightmarish possibility that the "coloured" races, especially the "yellow" races, might emerge as a new imperial power [136].

Early Australian invasion narratives, in particular, came to feature Asian invasions more prominently. Dixon suggests invasion stories reveal anxieties about identity because the nation was "new," particularly at the height of popularity for the genre in the 1900s, and its invasion meant that the invading country's race may weaken white people, for "the national self is constructed at its boundaries by the always ineffectual exclusion of its others, and nothing is more calculated to disclose the anxiety attendant upon that process than the invasion of boundaries" (135). With this in mind, Marsden's text is not a unique example of a literature of invasion. Marsden himself nominated as one of the inspirations for his novels that "Australia came close to [Japanese] invasion in World War II, with several cities and towns being bombed" ("PW Talks" 70). Rosemary Ross Johnston has suggested that Australia's national fears include the "fear of isolation"; while other countries such as Canada dread "proximity" (91). The anxiety in these novels, however, appears to encompass both isolation from allies and proximity to large and potentially hostile Asian populations.

Dixon writes that commentators and authors in the early twentieth century repeatedly argued that "because Australians are complacent, because they rely too much on British defence, because they have grown effeminate like the Asian races, they almost *deserve* to be taken over by them" (139). It is hard to miss the parallels between these fears and the arguments appearing in Marsden's novels. There is complacency: "ordinary people who hadn't taken enough interest" partly caused the war (*The Third Day* 160); defense treaties with other countries fail (*Tomorrow* 169–70); and Australia is weak and thus deserves punishment, as one character — a traitor — says: "We've become slack, we've become soft.... If you ask me, these people have done us a favour by invading. We can learn a lot from them. They're a disciplined organised force of well-led soldiers" (*The Dead of the Night* 119).

However, while some interpret Marsden's series as perpetuating fear and paranoia of an "Asian invasion," we can also see in the invasion theme another version of the ambivalent attitude Australians have towards land. At first the repeated assertions in the novels about how the characters belong in the bush appear to negate this idea. For instance, Ellie says that "this was where I belonged" (*Darkness* 39–40), even though it is a hostile environment:

> The cruel cold of the wind suggested it might be bringing something wild in. Beyond the furthest mountains we could see the tops of some thick white cloud. It seemed to be lying in wait.... [We] spent the time admiring the ferocious beauty of our home, in the last of the light. I could see why it had looked so frightening to me for so many years. Even now, when we knew it so well, it had the same look of potential violence that some animals in zoos manage to keep.... Hell was a vivid mess of trees and rocks, dark green and reddish-brown, grey and black. It looked like a dumping ground for the gods, a great smashed mess of living things that grew without help or guidance, according to their own wild rules. It was the right place for us [*The Dead of the Night* 77–78].

The protagonists live in an area of bushland called Hell, adjoining Satan's Steps, and the differences between these places and images of paradise and the promised land are stark. Hell is both dangerous and a "refuge" for Ellie (*Incurable* 181). The depiction of the bush as both savage and home for the teenagers demonstrates an underlying uncertainty that belies a simple equation of nature and safety.

Ellie's love of the land seems to position her as indigenous to the land. The description of the bush as Ellie's dreaming—"this was my dreaming" (*Darkness* 40)—appears to allude to Indigenous traditions. Catriona Ross notes this process and suggests that it is a "performance of white indigenisation, [in which] Marsden plays out the nativist sentiments begun in the early invasion novels" (96), where we see a "new white indigeneity that fully encompasses spiritual rights to the land" (94). Ellie's group thinks they are the first people to ever walk in their bush hideaway: "I wonder how many human beings have ever been down here, in the history of the Universe. I mean, why would the koories have bothered? Why would the early explorers, or settlers, have bothered?" (*Tomorrow* 31). In a genre with such potential for revealing new perspectives, the presence of Aboriginal characters or viewpoints in many apocalyptic children's fictions is negligible, although Wrightson's *The Ice Is Coming* is an obvious exception, given that she depicts Aborigines as the heroes, and whites — "Happy Folk" — as selfish and ignorant. However, many Australian speculative novels adopt clichéd images of Aboriginality that diminish Indigenous land rights and the impact of white colonization. In the *Tomorrow* novels, Ellie's references to Indigenous people are usually confined to admiring their knowledge of the land, such as bush remedies (*The Third Day* 150), Aboriginal trackers (*The Night Is for Hunting* 78; *Incurable* 50), and being able to "dig up roots using ancient Aboriginal knowledge" (*Burning* 172). Instead, Ellie calls Australia "my country" (*Tomorrow* 215), and the novels seem to depict the group as the rightful possessors of the land. For some critics, therefore, the novels attempt an "erasure of Aboriginality" (Bradford 32) where white people are "victims" (C. Ross 95). Indeed, Ellie and her friends seem to appropriate Indigeneity when one of the group compares the invasion with European colonization: "A disease of colonists had infected the countryside.... 'It must feel like the old days, when the whites first arrived, and all they could see was this huge country with no one in it who they cared about. So, after living in pokey little towns or on ten hectare farms in England, they could suddenly spread out ... a couple of centuries later, here's history repeating itself'" (*The Third Day* 17). Ellie also worries that the invaders will not respect and care for the land as they should (*The Dead of the Night* 259), an attitude that frames her group as an indigenous people who have lost their land. Attempts to liken the invasion in the *Tomorrow* series to the experience of European colonization appear to be constructing the teenagers as the new Indigenous people; they are suffering the loss of "their" land, and the loss of "their" dreaming, and this ultimately diminishes Indigenous history while reinforcing white possession of the land.

Yet several aspects of the series stymie attempts to read the books as simply perpetuating old racial fears or asserting white land rights. Johnston argues that the theme of invasion and reference to Indigenous inhabitation actually work to undermine the fear of Asian invasion by offering a "layer of indigenous perspectives [that] opens up deliberately provocative ideas about ownership of land" (97). Although the references to Indigenous groups are very limited, there is passing recognition of white colonial violence against Indigenous people when Ellie wonders: "maybe so many of them were murdered that a lot of stories were lost" (*Incurable* 193). In the post-invasion Australia of the second series, boundaries are vulnerable and border raids are rife, and all sense of belonging is undermined. These are but small pieces of the novels, yet together they do confuse notions of belonging, land rights, and cultural identities. We can see this particularly in relation to land when Ellie describes losing her sense of belonging. The invasion brings "a change in the feel of the land. It felt wilder, stranger, more ancient. I was still comfortable travelling through it, but I felt less important" (*The Dead of the Night* 11). After Australia cedes territory to the invaders in the peace settlement, Ellie finds formerly familiar places made uncanny:

> I'd thought I would find Rawson Road pretty easily, but something basic had changed. I don't want to sound too cosmic and psychic but because it wasn't our country any more it seemed almost impossibly different. How weird that was, to be in a foreign country.... I should have felt at home myself. But a new spirit had spread across the land and I trembled as I pushed forwards, knowing that although it felt like my land it was not. It smelt different. The energy was not the same. I was in alien territory [*Incurable* 56].

Although the characters have lost land once when their properties are redistributed following the settlement, Ellie chooses to lose her land a second time when she sells her family's farm to begin a new life elsewhere, at the conclusion of the second series. In some ways, therefore, Marsden's series does interrogate our ideas of land and identity, particularly the desire to belong in a place that is fraught with confusion over ownership and belonging. As much as Ellie loves her land, the invasion reminds readers that belonging is not so certain after all. Although some aspects of Marsden's work might give commentators cause for concern, his novels — and the other case studies in this chapter — are fundamentally concerned with the adventure narrative rather than exploring postcolonial issues and it may do more justice to the works to read them as speaking, even indirectly, to the difficulties of contemporary white existence in Australia.

Before leaving children's literature behind, I want to end this chapter with brief reference to a children's picture book that serves to transition into the next chapter with its focus on apocalypse and race. John Marsden and Shaun Tan's *The Rabbits* interrogates race and belonging using apocalyptic themes. *The Rabbits* allegorizes European colonization of Australia as an invasion of rabbits, and narrates from the perspective of the invaded. The invading rabbits do not "understand the right ways. They only know their own country," and while the rabbits' presence brings some benefits, it also entails sickness, conflict, environmental damage, and the loss of the colonized group's children. The book ends with pictures of a "bare and brown" land, then darkness, and finally the words: "Who will save us from the rabbits?" Throughout the book the invading rabbits' flag is a caricature of the British Union Jack, with four lines intersecting and ending in arrows pointing out, as if to imply the ever-spreading imperial and colonial greed of British interests. Some critics have dismissed *The Rabbits*, such as Bradford, who argues that the book conflates animal and Indigenous and "leaves the indigenous in a state of continuing (and, presumably, permanent) helplessness and lack of agency" (116). While the concluding words may suggest this, the visual conclusion of this picture book offers more promise: representatives of both groups sit facing each other, as if preparing to negotiate together as equals. The next chapter discusses two case studies where authors take the initiative in exploring paths to reconciliation, where Indigenous peoples are not helpless victims of white violence but powerful and influential in cataclysmic events, despite the apocalyptic events of colonization.

Apocalypse, then, allows writers of children's literature the latitude to adapt its imagery to suit a variety of messages. The works in this chapter offer dystopian scenarios where children must question rather than rely on adult authority. Underpinning the adventure narratives are familiar questions about belonging and land, colonization and white existence. These novels display the sense that Australians have not come to terms with their nation, for they frequently invoke the specter of colonization. Together, such works betray ambivalence about belonging and possession in a country that authors have long depicted as hostile, particularly to its juvenile inhabitants.

• FIVE •

(Re)Writing the End of the World
Apocalypse, Race, and Indigenous Literature

> My land! My land! What have the migloo [white people] done to you? They have bound you in chains of concrete and steel. They have raped you. How can you live with such terrible shame?
> — Sam Watson, *The Kadaitcha Sung* 132

The previous two chapters delved into apocalyptic landscapes and ideas about belonging in the context of colonization. In many of the representations of Australian apocalypse there is the notion of a great absence at the heart of the country: the "dead heart," the "nothing." Yet this has implications for Indigenous peoples. There is a long tradition linking Indigenous people with the outback, and this connects them with a convenient myth of disappearance.[1] It is just this strategy that commentators find problematic:

> More than any other geographical region, the desert was associated with the Aborigines. This was the last stronghold to which they had been effectively driven by the expansion of settlement from the coastal fringes, and since it remained the area most inimical to Europeans it was readily ceded to them until it began to acquire commercial and strategic value for mining or nuclear testing. This association between Aborigines and the desert was not, however, a simple empirical matter; it resonated with political and ideological implications in a bitter preview of the "land rights" issue that has continued to bedevil Australian history [Haynes 34].

If people link Indigenous groups with the outback, then representing the Australian desert interior as empty suggests that the Indigenous people are also missing. Speculative visions frequently literalize this sense of disappearance. Utopias, Darren Jorgensen notes, are often created from "colonial violence ... the conquest of a foreign land" (178). Science fiction and speculative texts that imagine future worlds without Indigenous peoples perhaps perpetuate this colonial violence. As Brian Attebery suggests, these exclusions are "a form of control" ("Aboriginality" 385) and "the fictional equivalent of the longstanding legal principle of *terra nullius*, by which the Australian continent was treated as if it had no ownership before white settlement" ("Aboriginality" 387).

This chapter addresses apocalyptic writing in the context of race, and specifically authors who rewrite Australian history as apocalypse to represent the impact of white colonization on Indigenous peoples. The disaster scenarios of apocalypse can allow minority groups to invent a new world in which to challenge and change dominant cultural constructions for widely differing agendas. The apocalyptic paradigm of revelation and disaster can work effectively to interrogate the history of colonization and relations between white and Indigenous Australians.

Yet there is critical debate over whether apocalyptic writing is inherently conservative or radical, and this chapter begins with these topics to contextualize the case studies that follow. Given the potential for critique, it is worthwhile to assess the works of two authors—Sam Watson and Archie Weller—who specifically use the metaphor of apocalypse to discuss the impact of colonization on Indigenous peoples. These writers also contest some of the frequent tropes of Australian speculative fiction such as the "dead heart" and a barren landscape. Instead, they use the genre to both propose spaces of hope for the future and re-inscribe the Australian landscape as a sacred place of restoration.

Apocalypse as Conservative

While some commentators note that apocalypse proves flexible for different agendas and conservative and radical ends (Seed "Aspects" 12; O'Leary 56), Malcolm Bull writes that authors do not always realize this potential:

> Unlike the religious variety, secular apocalyptic — which is found in many areas of popular culture, but most notably in science fiction, rock music and film — is not usually intended to effect personal spiritual transformation. It may be designed to influence public opinion in favour of social or political objectives ... but in many cases the language of apocalyptic is deployed simply to shock, alarm or enrage ["On Making Ends Meet" 4–5].

Yet Richard Dellamora argues that apocalypse is easily adaptable for negative ends, particularly against minority groups: "Among dominant groups apocalyptic narratives have often been invoked in order to validate violence done to others. Among subordinate groups apocalyptic thinking is frequently an effect of the pressure of persecution. Apocalyptic narratives have been mobilized to justify the imprisonment, torture, and execution of the subjects of male-male desire" (*Apocalyptic Overtures* 3).

Other critics have read apocalypse as a conservative genre or one that is open to the worst uses, displaying "rage" (Plank 36). Lee Quinby argues that apocalypse tends to be "hypermasculine" ("The Days Are Numbered" 97) and has a "patriarchal dimension" (98). Catherine Keller also reads apocalypse politically in terms of gender ideology, arguing that apocalypse is "a quintessentially male product" (28) that cannot be divested of its "toxic misogyny" (29), thus making it a problematic trope for feminist uses. Marlene Goldman claims that "violence" is at the "heart" of apocalypse (26) and thus enables the persecution of minority groups: "Revelation, in keeping with its name, unveils a secret, and that its hidden message, predicated on violence and absolute destruction, is politically charged ... the originary apocalyptic violence that engendered the nation-state typically involved the subordination and commodification of women, Native peoples, ethnic minorities, and the landscape" (25). Other critics (Kermode; Cohn) note that apocalypse may serve the ideologies of a number of groups, including the rhetoric of Hitler and Lenin.

In an analysis of Immanuel Kant in "Of an Apocalyptic Tone Recently Adopted in Philosophy," Derrida also discusses the persuasion and rhetoric of apocalyptic discourse. Derrida refers to the "narrative sending" of apocalypse, that is, the "ruses, traps, trickeries, seductions" (27) that apocalypticists use to convince their hearers. The apocalyptic tone persuades others of hidden things, of secret truths and revelations:

> Whoever takes on the apocalyptic tone comes to signify to, if not tell, you something. What? The truth, of course, and to signify to you that it reveals the

truth to you; the tone is the revelatory of some unveiling in process. Unveiling or truth, apophantics of the imminence of the end, of whatever comes down, finally, to the end of the world.... Truth itself is the end, the destination, and that truth unveils itself is the advent of the end.... Then whoever takes on the apocalyptic tone will be asked: with a view to what and to what ends? In order to lead where, right now or soon? The end is beginning, signifies the apocalyptic tone. But to what ends does the tone signify this? The apocalyptic tone naturally wants to attract, to get to come, to arrive at this, to seduce in order to lead to this.... The end is soon, it is imminent, signifies the tone. I see it, I know it, I tell you, now you know, come.... We're the only ones in the world. I'm the only one able to reveal to you the truth or the destination [24–25].

Derrida claims that "nothing is less conservative than the apocalyptic genre" (29) yet points out that the apocalyptic tone "can be mimicked, feigned, faked. I shall go so far as to say *synthesised*" (10). This implies that if anyone can use and adopt and fake apocalypse, it is open to any agenda, including oppressive purposes. Derrida suggests that because apocalypse is "an apocryphal, masked, coded *genre*, it can use the detour in order to mislead another vigilance, that of censorship" (29), hiding its message to evade detection: "We know that apocalyptic writings increased the moment State censorship was very strong in the Roman Empire, and precisely to catch the censorship unawares. Now this possibility can be extended to all censorships, and not only to the political, and in politics to the official" (29). However, apocalypse's ambiguities, the "mixing of voices, genres, and codes" (29), can result in multiple meanings and interpretations, and even the misinterpretation of the message. As Dellamora points out, Derrida's argument has two significant aspects, the "analytic" which insists that we must examine apocalypse in order to "resist the manipulative use" and the "affirmative" which facilitates the use of the genre "on behalf of subordinated individuals and groups" (*Apocalyptic Overtures* 26). In this way, apocalypse again offers vast potential for any number of motivations but warrants scrutiny.

For some commentators, apocalypse is a specifically racist mode. Edward James points out that the holocaust scenario appears utopian to some readers, who see in such survivalist fictions the opportunity to "cleanse the world of its corrupting forces (liberals, feminists, homosexuals, and blacks) and restore the good old masculine values" (53). James notes that such literature "has the advantage of allowing the author to recreate the world as he or she wishes ... Holocaust wipes out the problems of the present, to create a new, possibly simpler and, from the point of view of both author and characters, more manageable world.... The author can work out his or her social and political ideas on a clean slate" (52). A new and simpler world that eliminates the "problems of the present" can, of course, result in racism, and W. Warren Wagar also writes that the evolutionary and natural selection tenets of science meant that fictions could "rationalize warfare between the races of mankind, or the extermination of inferior races.... Once the idea was abroad that great life-and-death conflicts are inevitable and, for that matter, enjoined by laws of nature, imagining racial, class, or national wars of eschatological proportions was an easy next step" (*Terminal* 109). Ken Cooper, meanwhile, calls apocalyptic fiction a "curiously liberating genre" which displays "repressed racial fantasies" (83):

> Postholocaust novels — fables, really — propagated flagrant, blood-will-tell stereotypes that were inflammatory ... blacks reverting to cannibalism after nuclear war, while others envision Caucasian holocaust survivors joining noble bands of Native Americans and adopting their ways, frequently with sexual undertones ... a nuclear attack would actually regenerate a Midwestern city by enabling a suburban "world brand-new" to rise from the ashes, but only after the bomb exploded — not coincidentally — above the Negro district [83–84].

Cooper suggests that such fantasies play on the idea that white people will survive and ethnic populations will not, because the nuclear bomb was built by white people to protect themselves (81).

Apocalypse as Subversive

Even as some critics are divided as to whether apocalypse is inherently conservative, negative, or simply open to oppressive practices, others insist that the genre is highly subversive, allowing minority groups to present radical critiques of society. Despite its negative aspects, Christopher Rowland argues, apocalypse has nonetheless "expressed a critical response to the injustices of the world, frequently on behalf of the powerless, and opened eyes closed to realities which have become accepted as the norm" (56). James Berger claims that reading apocalypse as conservative ignores "how profoundly hostile most apocalyptic imagination is to the versions of hierarchy, truth, and morality currently in power" (223). For Berger, "apocalyptic and post-apocalyptic representations serve varied psychological and political purposes. Most prevalently, they put forward a total critique of any existing social order" (7). Berger suggests that apocalypse can be appealing to a range of anti-authoritarian stances:

> The desire to see the old order disintegrate links such religiously and politically disparate apocalypticists as the romantic anarchist Henry Miller, the poststructuralist theorist Michel Foucault, 1970s Punks, more recent cyberpunk science fiction writers, and Christian New Right theologians like Hal Lindsay. For all of these, the world is poised to end and is so suffused with moral rottenness and technological, political, and economic chaos and/or regimentation that it should end and must end, and it must end because in some crucial sense it *has* ended. This weird blend of disgust, moral fervor, and cynicism helps explain the enormous, ecstatic, fascinated pleasure many people in late-twentieth-century America feel in *seeing* significant parts of their world destroyed [in disaster films] [7].

John Walliss similarly argues that apocalyptic works are "inherently critical of the contemporary social order" (85).[2]

Lois Parkinson Zamora, meanwhile, points out that apocalypse is open to radical purposes because "novelists who use apocalyptic elements, like the Biblical apocalyptists, are often critical of present political, social, spiritual practices, and their fiction entertains the means to oppose and overcome them" (3–4). Such writers are less interested in characters than metaphysics: "Their awareness of the historical forces conditioning and constraining individual existence suggests a dissenting perspective" (3). This reflects back to Revelation and the "subversive vision" of the narrator who is "outside the cultural and political mainstream" (2). Zamora implies that times of change create an environment that is particularly conducive to social critique, noting that "apocalyptic modes of thought and expression increase during times of social disruption and temporal uncertainty" (177). Apocalyptic tales of the future, then, can be susceptible to racist attitudes, yet this is arguably a perverted use of a literature that itself emanated from the persecuted Jewish and Christian groups who often faced oppression from the ruling authorities of the day. While dominant systems have since appropriated apocalyptic rhetoric, apocalypse was originally a narrative for the oppressed and therefore profoundly critical of the major powers in society.

For some theorists, apocalypse has significant links to issues of empire and colonization.[3] Frank Kermode argues that the themes of apocalypse include decadence and renovation, progress and catastrophe, and empire (29). He suggests that there is a strong connection between apocalypse and the idea of imperialism (10), where apocalyptic "doctrines of crisis, decadence, and empire" (14) allow societies to read nations, wars and empires in terms of the end of the world. Goldman notes that apocalypse is highly critical of imperialism because "Revelation's fundamental aim lies in challenging its readers to resist the Roman Empire and to remain faithful to the teachings of Christ" (17). She writes that apocalypse is a central theme in specifically Canadian fiction because it provides an appropriate template for that nation's experience, although Canadian writers tend to challenge and "rewrite" the apocalyptic narrative rather than celebrate it, presenting instead an adaptation of apocalypse where "Canadian exploration more often invoked apocalyptic visions of hell than of paradise" (3). Goldman suggests that "Canadian writers, recalling the visions of apocalyptic writers at mid-century ... stress the links between apocalyptic violence and the creation of the Canadian nation-state" (25). She notes that the apocalyptic "Canadian perspective" is "ex-centric" (27), focusing on the damned rather than the elect. Reading Revelation in terms of the Roman Empire, Goldman calls early apocalypses "disaster narratives registering the impact of Roman imperialism and colonialism" (17).

Yet Revelation is part of a prophetic tradition that is strongly intertextual and interdependent. The ambiguity, allegory, and symbolism in Revelation and its openness to multiple interpretations appear to discourage reading the text only in terms of the threat of the Roman Empire. Revelation also closely follows in the tradition and themes and visions of prior prophecies in the Old Testament — for example, Daniel and Isaiah — that were not necessarily speaking to the Roman Empire, although some Biblical commentators read Daniel in relation to Rome (Whitcomb 292). The long-term perspective of the prophetic tradition in the Testaments suggests that overly narrow interpretations can be problematic. Yet even if the Roman Empire were not the only target of Revelation, Goldman's point about the imperialist discourse remains significant, for earlier Biblical apocalypses (for instance, in Daniel) are very much concerned with empires and invasion and critical of imperialism.

Given these associations between Biblical apocalypse and empire, therefore, we can read Australian apocalyptic texts in a similar way. Writers may use an apocalyptic discourse to speak against imperialism or to justify conquest. Australian speculative writers have drawn on both options, and many of their apocalypses address problems of colonization either explicitly or by inference. In this manner, Biblical texts prove enormously influential because they demonstrate a deep concern with the effects of colonization, and secular writers may therefore deploy apocalyptic themes for highly political purposes.

Apocalyptic themes can thus be an empowering tool for Indigenous authors. In the Australian context, the people indigenous to the land can speak out and interrogate the fiction that the land is empty. The revelation of new perspectives and hidden truths shows that the writers possess more knowledge than their readers. Lydia Wevers argues that Indigenous writers can challenge a white audience because their novels give readers "new and different knowledge" (127):

> [White readers] have to participate, to cede agency, accept concepts, landscapes and actions that challenge not just power relations but also their apprehension of what history is and how it is understood, that challenge also their epistemologies, taxonomies and contingencies. Part of the attraction of indigenous texts ... may be the revisioning they force, and the hope they offer of imagining the world locally, specifically, but also radically redrawn [127].

The writer reveals, the reader learns. Apocalypse offers an opportunity for Indigenous writers to re-inscribe the unwritten future with themselves as a significant part of the landscape. Indigenous commentators have emphasized the importance of having the right to speak for themselves. Michael Dodson notes that "in all these representations, these supposed 'truths' about us, our voices and our visions have been notably absent.... Nearly suffocated with imposed labels and structures, Aboriginal peoples have had no other choice than to insist on our right to speak back" (4). Indigenous writer Alexis Wright also speaks against being silenced:

> I do not like the way we are being treated by successive governments, or the way our histories have been smudged, distorted and hidden, or written for us. I want our people to have books, their own books, in their own communities, and written by our own people. I want the truth to be told, our truths, so, first and foremost, I hold my pen for the suffering in our communities ["Breaking Taboos" n.p.].

Wright laments the "damage" that Indigenous people suffer because of misrepresentation, when dominant groups have silenced or misconstrued Aboriginal voices ("An Interview" 120).

Five • (Re)Writing the End of the World 143

It is easy to understand why apocalypse can prove so fruitful a mode for writers to address race and colonization. Their secular apocalyptic texts can reveal new perspectives, and provoke readers to question their own ways of thinking. Apocalypse can interrogate colonial practices, tease out the rhetoric about new worlds and remind readers that postcolonial literature is apocalyptic both because of its language, which resonates with themes of the end of the world and annihilation of tribes and cultures, and also because the colonial search for "new worlds" inevitably involves the ending of one (Indigenous) world and the imposition of another (white) one. Rewriting history transforms traditional beliefs about white-Indigenous relations, and speculating about the future allows new visions of renewal and reconciliation.

These themes recur in a number of apocalyptic texts that address Indigenous history. Peter Weir's film *The Last Wave* focuses on a white lawyer, David, whose dreams and interactions with Aboriginal characters convince him that the apocalypse is coming, as an end to another Dreamtime cycle. A white character summarizes European colonization this way: "We destroyed their languages, their ceremonies, their song, the dance — and their tribal laws." Keith Willey's non-fictional account of colonization carries the apocalyptic title *When the Sky Fell Down: The Destruction of the Tribes of the Sydney Region 1788–1850s*, while Werner Herzog's film *Where the Green Ants Dream* explores the dangers of mining sacred sites and environmental disaster. Similarly, the documentary *Land of the Apocalypse* warns that there are catastrophic consequences of mining sacred areas in Kakadu.[4]

Mudrooroo revisits the colonial experience in several of his novels such as *Master of the Ghost Dreaming* and *The Undying*, which use the vampire motif to symbolize European colonization, and *Doctor Wooreddy's Prescription for Enduring the Ending of the World*, which explores the devastating effects of colonization on Tasmanian Aborigines. The latter text rebukes passive acceptance of escalating disaster:

> Mangana, he had heard, on hearing of his wife's murder, had only shrugged his shoulders and muttered: "It is the times." His words summed up the general mood of the community. No one had any trust in the future and they accepted a prophecy that passed among them: fewer babies would be born to take the place of the adults dying ever younger; fewer babies to be born, to be weaned, to die — and this meant fewer mature adults to keep and pass on the traditions of the islanders. Thus it was, and it was the times. Everyone

knew this and accepted it. Wooreddy alone knew more. He knew that it was because the world was ending. (9)

Wright's *Plains of Promise*, meanwhile, draws on magic realism to narrate several generations of an Indigenous family who are removed from their country and each other.[5] Wright's novel uses explicitly apocalyptic language to describe the process and consequences of this separation, and the work militates against white practices that have had a catastrophic effect on Indigenous people, such as missions and assimilation: "Protection. Assimilation ... different words that amounted to annihilation" (74).[6]

The novels of B. Wongar, meanwhile, concern themselves with the impact of nuclear testing in the Australian desert on Indigenous peoples.[7] Wongar's preface to *Manhunt* begins: "I wrote *Manhunt* during the time of the Vietnam War. Some years earlier the British Government had carried out a series of nuclear tests in the remote Australian outback which decimated the local Aborigines and destroyed much of their culture" (5). *Manhunt*, while published in 2008, is the first novel in Wongar's "nuclear quintet" and not only addresses nuclear testing but also interrogates cultural and ethnic identities through the eyes of its Vietnamese-born protagonist, Dao Ba Rhang. Dao's attempts to assimilate to the Australian lifestyle are accompanied by paranoia about being discovered to be different, and his physical appearance slowly transforms into an Indigenous character, implying a shared identity between migrants and Indigenous as outsiders in an oppressive Australia that will only tolerate those who conform to a narrow-minded, white identity. *Karan* is similarly dedicated "To the unknown tribesman, victim of nuclear testing in Australia." Robert L. Ross writes that the Serbian-born Wongar identifies with Indigenous groups because of a shared sense of displacement; Ross also refers to Wongar's post-apocalyptic nuclear novels as regenerative for readers.

From this introduction, we can move forward to the specific case studies of this chapter: Sam Watson's *The Kadaitcha Sung* and Archie Weller's *Land of the Golden Clouds*.[8] Both novels deploy apocalyptic motifs and language to challenge the enduring myth of Australia's dead, empty spaces, by revisiting and retelling colonial history, and re-inhabiting the vacant heart of the country. They expose Australia's European settlement as an apocalypse, the ending of the world, and also explore paths to reconciliation in the future.

Sam Watson: The Kadaitcha Sung *(1990)*

Sam Watson's *The Kadaitcha Sung* spans multiple times and places in Australia and includes elements of magic and realism in its narrative. Watson's novel interrogates several apocalyptic themes that this book has so far outlined, including the concepts of disaster, a dead heart, and a dystopian land of monstrosity. *Kadaitcha* rewrites the coming of British colonizers to Australia as an apocalypse, deploying imagery of paradise and destruction to show a pre-colonial Australia that is an idyllic sanctuary. Watson's rendering of Australia as a utopian place prior to colonization directly contradicts the dystopian tradition that constructs the land as a place of monstrosity and strangeness. Instead, *Kadaitcha* creates a new apocalyptic "map" of Australia where the land is fruitful and idyllic until white people arrive. In language that echoes Biblical accounts of Canaan as the site of the promised land, the narration extols the landscape as a paradise: "One god, a greater being, made his camp on the rich veldts and in the lush valleys of the South Land" (1). The god, Biamee, had "chosen" the land for his own camp, and it was not desolate but "rich and brown ... bountiful in life" (32). A "veil of mists" covered the land to protect it from the "savage" world (1), paralleling the protection of the Garden of Eden by powerful angels. This south land is a garden (3), the "wealthiest land on the earth," even "the promised land" (203).

The Australian landscape, the subject of so much angst and horror in many other speculative fictions, is dystopian not because of its essential nature but because it has witnessed colonization and invasion. Watson contends that white convicts and settlers did not arrive to find a punishing land, but that it was their arrival that made the land hostile: "The evil one caused the mists to lift from the land and other mortals saw its wealth and abundance.... The fair-skinned ones laid waste to the garden and the chosen people" (3). Following colonization, the land became dystopian. In *Kadaitcha*, characters refer to the land using the same language of any number of post-apocalyptic texts: "Only a few years ago this land was untouched.... Look at it now! It's a bloody wasteland!" (156). Watson describes land in language that evokes possession and domination and violence. White people "rip up the land! They pull down the trees and change the courses of our rivers. This land will be devastated even within our own generation" (132), and "the entire land was conquered and bound to their needs and desires" (35). In language that recalls Biblical apocalypse, the white people in *Kadaitcha* are "the evil ones" (204); they are "a terrible plague that had come upon them with an evil suddenness" (62). Colonization was a violent battle: "The mass murderers of the NMP reminded the rest of Australia that colonisation in the north had been a vicious and bloody process ... the great native wars" (41).

This apocalyptic event of colonization forms the crux of the plot, which is largely set in contemporary times. The protagonist is Tommy Gubba, whose task is to seek an Indigenous Kadaitcha (sorcerer) named Booka who has betrayed Indigenous groups by joining white men. Tommy succeeds in his quest, and his death at the conclusion of the novel positions him as an apocalyptic savior figure. The novel does not suggest that all has been restored, however, for Tommy warns of the consequences of the disaster of colonization: "You will be doomed to the end of time to wear the blood of my people.... The blood is upon the land until the end of time, and it is upon you until the end of time" (311). As apocalypse reveals, its disclosures can be warnings of judgment, as in Revelation, and Watson's novel warns that the time is coming when whites will suffer punishment for their crimes against the Indigenous people and land. Tommy demands that the god Biamee grant his request that "for every one hundred migloo, there had to be one that would know depthless tragedy and sorrow. That chosen one would be ridden by a hunger that could never be satisfied, that single life would be a lasting sacrifice to the land of the people" (310). The violence of colonization is a sin that can "never be expiated" (241), and the punishment motif reflects the judgment warnings in Revelation if the guilty do not seek forgiveness. These apocalyptic ideas of evil and judgment recur in the novel. Tommy says, "No migloo who walks on this land is innocent. They are all guilty! And they shall all be punished for what they have done" (131).

Colonization is an apocalypse in *Kadaitcha* because it involves the ending of culture, of language, of whole tribes. Tommy worries about the loss of culture when Aboriginal children abandon their traditional languages: "The tribes had always measured their wealth in the health and

Opposite: In *The Kadaitcha Sung*, apocalypse operates as a literature of protest against white colonization on Indigenous Australia. The novel describes a supernatural battle to restore and heal the land. *The Kadaitcha Sung*, Sam Watson. Ringwood, Vic.: Penguin, 1990.

The Kadaitcha Sung

A seductive tale of sorcery, eroticism and corruption

A NOVEL BY   SAM WATSON

abundance of the next generation, who were the guardians and warriors of tomorrow. Yet children like Poddy had never walked upon their own land and they spoke English too fluently. Their own language was beginning to fade and they knew nothing of their own Dreaming" (261). *Kadaitcha* is part of a body of Indigenous literature that emphasizes this apocalyptic sense of cultural loss. For instance, Wright's *Plains of Promise* is a tale of loss: loss of country, language and tradition. Wright's novel is also deeply concerned with the disappearance of Indigenous children in a government scheme that separated Indigenous children from their families.[9]

The systematic removal of children has apocalyptic consequences. As Rebecca La Forgia points out, the United Nations definition of genocide includes the practice of "*forcibly transferring children of the group to another group* with the intent to destroy, in whole or in part, their national, ethnic, racial or religious grouping" (193). Joan Gordon also notes that for Indigenous people globally "annihilation may occur through familiarization: by assimilating or by 'passing,' by absorbing or being absorbed by the dominant culture. That is the peaceful method. Or the annihilation may occur through erasure: by expulsion or killing" (205). Losing children, cultural traditions, and languages is tantamount to the end of the world.

Despite recognizing such losses, *Kadaitcha* upholds Indigenous groups as powerful and influential. They are superior to whites, for instance, in their peaceful ways. In this way Watson's work subverts common, racist colonial beliefs about non-white people as monstrous, immoral and savage[10] to reveal that it is white people who are truly violent and brutal. Whites are "driven by a blood lust that was never far from the surface" (61) and have a "mindless savagery" (62). Such descriptions invert colonial ideas and reveal the white person as the real savage. It is not difficult to see the implications of Booka's disguise amongst white people: he blends in with their violence. Although, as Gelder and Jacobs point out, the novel also narrates violence between Indigenous people who adhere to tribal laws and those who do not (111), white violence is generally alien to Indigenous people. The "camps of the innocent" belong to the Indigenous population, while the white people have a "love for blood" (204). We are reminded here too of the anxieties expressed in previous case studies over belonging in Australia, as we see in Watson's novel that it is white people who do not belong, who are aliens in every conceivable way: "Their words, their clothes ... everything about them. They don't belong to this land" (132).

Five • (Re)Writing the End of the World

White people are foreign, alien, and outsiders, the Other, a distinction that Watson reinforces with his use of "migloo" to designate whites: "The migloo ways — their language and their violence — were foreign to the land of Uluru" (62).

Watson therefore positions white characters — and readers — as outsiders. Terry Goldie has argued that the presence of Indigenous people can make whites feel uncomfortable and undermine their sense of security and possession. He comments that in the Canadian context: "The white Canadian looks at the Indian. The Indian is Other and therefore alien. But the Indian is indigenous and therefore cannot be alien. So the Canadian must be alien. But how can the Canadian be alien within Canada?" (12). As Chapter One discussed, Gelder and Jacobs have pointed out that conflict over land rights creates an "uncanny," uncomfortable situation over the issue of possession and belonging. The competition between Indigenous and white land rights positions both groups with justifiable claims, where "what is 'ours' is also potentially, or even always already, 'theirs': the one is becoming the other, the familiar is becoming strange" (23).

Kadaitcha also directly contradicts the notion of a dead heart in Australia. The novel reveals that the interior is actually a place of healing and power. Booka has stolen the "heart of the Rainbow Serpent from the fountain of life" (33) from its place in Uluru, a location that is a "most sacred altar, in the vast red rock that sat upon the heart of the land" (1). If Tommy completes his mission to find this "sacred heart" (35), the land will be healed from the ravages of colonization and restored under Biamee's authority (34). Tommy journeys there for his final initiation as a Kadaitcha, and he reacts with "reverent awe" (23) at the power in Uluru. Inside the rock, Tommy travels through the "passage of life that lay between the world of men and the Dreaming Time" (24) and becomes a spirit, witnessing the creation of the world (31). Watson thus depicts the Australian interior as a sacred and holy place of power. When Watson writes that Booka's seat of power is Brisbane and "the further he drifts from the mysteries of the land, the faster he loses his strength" (37), this also implies that Booka, who walks in the skin of a white man, also loses his strength as he drifts from his Indigenous identity. Noting *Kadaitcha*'s emphasis on the outback and Uluru in particular as a sacred place, Ken Gelder and Jane M. Jacobs have argued that *Kadaitcha* is a "'national fiction,' playing out both a mythical and a modern battle for the nation's soul ... Uluru stands at the centre of all this, drawing characters into its frame no matter how far away they may be" (112). Thus, far from being hostile, a dead heart, or a "nothing," the land — the outback — is a sacred place of power, restoration and strength.

Indigenous people are therefore significant and powerful in *Kadaitcha*. They have the agency to restore the land. *Kadaitcha*'s use of apocalypse in both its content and language to challenge the dominant version of Australian history thus recalls the effectiveness of the apocalyptic mode as a tool for critique of dominant systems. Watson's work aligns with Berger's claim, noted earlier, that apocalypse can militate against "the versions of hierarchy, truth, and morality currently in power" (223). Watson rewrites Indigenous people not simply as victims but as influential figures in a supernatural drama in which white people are ignorant and powerless. He also extends his claims against dominant social systems to include other groups as fellow minorities who must support each other. These include African groups (162) and American Indigenous peoples, such as when Tommy rejects one character's admiration of the cowboys in American Western films, because "you backing the wrong mob there. Those same Indians now, well they our countrymen and we the same blood as that mob.... You want to back those red fullahs up, boy" (260). Elsewhere, Watson has linked these groups: "those who have been marginalised in society, including Aborigines, disadvantaged women, gays and lesbians, and migrants" ("Aboriginal" n.p.). Knudsen points out that "the only whites in *The Kadaitcha Sung* who are tolerated [by Tommy] ... are those who are themselves, in however small a way, outsiders to mainstream society" (280).

Lest this sound like a militant treatise against white Australians that halts the apocalyptic paradigm before it can reach the stage of renewal and new worlds, *Kadaitcha* does offer some sense of reconciliation and ways forward. While Wevers notes that "there is nothing optimistic about *The Kadaitcha Sung*" (126), we can nonetheless find some points of hope. Tommy does succeed in his quest, and he is himself a symbol of reconciliation. As court interpreter, and as the child of a Kadaitcha and a white woman, he is from "two camps" (182). For Attebery, the figure of Tommy in both modern and ancient contexts "asserts the continuity of Aboriginal tradition within modern urban Australia" ("Aboriginality" 400). Gelder and Jacobs also point out that Tommy's name, Gubba, is an Aboriginal abbreviation of government meaning a white person (110). Tommy's racial identity, then, is not limited and he is able to represent both groups at different times, even if both groups deny him the right of belonging at times. Indeed, Watson singles out Tommy's white mother in particular as a reason for his ability to defeat his enemy: "But Koobara's son had been born of a white woman, and Biamee promised his people that the Kadaitcha child would deliver them" (4). The particularly unusual aspect of this is that even while Tommy's hatred of white people has punctuated virtually every page of the novel, his mother has been chosen because her "blood reaches back to sorcerers from the northern lands. They worshipped stones, great standing stones, and their powers are equal to those of the Kadaitcha" (228). It is this English blood that the novel credits with unlocking the sacred heart (229). The final association of English sorcerers with the Kadaitcha suggests that the two groups are, in fact, equal and must work together to bring restoration and healing to the land.

This equivalence of black and white groups seems significant in a novel that is otherwise hostile to white people, suggesting as it does that there may be hope for a new world in which reconciliation and racial equality are possible. Elsewhere Watson has called for a treaty between white and Aboriginal groups as a way for white people to "right the wrongs" ("Treaty or Ghost Dance" 15). If there is no treaty, a "racial holocaust" will occur and the nation will begin "a time of terrible darkness" ("Treaty or Ghost Dance" 15). In *Kadaitcha*, however, the implications of equality and kinship between white and Indigenous rest uneasily alongside the overwhelmingly negative constructions of white people, achieving a portrayal of hope and reconciliation that is ambivalent at best.

Watson's purpose in writing *Kadaitcha* is admittedly didactic. He has described his writing as "a hard-hitting message and that's the way I write. I don't apologize for it" ("I Say This to You" 595). He writes "to make a statement and I wanted to get into the hearts and minds of the great unwashed, white Australian masses" ("I Say This to You" 589–90).[11] In interview, Watson places great value on the process of storytelling: "Aboriginal people were the original storytellers. Our culture is the oldest surviving culture on the face of the Earth, and every generation, even though we now have the written page, we now have the internet, we now have so much technology available to us, the basic communication dynamic within our culture is still the spoken word, it's still the story" ("Our Dreaming Stilled" n.p.). The story in *Kadaitcha* has obvious apocalyptic overtones.

Watson uses the tropes of apocalypse — revelation, destruction, judgment and hope — to comment on Australia's history and offer new perspectives on colonization, the devastation that white people caused, and their coming judgment. In this way, he rewrites the end of the world to give readers a new perspective on the society in which they live.

Archie Weller: Land of the Golden Clouds *(1998)*

Archie Weller adopts a conventional post-apocalyptic framework in *Land of the Golden Clouds* and addresses themes of diversity and unity amongst multicultural groups. The post-nuclear setting is a future Australia three thousand years in the future. The protagonist, Red Mond, gathers representatives of diverse ethnic groups to lead an attack on their enemy, the Nightstalkers, a group of cave-dwelling humans who emerge at night to attack and eat other people. Weller's use of the apocalyptic paradigm focuses more on the possibilities for restoration than devastation, and he reveals a future where reconciliation is not only possible but mandatory for survival.

The nuclear event that shaped this world was apocalyptic; it was "the wrath" (20) and "Armageddon" (211). Weller shows that this land is now a difficult place to live: it is the "dry, hard land" and "dead plains" (20), "dead country" (4), and the "inhospitable land" (68). The Visitors, one of the groups from different races that Red Mond gathers together, come from Jamaica, a land that contrasts favorably with Australia because it is a paradise, a "land as green and full of trees and waterways as this land is barren and dead" (78). In contrast, Red Mond's group visit Melbourne, a "dead city" (324), "a desolate place of death and emptiness" (320). Weller also uses "wasteland" to describe the Australian interior in *Land of the Golden Clouds*, a word so frequently occurring in post-holocaust texts that it is virtually synonymous with apocalypse: the country is a "desolate red wasteland" (34).

Weller's novel does have several points of similarity with Watson's *Kadaitcha*. We saw in *Kadaitcha* that Watson challenged the concept of a "dead heart" in Australia, and Weller's novel also disputes this notion, though less directly. On the edges of the Ilkari (the white tribe) country are the Purple Plains, "the dead country where no one ever ventured," but it is not vacant, because "hardy" Keepers of the Trees (an Indigenous group) live there (4). Weller's novel, therefore, rejects the notion that Indigenous people are missing or that there is a dead heart in Australia. These Keepers of the Trees are a powerful and respected group. In fact, as Sargent notes, the novel "presents the groups that are closest to the Aboriginal way of life most positively" ("Australia as Dystopia" 117). In another parallel with *Kadaitcha*, the Indigenous groups in *Land of the Golden Clouds* are peaceful, in contrast to the violence of white people:

> It was known by every Ilkari that the Keepers of the Trees had sprung from this land like the rocks and rivers and trees themselves. They were a part of this country — every grain of it — and they knew all its secrets. They kept out of the way of the white people and their ways, for it had been the white people who had annoyed the spirits and caused the High Ones to walk upon this earth, bringing not sustenance but destruction. So they kept to themselves, these remnants of the oldest Tribe, with their own language, laws and customs [4–5].

During an attack, for example, the Keepers of the Trees refuse to interfere because brutality is foreign to them and it is seen as "white man's business. They had been killing each other forever and when they were tired of that they had turned on the Keepers of the Trees and had killed them as well" (139). Readers learn that the Keepers "disliked anything to do with warlike white men who used their aggression without reason. They knew many stories of past atrocities perpetrated upon their people, that lost none of the horror just because they were only stories now" (286).

Again, where *Kadaitcha* suggested that white people have wrought destruction on the land, *Land of the Golden Clouds* also shows that white violence has damaged the environment: "The general feeling in the caravan was one of unease.... Even the gentle Kareen could offer no comfort to the land all around her. It was in great pain, she told her cousin. There were certainly enough signs of the turmoil that had erupted here at the time the High Ones had walked upon the earth" (308). The shame and sins of the past cry out from the very earth in Weller's novel and the land demands restitution. The Keepers of the Trees feel this pain as they travel over the land: "They could sense the result of this destruction on these desolate pages of the landscape they had just passed, where not a single tree stood to hold the spirit of an ancestor close to the earth. It was a forgotten land — an unhappy land" (139). The Keepers avoid relics of European buildings because "often uneasy, restless spirits frequented the ruins of their home" (304). These spirits function as a kind of postcolonial haunting.

Land of the Golden Clouds critiques colonial practices such as mapping and naming places. When colonizers, the outsiders, assign British names to sites and dictate a foreign language as the only language to be spoken, this effectively reverses their own status as aliens and establishes the Indigenous people as the new outsiders, aliens in their own land. *Land of the Golden Clouds* describes the practice of anglicizing place names as "white man's desire to establish some prestige that made him touch with a finger a million years of history, then claim it as his own" (82). Edward Said has called imperialism "an act of geographical violence through which virtually every space in the world is explored, charted, and finally brought under control" (225). For Said, the imperial process of exploration, mapping, and colonization results in a "loss of the locality to the outsider" (225). Simon Ryan has argued that mapping a place positions the land as a text, which colonists can inscribe and thus dominate (126). Cartography can become an assertion of power and control. White people's attempts to exert control and authority over the land in such ways are thus unsuccessful attempts to impose themselves on a place that is not theirs, and to pretend that they are the rightful possessors.

Mapping a place also implies that it is a tabula rasa and only from that time does it have existence and history. This practice erases Indigenous history. Colonization, after all, entirely rejects history for new beginnings. It is an ending for the colonized people but a start for the colonizers who begin a "new world" as if nothing has gone before. Bradford, Mallan and Stephens note in their discussion of Kelleher's *Red Heart* that "selective naming erases the past and reinforces the narrative proposition that a new world has replaced the old" (354). Maps are therefore often associated with colonial practices of erasing Indigenous existence. John Rieder notes that the map is also a common trope in lost-race narratives and, in some cases, may even infer European superiority: "the map that instigates the adventurers' expedition, often pointing the way to a hidden treasure, indicates the way that European knowledge gives the adventurers both the means and the right to claim the hidden treasure as their own" (*Colonialism* 23). Outside lost race romances, we can see that the same process of knowledge and power operates in any colonial mapping. Gibson has written that "any space which did not seem to have meanings invested in it was alluring because its first inscribers could imbue it with their own meanings, their own knowledge and beliefs.... The world was being written into European history" (*South* 5). Simon Ryan has suggested that in imperialism, the practice of cartography engenders a dismissal of the past because it ignores history and favors the future (127). The dismissal of Indigenous history is evident in national accounts that solely focus on the country's colonial past, such as the "birth" of the nation Australia after the arrival of the First Fleet, and its bicentenary in 1988.

While Lyman Tower Sargent writes that Australian utopian writing has typically presented Indigenous characters as "sub-human" ("Australia as Dystopia" 116), Brian Attebery suggests that Australian science fiction writers have usually used one of three main ways to depict Indigenous people:

> During the Bad Old Days [1890s–1970s], Aboriginal peoples were seen primarily as a problem: holdovers, like the marsupials, from some earlier stage of evolutionary history, and, like the Tasmanian tiger, unlikely to survive the arrival of more advanced competitors. Next was the Hopeful Moment, a brief period in the 1970s ... of an Aboriginal civil-rights movement.... Finally there is the Troubled Now, a time when which there is no safe way for a non–Aboriginal writer to tackle Aboriginal issues and yet when the discourse of sf offers a number of innovative ways to reframe ideas of race and cultural difference ["Aboriginality" 387].

Attebery classifies works such as Weller's *Land of the Golden Clouds* and also Watson's *Kadaitcha* in the third period because their novels engage with the problems of reconciliation and offer different ideas or solutions to the difficulties that contemporary society faces.

Indeed, if Watson's *Kadaitcha* implies that some reconciliation between Indigenous and white might be possible, Weller's novel is predicated on this very fact. The themes of inter-racial peace in *Land of the Golden Clouds* permeate every aspect of the novel from its structure to its characters. The novel features each of the main characters' perspectives in turn, and thus gives equal weight to their diverse beliefs and attitudes. An explanatory note prefacing the novel outlines the use of languages in the novel: Nyoongah, Koori, Gypsy, Spanish, a "type" of Hebrew and a "type of hybrid English" (viii). The combination of different languages between the groups, the changing perspectives, and also the shift between past and present tense all contribute towards a breakdown of boundaries and distinctions, of past and future, particularly given that some of the languages are themselves impure types, "hybrid" mixings of several distinct languages. The references within the text such as Bob Marley, the Bible, and poet John Bartlett reinforce the theme of multiple cultures converging. The formal characteristics of the novel reflect the integration of the different groups within the novel. The Keepers of the Trees are the "remnants of the oldest Tribe" (5), distinct from the other groups, separate and never fully involving themselves with different races. Yet despite being set apart, Weller shows that the Keepers are willing to protect the white people. The "past atrocities" do not lead to irreconcilable conflicts. Instead the Keepers are prepared to sacrifice their lives for the greater purpose of defeating a common enemy, offering their assistance to the other groups in the battle:

> [Weerluk] knows what he must do. All his life he has lived apart from others except his own kind and adhered strictly to his laws. But this is *his* land and it is crying out for him to save it now. Grabbing up the foreign horn, he leaps noiselessly into the waters and heads for the outside world. It will be *his* lips that summon the Asian people, foreigners — and yet friends — of the Keepers [363].

Red Mond falls in love with S'shony, a woman from the Nightstalkers, a tribe his own people had hated and feared, and different cultural groups combine their skills to work together and save each other: "the worst wounds of S'shony were healed by Chinese ingenuity, Aboriginal bush lore and Laelia's magic" (367). The convergence of multiple languages, characters, and structural elements reinforce this utopian plot for peace and reconciliation.

The conclusion of *Land of the Golden Clouds* neatly brings together the final elements of apocalypse, stitching together destruction and renewal to focus on the new world. Weller's novel collapses differences between the groups in an apparent rhetorical strategy to demonstrate that the only path forward and chance for a better world is to focus on common areas. The future is only made possible by the co-operation of a plurality of ethnic groups. "We come in peace to do battle with our common enemy. Even though we all have different beliefs we all have the one enemy" (323). Red Mond's speech at the conclusion of the final battle repeats this philosophy, echoing apocalyptic imagery in that destruction leads to a new world:

> The time for war is over.... For the purpose of all this death and the loss of our compatriots was not to continue the killing but to end it all. You see the woman I love — who has saved my life twice and who almost died by my

side—is one of the enemy. We see cave people who are hated and despised and killed by cave people. Above, there are many different people, all of whom hate each other, and yet we banded together. So who can say who is an enemy? Let us embrace our enemy and all be friends and I will lead you out of our dark world! [368].

While such a conclusion may be overly simplistic for some readers, Weller's utopian aims in *Land of the Golden Clouds* for reconciliation between the various cultural groups cannot be denied.

Red Mond's leadership speech for unification is particularly resonant given his racial identity: he is white, while his name suggests "red world" or even "red man." The group of travelers comprises people from around the world and of various ethnic backgrounds, but a white person leads them. This seems to be a curious choice for a writer who has previously identified himself as Aboriginal. This white leadership may seem troubling, although an alternative way to read this is to understand that Red Mond's own beliefs had to change as he realized that the old divisions between groups no longer mattered. Perhaps, as in Watson's *Kadaitcha*, where Tommy has white heritage as well as Indigenous, this asserts that reconciliation cannot be accomplished by one group alone; there must be representatives of both groups before change can be effected. Using a multiracial or white character as an agent of restoration may be a recognition of the potential for reconciliation in that white groups must take responsibility for the tragedy in the past and participate in exploring ways forward in the future. Weller's novel suggests that any vision for the future must be predicated on the coexistence and co-operation of Indigenous and white characters, as well as those of other cultural backgrounds.

These two case studies suggest that there is indeed ample room for writers to use the language and paradigm of apocalypse to present subversive and radical critiques of dominant cultures. Both texts refuse to conform to traditional versions of white history, instead presenting narratives that rewrite Australia's history in ways that highlight the catastrophe of colonization on Indigenous groups and the Australian landscape. In the establishment of a "new world," colonial practices such as assimilation, cartography, and the removal of children contribute to the ending of Indigenous groups, cultures, and languages. The writers contest the notion that the Australian landscape is an empty, dead space. Instead, it is a sacred place, and Watson and Weller populate it with powerful, respected Indigenous figures.

These two case studies also implicitly warn their readers not to imagine Indigenous characters as victims or helpless sufferers of great tragedy. Watson's novel brims with the power and triumph of Indigenous characters in a supernatural narrative that takes place against an unsuspecting white society, while Weller characterizes his Indigenous characters as central to the project of reconciliation in his novel. Watson's *Kadaitcha* ends with some ambiguity, simultaneously upholding a sustained critique of white society while attempting to demonstrate the kinship of white and black groups, most obviously represented through Tommy's mixed heritage. Weller's work more clearly focuses on the imperative for reconciliation, presenting a determinedly utopian vision of the potential for inter-racial restoration. Rewriting the end of the world, rewriting history, and rewriting power relationships, these novels show that apocalyptic destruction in the context of Indigenous history in Australia can be followed by renewal and hope for a better future.

· Six ·

The End of the Human
Apocalypse, Cyberpunk, and the Parrish Plessis Novels

> Judgement Day was getting a fair whipping. Punters had already lined the beach dunes to catch the spectacle.
> Marianne de Pierres, *Code Noir* 11

It is clear that apocalypse can provide a powerful means for writers and filmmakers to engage with a number of topics including nuclear war, environmental damage, colonization, and race relations. The previous chapters have discussed how authors have achieved this in science fiction, fantasy, children's dystopian literature, films, and novels. Yet in one particular mode of speculative fiction, the influence of apocalypse is disputed. Critics such as Bruce Sterling and Veronica Hollinger have described cyberpunk as an anti-apocalyptic mode because it rejects fearful constructions of disaster and produces nonchalant attitudes to the prospect of catastrophe. Sterling and others, such as Claire Sponsler, have also claimed that cyberpunk is a globalized genre that transcends borders and local concerns, and dissolves languages, ethnicities and even human identity into such a mélange that it effaces nation, race, and sense of place.

Given these claims, cyberpunk offers space for Australian writers to reject the enduring national apocalyptic themes and imagery, particularly the apocalyptic map that preceded colonization. The question of whether or not this is indeed what happens becomes the focus of this chapter. The following discussion offers a brief summary of cyberpunk globally and in

Australia and then, within the framework of Australian apocalypse outlined so far in this book, examines Marianne de Pierres's Parrish Plessis novels to determine one approach to the sense of location and apocalypse in Australian cyber narratives. De Pierres sets her novels in a future Australia but describes a mixed cultural and linguistic environment that appears to constitute a generic global space. Yet her representation of the hostile and harsh landscape indicates specifically Australian themes. De Pierres's use of eschatological motifs as well as the textual anxieties about posthumanism and the end of authenticity also belie cyberpunk's indifference to apocalypse.

Cyberpunk

Critics usually identify William Gibson's *Neuromancer* as the first or archetypal cyberpunk work. Hollinger has written that *Neuromancer* is the "quintessential cyberpunk novel" ("Cybernetic" 30), influencing numerous texts that followed. Commentators have also cited Gibson's "Johnny Mnemonic" and Ridley Scott's film *Blade Runner* as early, definitive examples of cyberpunk (Baccolini and Moylan, "Dystopia" 2; McMullen and Dowling). Over the decades since the birth of cyberpunk in the early 1980s, authors such as Bruce Sterling, Pat Cadigan, and Neal Stephenson have all produced their own interpretations of the genre and provoked critical discussion and debate. More recently, *The Matrix* and its two sequels have become arguably the most well-known cyberpunk texts for a mainstream audience.

Discussions of cyberpunk often link the emergence of the genre in the 1980s with the political and cultural circumstances of the time. Jameson writes that cyberpunk is "the supreme *literary* expression if not of postmodernism, then of late capitalism itself" (*Postmodernism* 419), while Baccolini and Moylan argue that the genre "generated a usefully negative if nihilistic imaginary as the impact of the conservative turn of the decade began to be recognized in both the social structure and everyday life" ("Dystopia" 2–3). Critics often emphasize the genre's focus on capitalist developments such as multinational corporations and globalization. For instance, David Seed points out that the experience of America in the 1980s influences Pat Cadigan's cyberpunk fiction, with its "business conglomerates, the increasing sophistication of electronics in the entertainment industry, and above all the growth of virtual reality technology ("Cyberpunk" 70).

In his oft-cited Preface to *Mirrorshades: The Cyberpunk Anthology*, Sterling describes the growth of cyberpunk and discusses the countercultural influences and the themes that define it as a genre. Sterling calls cyberpunk "a new movement in science fiction" (vii), a "product of the Eighties milieu" (viii) with a definitive emphasis on style and fashion from its writers: "they prize their garage-band esthetic. They love to grapple with the raw core of SF: its ideas" (viii). Sterling suggests that one of the key characteristics of cyberpunk is a combination of a revolutionary sentiment with the latest advances of science: "a new kind of integration ... the realm of high tech, and the modern pop underground" (ix), "an integration of technology and the Eighties counterculture. An unholy alliance of the technical world and the world of organized dissent — the underground world of pop culture, visionary fluidity, and street-level anarchy" (x). The development of new technologies and the effects of such growth on society are key aspects underlying the genre. Sponsler describes cyberpunk as "a fusion of high-tech and punk counterculture characterized by a self-conscious stylistic and ideological rebelliousness ... a reinterpretation of human (and especially male) experience in a media-dominated, information-saturated, post-industrial age" ("Beyond the Ruins" 251). In its context, born of 1980s consumerism and globalization, and also its content, focusing as it does on subcultures, cyberpunk is a self-designated intensely political genre, a fiction of protest.

To portray the sinister effects of a world dominated by multinationals, cyberpunk often employs a dystopian setting, almost invariably imagining a world worse than today. Cyberpunk is usually bleak, as Kevin Pask has written:

> In its early formulation as the description of scientific and technological utopia, science fiction was a pendant to such "grand narratives," and in fact "cyberpunk," a popular mode of science fiction in the past decade, announces its break with earlier versions of the genre as the decommissioning of a utopian vision of the future. Dystopia has long played a role in science fiction, but it is difficult to imagine cyberpunk without it [182].

In a discussion of the film *Blade Runner*, Giuliana Bruno cites the film's "aesthetic of decay" which emphasizes "disintegration" and "the dark side of technology" (239). Decay and desolation are common features of the cyberpunk landscape. Sponsler suggests that the environments of the genre are post-apocalyptic: "the physical settings of most cyberpunk stories nonetheless look strikingly like the setting of any post-holocaust story: blighted, rubble-strewn, broken-down cityscapes; vast terrains of decay, bleakness, and the detritus of civilization; and the nearly complete absence of a benign or beautiful nature" ("Beyond the Ruins" 253). Phillip E. Wegner writes that "the blasted urban landscapes ... of cyberpunk fiction [are]: post-industrial cores, filled with abandoned buildings, decaying factories, and the waste products and 'throwaway' populations of twentieth-century capitalist culture" (174). Cyber texts, then, not only undermine positive and optimistic constructions of the future, but also tend to link the capitalist world with the devaluation of human life.

If, as some critics claim, cyberpunk displays an anti-authoritarian political engagement, there are others who argue that it has failed in this respect. Preoccupied as the genre is with dystopian settings and bleak scenarios, it is perhaps fitting that writers and critics have touted the end of cyberpunk for years, often in apocalyptic language. Jameson reads cyberpunk as a "doomed attempt at a counteroffensive" to the increasingly popular genre of fantasy; it is "SF's ... final effort to reconquer a readership alienated by the difficulties of contemporary science, increasingly hostile ideologically to the radicalism of more social SF (now generationally distanced by the youth culture), and frustrated by the diminishing production of new yet formulaic easy reading in the SF area" (*Archaeologies* 68). In "William Gibson and the Death of Cyberpunk," published in 1995, Sponsler not only declared the genre dead but also argued that cyberpunk had arrived "DOA — dead on arrival," failing completely as a radical literature (47). In an earlier essay, "Cyberpunk in the Nineties," Sterling had suggested that the increasing respectability of the genre and the ageing demographic of the early cyberpunk writers, along with an attendant loss of vision and rebellion in the genre's content, combined to render the genre entirely ineffective, if not dead. Hollinger has noted a similar point, arguing that the commercialization of the genre resulted in its "final implosion" with cyberpunk "self-destructing under the weight of its own deconstructive activities" ("Cybernetic" 42).

While some critics insist cyberpunk met its demise shortly after its much-heralded beginning, others suggest its "death" was only temporary. P. Chad Barnett argues that *The Matrix* single-handedly resuscitated "the corpse-cold body of cyberpunk" (360). *The Matrix*, Barnett claims, was the first authentic cinematic expression of cyberpunk (360), although other critics, notably Slavoj Žižek, were more dismissive.[1] Despite the dire pronouncements of its early proponents, cyberpunk continues to reappear in or inform science fiction texts of today. Sponsler has written that while cyberpunk is "over" ("Beyond the Ruins" 251), its influence is seen in authors who either write against the genre or regurgitate its themes and clichés. In 1994, Sean McMullen and Terry Dowling suggested that "real-tech, a type of rigorous, hard SF" exemplified in the writing of authors such as Greg Egan and McMullen had superseded cyberpunk (n.p.). Elsewhere, Lawrence Person argued that one may characterize "postcyberpunk" works by their optimism rather than dystopia, and conformity rather than rebellion, where protagonists are socially integrated members of the middle class rather than isolated misfits.

Given cyberpunk's interest in dystopian societies in a globalized setting, it is worth considering how Australian writers have approached the genre. Around the time when theorists were pronouncing cyberpunk dead, local critics questioned why the genre had failed to even make any kind of impact in Australia in the first place. In 1998, when Paul Collins's *The MUP Encyclopedia of Australian Science Fiction & Fantasy* was published, cyberpunk did not warrant an entry of its own. McMullen and Dowling have discussed the small amount of cyberpunk that Australian authors produced, listing Egan, Russell Blackford and Gillian Rubinstein among the relatively few examples.[2] McMullen and Dowling note that their inclusion of Rubinstein's children's novels *Space Demons* and *Skymaze* (and the later *Shinkei*) acknowledges only her use of computer themes rather than the style of cyberpunk. The novels, in which the child protagonists enter virtual worlds of computer games — much like the child heroes of the television programs *Pirate Islands 1* and *2*— also lack the essential thematic interests of cyberpunk, so cannot reasonably be associated with the genre.

If there have been few Australian texts that exemplify Gibsonian cyberpunk, there are still writers in Australia who have adopted the themes or style of the genre. For instance, cyberpunk short stories include Blackford's "Glass Reptile Breakout" and "The Soldier in the Machine," Paul Collins's "Wired Dreaming" and Egan's short story collection, *Luminous*. Some of the Australian cyberpunk or cyber-themed novels include Paul Collins's novel *Cyberskin*, Sean Williams's *Metal Fatigue*, and several by

Egan, including *Quarantine*. Egan's *Permutation City* focuses on technologies and artificial realities even though the stylized narrative of cyberpunk is absent. Ian Irvine's Human Rites series (*The Last Albatross, Terminator Gene, The Life Lottery*) imagines a world controlled by the media, the Net, although, again, one can only very broadly characterize the novels as cyber-themed rather than cyberpunk. More recently, Marianne de Pierres's Parrish Plessis series has emerged as another local example that is written in the style of cyberpunk. While one could argue that de Pierres's novels may not technically be cyberpunk, the genre's themes and especially its style have had an obvious influence on her writing. The series adopts the stylistic features, decaying urban setting, and technology-infused bodies that characterize cyberpunk, and it is a popular, recent example of the way that writers can adapt the genre in Australia. The novels are useful to examine because of the way they negotiate and reject cyberpunk's supposed construction of a globalized world and its indifference to apocalypse, ultimately articulating a vision of the future that is particularly Australian.

Marianne de Pierres: Nylon Angel, Code Noir, Crash Deluxe *(2004–2005)*

Marianne de Pierres's three Parrish Plessis novels are set on the east coast of Australia many years into the future.[3] In this future dystopia, the Media comprise several powerful and corrupt organizations and their famous reporters who essentially control society, and class divisions separate society into the rich, who live in Viva, and the poor, who live in the slums of The Tert, outside the city. The Media are "frigging royalty in this hemisphere" (*Nylon* 55), more powerful even than law enforcement. The narrative follows the story of Parrish, a bodyguard for Jamon Mondo, an abusive and violent underworld figure. She becomes involved with the Media when she assists two men to escape custody who are accused of the murder of journalist Razz Retribution, a celebrity on the Net. The Media then target and frame Parrish for the murder. In her efforts to escape Jamon's control and solve the crime she discovers that the Media have funded a secret genetics project called Code Noir, a malicious experimental scheme to create grotesque human/machine hybrids in an attempt to boost media ratings. During Parrish's travels through The Tert, she accidentally

Six • The End of the Human

consumes the blood from a feather totem and becomes infected with an alien parasite called the Eskaalim, a race that has been infecting humans for thousands of years. The parasite's growing power over Parrish manifests itself in visions and increasing violence as she attempts to stop the Code Noir project and the Media organization behind it.

The urban setting of de Pierres's novels is bleak and dystopian. Much of the narrative occurs in slums and ruins, in places of poverty and lawlessness. The first novel, *Nylon Angel*, highlights the degradation. Parrish lives in The Tert, which is "outside the city limits. A leftover strip of toxic humanity where, it was rumoured, you could survive on your own terms" (2). Society has abandoned and forgotten the people in The Tert, and life there is harsh and violent. The Tert is the opposite of Vivacity, "an exquisite, neat, expensive carpet of humanity" (150), which is "one of the world's carnivorous super-cities, spreading down the east coast of Australia" (12).

While the dystopian environments in cyberpunk appear to suggest that the genre is closely connected with apocalypse, critics have argued that it is actually anti-apocalyptic. Sterling claims that while the issues of social change led some science fiction writers to overreact and warn of disaster, a "distinguishing mark" of cyberpunk is its "boredom with the Apocalypse" ("Preface" to *Burning Chrome* xi). Lauraine Leblanc characterizes cyberpunk as non-apocalyptic, while Sponsler argues that cyberpunk differs from other apocalyptic fiction because it dismisses the idea that apocalypse ultimately produces a better, often idyllic, society and instead adopts a "profound indifference" to apocalypse, where catastrophes are of no account, "neither good nor evil" ("Beyond the Ruins" 253) and are, in fact, "taken for granted" (254). Sponsler writes that cyberpunk removes the "crisis and climax" of apocalypse ("Beyond the Ruins" 260) because survivalism and nuclear fears are no longer valid factors in the genre. In "Apocalypse Coma," Hollinger suggests that "Cyberpunk, at least in Gibson's original version, demonstrates a kind of postmodern ennui with the narrative conventions of earlier apocalyptic fictions" (164), such as in the post-nuclear period. Hollinger writes that the "anticlimactic" millennium with decreased nuclear threats and the continued unfulfilled predictions of doomsdays have produced boredom with, rather than an accumulated fear of, apocalypse (164). Instead, she argues that cyberpunk tends to work against apocalypse: "The cool antiapocalypticism of cyberpunk not only challenged the deep-seated apocalyptic tendencies of genre sf as a whole but, as the

MARIANNE DE PIERRES

"A COMPELLING BLEND OF MAD MAX AND DARK ANGEL." *THE MELBOURNE AGE*

Nylon Angel

official end of the millennium approached, served as a continuing site of resistance to the growing tide of eschatological sentiment in both genre fiction and mainstream cultural analyses" (165). In "Cybernetic Deconstructions," Hollinger notes that cyberpunk demonstrates a "coolness, a kind of ironically detached approach" to its content, including apocalyptic themes (38). Apocalypse is "no longer a favored narrative move," in part because "a kind of philosophical apocalypse has already occurred" (38).

It does appear that the prevailing sentiment in many examples of cyberpunk, including de Pierres's work, is cynical and closer to skepticism rather than a fear of the end of the world. In the Parrish novels, references to apocalyptic terms such as holocaust — a bar has "holocaust decor" (*Crash* 20) — and Judgment Day are deliberately casual and appear to be mere words divorced from their significance. For instance, the opening of the second novel, *Code Noir*, implies a blasé attitude to apocalypse:

> The whole of One-World was crawling with meteorologists sprouking about how it would be the biggest tide in the Southern Hem's history. Close to thirty metres due to the full moon and some other tongue-tying stuff that they couldn't explain sensibly in a news grab. It had brought the closet crazies out, and given the confessed ones carte blanche. Judgement Day was getting a fair whipping. Punters had already lined the beach dunes to catch the spectacle, while others had fled to the borders of the Interior [*Code* 11].

Yet even if cyber texts have a tendency to avoid the gravity and earnestness of prior dystopian texts, the apocalyptic undercurrents of the genre remain strong, particularly in works such as de Pierres's novels. An ironic or indifferent attitude to apocalypse does not make the genre anti-apocalyptic, for the genre still trades on the themes, imagery and language of apocalypse, even when subverting them. Cyberpunk often narrates the end of the human, if not the world, in order to expose the greed and abuse of power of multinationals and capitalist structures, as well as depicting in many cases a future world after disaster where a lone figure strives to "save the world."

Rather than reproduce an anti-apocalyptic stance, de Pierres's trilogy specifically references apocalyptic themes. This is evident both in Parrish's

Opposite: Nylon Angel is the first of three novels set in a future dystopian Australia. Despite the bleak setting, the series suggests the utopian possibilities of apocalypse. *Nylon Angel*, Marianne de Pierres. Parrish Plessis 1. London: Orbit-Time Warner, 2004. Artist: Larry Rostant.

attempts to avert disaster as well as her fears of technologies leading to the end of the human and the "real." Despite Parrish's cynical first-person narrative and her dismissal of holocaust as mere "decor" or Judgment Day as a "spectacle," the series' tone is eschatological. The novels are full of prophecies, warnings, proclamations of destiny, appointed times for catastrophe, world-affecting events, and messianic figures. When Loyl-me-Daac, Parrish's occasional lover and nemesis, says that trailing Parrish is "like slipstreaming the end of the world" she warns him not to "joke" about such things (*Code* 131). Geological disturbances and other events such as "King Tide" threaten society and there are also reports of rising sea levels and a cycle of birth and death (*Code* 244). This is not the only imminent disaster, however, for war between The Tert and Viva is also looming at the conclusion of *Crash Deluxe*, and characters view the Code Noir genetics project and its misuse and abuse of technology in catastrophic terms.

Within this framework of disaster, de Pierres creates Parrish as a messianic figure. The conclusion of *Code Noir* affirms Parrish's status as savior when she decides to sacrifice herself to the parasite in order to save her people; at one point the narrative describes her hair as "styled à la crown-of-thorns" (*Code* 301). The people of The Tert proclaim that Parrish is the "female orisa—spirit power. They have a *long-tell* story. *Whoever the Feather Crown chooses will protect their future time....* Now they want to follow her into battle" (*Nylon* 85). In the "legend of Oya," Oya brings about "great changes" (*Nylon* 288). Parrish's cynical reactions work to undermine the integrity of the apocalyptic discourse: "It seemed likely they'd somehow worked me into some old myth. Punters needed heroes—didn't matter what religion they gigged to. Muenos were worse than most. It had something to do with their particular mash of Catholic, voodoo, tek worship. God's in the heavens, the animals *and* the machine! Crowded, huh!" (*Nylon* 77). Yet even while Parrish adopts an ironic stance, her heroic role gives credence to the prophecies as the story progresses.

The positioning of Parrish's story inside the myths and legends and prophecies necessarily invokes apocalyptic discourse. The parasite has associations with apocalyptic figures from religion and mythology. The Eskaalim appears to Parrish in the form of an angel, its wings "a swarming, crawling mass of data. Scrolling past at a frantic rate" (*Nylon* 258). In the data, Parrish sees various names and stories of figures from Greek mythology and Christianity, including "Jesus, Thor, Zeus" as well as "Mamba.

Satan" (258). Eventually, if the parasite is unchecked, it will erode the human self: "It's a parasite, Jamon. Using you for food. It'll leave you nothing. No 'self'" (*Nylon* 306).

The novels evidence apocalyptic themes not only in the messianic discourse but also in Parrish's attitudes to technology, and this betrays an ongoing suspicion about the impact of machines in society. Invasive mechanical intrusions into bodies as well as the all-pervasive Media threaten the "real" and the human, manipulating and distorting reality and deceiving people; in its worst form, technology literally feeds on the flesh and blood of human bodies. J. P. Telotte argues that the figures of the cyborg or artificial human in cyberpunk texts address "our ambivalent feelings about technology, our increasing anxieties about our own nature in a technological environment, and a kind of evolutionary fear that these artificial selves may presage our own disappearance or *termination*" (26). Wagar has written that "terminal visions bring emphasis of a special kind to the prophet's cry of woe and warning. They attack us at our most vulnerable point: our sense of mortality, and our fear of non-being" (*Terminal* 205).

One of the recurring themes of cyber texts is this anxiety about human identity and the "fear of non-being," although in many cases cyberpunk texts articulate and then dismiss or even celebrate this possibility. A cyber apocalypse suggests the idea that humans are dying out and their replacements and successors will be robots, cyborgs, artificial intelligence or virtual selves. The enduring concerns of cyberpunk — biomechanics and technological surveillance and manipulation — support an apocalyptic reading of the genre. Sterling lists two main themes of cyberpunk: technological invasions of firstly the body and secondly the mind. These two kinds of invasions are seen in "prosthetic limbs, implanted circuitry, cosmetic surgery, genetic alteration ... brain-computer interfaces, artificial intelligence, neurochemistry" ("Preface" to *Mirrorshades* xi). Many critical discussions about cyberpunk echo Sterling's assertion about the integration of human and machine. Scott Bukatman, for example, has suggested that one can characterize cyberpunk by the breakdown of divisions between human and machine, and he argues that cyberpunk of the 1980s was "concerned with the intimacy of the contemporary interfaces that exist between human subject and electronic technology" (84).

The Parrish novels articulate the fear of the end of the authentic human self due to technologies through descriptions of Parrish that assert the boundaries between human and technology. De Pierres depicts Parrish in a way that emphasizes the alienating differences between the machine and the human: "Most babes are chocked up with enhancements. Wired so tight their buns act like capacitors! I've got different ideas. Sure, some things you can't live without — compass implant and olfactory augmentations (*olfaugs*) — but the rest is pure me. Nearly two metres of well-honed skin. In hand-to-hand combat I can match anyone" (*Nylon* 8). Parrish's rejection of inorganic material makes her unlike "most babes" and the opposition of the physical body ("pure me") and technology ("enhancements") reinforces the machine-human distinction.

Cyberpunk closes the distance between human and machine, and this has the potential to signal the end of the human. Stableford has written that the threat of machines occurs in one of two ways. In the first event, the machine becomes a danger when those in power use it to maintain their position and control the population. The second occurs when "the machines themselves are the manipulators and oppressors, and sometimes the destroyers of humankind" (115). Jameson has argued that this shift from benign robot to actively menacing machine occurs when "the purely mechanical robot is transformed into the at least partially organic android" (*Archaeologies* 114). However, the integration of machine and human also threatens the death of humanity, and one can add this machine-human hybrid to Stableford's categories as a third threat. As Sterling points out, the "integration" of technology and human has the effect of "radically redefining the nature of humanity, the nature of the self" ("Preface" to *Mirrorshades* xi). In cyberpunk, human existence and identity are under an apocalyptic threat of extinction or erasure, where freedom and privacy are lost, and where the merging of machine and human can result in the disappearance of the human entirely. The loss of self, the fear of the self ending, causes an apocalyptic anxiety, and Wagar identifies this general concept as one of the fears prompting "every story of the world's end [because it] draws power from, and illuminates in one way or another, the ends and beginnings of the self" (*Terminal* 67).

As Sponsler points out, human identity is problematic in cyberpunk worlds where characters can easily change bodies and faces:

> Identity in this milieu is cast onto the surface of the body, but where the body can be so readily redesigned and customized, conventional notions of individual uniqueness become meaningless. Chameleon-like, the body imi-

Six • The End of the Human

tates and even becomes its environment, but no longer really offers a mirror for an autonomous interior subjectivity. While physical being no longer determines the self, neither does personal experience ["Death" 49].

Yet in de Pierres's work, the physical does determine the self. For instance, the opening pages of *Nylon Angel* introduce Parrish as someone who would "never make the front cover of a glossy" and refuses to be "fixed up" because her flaws serve as a reminder "of what I'd left behind" (2). Parrish's body thus has an intimate connection with her "self"; changing her appearance equates to changing her identity. Naomi Jacobs writes that the "natural" is at risk in human-machine integration:

> Individuality can be modified by appearance-altering surgeries, cyber-prostheses, and even the repair of defective genes. Many fear that a new servitude awaits the product of these new technologies, which augur the obsolescence of the "natural" human.... Even the erasure of the physical limitations of the human body can seem to entail the erasure of humanity itself, or at least of some fantasized essence for which despite ourselves we feel a certain nostalgia. The posthuman body, like the posthuman subjectivity it concretizes, seems to bode a self so vulnerable, so permeable and unstable, that it will be incapable of agency [93–94].

Jameson has suggested that the merging of human and mechanical is not usually an even integration because technology is often the predominant partner, overtaking the human. When there are no boundaries between human and machine

> the tug of war between organism and machine increasingly inclines to the preponderance of the latter, in genetic engineering and in the promotion of biology over physics as the prototypical science. The reincorporation of organic material in the imagery of the cyborg or of intelligent computers, however, tends to transform the organic into a machine far more than it organicizes machinery. Thus, postmodern or cybernetic technology becomes if anything even more "unnatural" than the older heavy-industrial kind [*Archaeologies* 64].

Hollinger has argued that while science fiction also features integration between the human and the machine, cyberpunk differs in that unlike science fiction it no longer places the human in the "privileged place at the center of things"; the integration can come at the cost of the human, and this therefore makes cyberpunk "anti-humanist" ("Cybernetic" 30).

Parrish's attitude to other characters with artificial elements, such as Pets, clearly shows the suspicion that technologies threaten reality and the self. She is "uncomfortable" around Pets (*Code* 53), who are made up of varying degrees of both human/organic and mechanical parts. They are unnatural and their lifespan is short; Pets decay and die young because of the negative effects of the fusion of machine and body. Elsewhere Parrish uses "plastic" as a derogatory description for those who are not natural (*Nylon* 31), and admires Daac for his "natural" features: "He was attractive, in a *natural* sort of way. Not synthetically perfect like the genetically engineered" (*Nylon* 31). This society privileges the authentic human over technological improvements, where "natural body hair and real nipples" are "worth a mint" (*Nylon* 38). In contrast, Parrish's hologram "diary," Merry 3#, a perfect, flawless version of Parrish, ultimately proves unreliable. Baudrillard writes that the "holographic reproduction" has a "transgressive truth" that can lead to unsolicited consequences, for instance when "twins were deified, and sacrificed, in a more savage culture: hypersimilitude was equivalent to the murder of the original" (*Simulacra* 108). De Pierres's novels repeatedly assert the differences and boundaries between the artificial and the natural, authentic humans.

For some critics, the posthuman figure is one of potential rather than threat. Bukatman writes that "the post-alienation discourse of cyberpunk produced a range of techno–Surrealist mappings of technology onto the form of the human. Organism and machine dissolved their boundaries in an ecstatic act of cybernetic-neurological fusion and redefinition" (85). Commentators have read the dissolution of boundaries as offering utopian possibilities that allow writers to challenge and resist traditional gender and racial stereotypes.[4] Jacobs writes that "the posthuman subject and body can also carry a more utopian valence" because it "need no longer be confined to one gender, one sexuality, one race, one subjectivity.... In its cyborg wisdom the posthuman body refuses fixity, definition, boundaries" (94). Barbara Creed suggests that "the global self does not see others in terms of classical oppositions such as male/female; white/black; straight/gay; global/local. Rather, the identity of the global self is multiple, fluid, malleable and multisexual. The global self morphs across boundaries into unknown spaces" (3). Creed believes that cyberspace and virtual reality create opportunities for "flexibility, fluidity, fantasy" (2). For Russell Blackford, the real world is already grappling with issues — and positive opportunities — of machine-human integration, given the many technologies already coexisting in human bodies:

Six • The End of the Human

To some extent, we are already mutants and cyborgs. Through vaccination, we have used technology to enhance our natural immunity to certain diseases. The contraceptive pill alters the functioning of the female reproductive system by artificial means. Moreover, we have blurred the boundaries between our bodies and the inorganic world with contact lenses, tooth fillings, implanted teeth, pacemakers, prostheses and numerous surgical devices. I expect we will go much further ["Mutants" 17].

Žižek argues that cyberspace offers a "radical ambiguity" that allows both heightened experience as well as manipulation (22). Robert Galbreath has also argued against the idea of the machine as threat, suggesting that only occasionally do texts present the machine and human integration as signifying "the end of the human species" (64).

Yet posthumanism is the object of satire and suspicion rather than admiration in the Parrish novels. In a departure from the recognition of technology as offering radical potential, the texts explicitly mock posthumanism:

> Wom (corrupted to Wombat by some joker) was a nerdie-boy back twenty years who'd preached the beauty of post-humanism and the like. He tried to upload himself into his microwave on prime time Common Net — got electrocuted instead. His ridiculous stunt raised him to iconic status. People short on deities and big on irony adopted him. These days he was more a kinda idiom, and praying to an idiom suited my chic [*Code* 51].

The repeated use of *idiom* suggests *idiot*, and later Parrish refers to Wom as "an idiot prophet" (*Code* 171). Wom's obsession with posthumanism projects results in experiments that fuse human and machine, organic and mechanic, with results that are grotesque, bizarre, and unnatural: a "shop of post-human lunacy" (*Code* 191). De Pierres presents posthumanism in its extreme forms, and always contrasts it with Parrish's own tenets: "They chanted in practised accord, '*Famlee's a dysfunc'nal kustom. It's got no use in pos 'humanity'*" (*Code* 171). Wom is also known as Dr Del Morte (Dr Death), and his involvement in posthumanism emphasizes the destruction of the human that his projects and technologies entail.

The concern over the loss of the real is also notable in the construction of a society that is addicted to images and simulation. The novels' criticisms of a world interested only in its entertainment and the maintenance of the "good life," complacent and careless, echo the works that Chapter Two discussed, such as Turner and Shute's novels, which are intent on revealing the idyllic (Australian) life to be a façade. In an oblique reference to films such as *Dark City* and *The Matrix*—both of which were filmed in Sydney—Parrish makes a distinction between the real and the image that privileges the former:

> It reminded me of those old movies that were so popular fifty years ago, where at the end of the story they all realised they weren't living on a planet but under a glass dome floating through space. If the whole of Viva woke up tomorrow and found out they were on a comet scooting through the Perseus Spur, I doubted they'd care. As long as the streets were clean, the cafés served cappuccino and *One-World* was in their bedrooms and living rooms to greet them when they woke, who'd give a rat's? [*Nylon* 154].

Parrish despises the neuroendocrine simulation that addicts users such as her mother, and she rejects drugs as "chemical entertainment" (*Code* 63); simulation and drugs alter reality and cannot be trusted.

Cyberspace itself, with virtual reality and avatars and user IDs, might be said to discourage authenticity and individuality. Parrish feels claustrophobic and uncomfortable in "vrealspace" (virtual reality): "It was the thing I hated most about net-vreal. Human imagination. There was no accounting for their weirdness and opportunism" (*Crash* 11). The "imagination" and "weirdness" of cyberspace allows people to create new worlds outside reality, and this is portrayed negatively. Jameson has written that cyberspace is "an enclave of a new sort, a subjectivity which is objective ... but also like the structuralism and poststructuralism which preceded it, once more does away with the 'centered subject' and proliferates in new, post-individualistic ways" (*Archaeologies* 21). Yet Sterling has argued that one of the features of cyberpunk is its reliance on detail: "its telling use of detail, its carefully constructed intricacy ... sensory overload that submerges the reader in the literary equivalent of the hard-rock 'wall of sound'" ("Preface" to *Mirrorshades* xii–xiii). Matthew Conn has questioned this use of excess detail, and suggests that it in fact works to evoke place: "Why does a literature concerned with a place that has no textures of the *mise-en-scène*, but just text (in the form of ones and zeroes), have to create and be so concerned with texture and sense of place? That is, why are we trying to make cyberspace as close to the 'real' world as possible?" (209). Conn's point is that a key element of many cyberpunk texts is indeed a "sense of place" and that the evocative language writers use to describe richly detailed environments ultimately serves to assert location. De Pierres's work always describes and grounds Parrish's encounters in cyberspace in physical terms, in an apparent attempt to remind the reader always of the physical, real world. Hackers appear as "weird" characters who suffer from "brain-fry," far from "the popular, glamorous pastime it had once been" (*Crash* 25). Merv, the main example of a hacker, is a stuttering, dirty, "withered" and "ugly" person whose only confidence is inside cyberspace (*Crash* 77).

Technological enhancements to bodies and dependence on virtual reality are not the only threats to the end of the "real" in the Parrish novels, because the Media pose another danger. The Media obscure the distinctions between reality and the image. Whether powerful figures use technology to watch and control citizens or manipulate the internet and media for deplorable purposes, the loss of freedom, privacy, and trust in the dominant technologies has a dehumanizing effect. The popularity of the Media has created "a whole generation who couldn't tell reality from production" (*Crash* 159). As Peter Fitting asks, in his discussion of science fiction cinema, "How is the virtual reality of our present as offered by the machines [in *The Matrix*] different from the imaginary satisfactions of the illusory false utopias offered us by the media, which, like the machine dreams of the film, acclimatize and blind us...?" (161). The Parrish novels refer to the Media distortion of the truth as "reality-murdering" (*Code* 20), with viewers unable to distinguish between a real televised event and a fictional one: "If *One-World* decided you were the perp, then you were. The truth wasn't relevant" (*Nylon* 147). The Media influence on people is negative, feeding audience desire for destruction in order to increase profits: "Nothing like a stack of burning, expendable bodies to boost the ratings! Priers— pilot/journos and their intrusive cam-cording 'Terrogators in fruited-up 'copters — supervised the whole affair jostling their Militia lackeys out of the way for the best close-up footage. Image scavengers!" (*Code* 18).

Parrish and Merv believe that an editing program called Brilliance has evolved into an artificial intelligence choosing what airs, effectively controlling everything people watch. However, Parrish discovers that Brilliance is not an AI but a human mind that has become linked with the editing software. She attempts to destroy the Media by overloading Brilliance with too much information, causing the human element to fail. A return to a government-run State will then replace Media control over society, with "basic technology" and "genuine free information" (*Crash* 190). Parrish's on-air revelation of the Media's facilitation of the horrors of genetic experimentation, however, risks the audience interpreting it as merely another story, another production. De Pierres's novels, then, highlight the loss of clear boundaries separating truth and media fictions and instead insistently and repeatedly draw the line between the real and the image, the human and technology.

The question of whether de Pierres's adoption of a globalized setting negates the apocalyptic "map" of Australia is also worth exploring. Critics have claimed that cyberpunk speaks from a globalist perspective, where local boundaries and concerns are irrelevant. Sponsler has described William Gibson's imagined worlds as constituting a "pan-culture that has by and large effaced all local or ethnic differences" ("Death" 48), and the same argument could be made for the majority of post-apocalyptic texts where a future world collapses traditional cultural and national differences. Creed notes that the virtual worlds of new technology discourage a sense of place and distance, where people may challenge and redraw borders and boundaries of the traditional media, for "the virtual media ... offer the possibility of traversing boundaries altogether" (4): "A crucial difference between earlier media formats and the new virtual ones is the relationship of each to 'distance.' Whereas the older media forms always maintained a distance, or gap, between the user and the medium in question, the newer forms promise to obliterate that distance, to 'jack in,' to close that gap forever" (2). The implication is that in cyberpunk, where virtual reality and cyberspace are key components, location no longer matters — and one can argue the same about geographical spaces and boundaries. Sterling also echoes the common refrain that cyberpunk diminishes nation, instead favoring a global viewpoint. He notes that "cyberpunks aim for a wide-ranging, global point of view," a globalized world where nation has little meaning, for "Cyberpunk has little patience with borders" ("Preface" to *Mirrorshades* xii). This feature of the genre is of particular interest in the Australian context, offering the potential for cyberpunk writers to transcend local concerns and anxieties.

The Parrish novels initially appear to use the global and open possibilities of cyberpunk to break away from the apocalyptic discourse that frames the Australian landscape as threatening and deadly, because they feature an urban, multicultural society that one could seemingly transfer to any other national setting. For instance, de Pierres intermingles specifically Australian references — moleskins and R. M. Williams, dingoboys and Packer-Murdoch media families — with shamans, voodoo and Chinois,

Six • The End of the Human

while the city and place names are generic rather than specific to Australia. In "Dis-Imagined Communities: Science Fiction and the Future of Nations," Istvan Csicsery-Ronay, Jr., discusses the place and portrayal of nations in futuristic science fiction, suggesting that in many cases, particularly in post–World War II years, speculative fiction eliminates traditional models of nations. Instead, "writers began to imagine the deterioration of their own societies, which disqualified even their own milieus as potential models for national futures" (223). Csicsery-Ronay, Jr., argues that cyberpunk in particular applies a "slum globe" (223) perspective rather than displaying any interest in nations per se:

> In cyberpunk, especially, the concept of nation, with its implication of some historical homogeneity through time, has been made obsolete by the dramatic heterogeneity of human, primarily urban, society. There is no national community to legitimize a state, nor is there a state that might consolidate a national constituency. The privileged setting for all significant action in the future is the postmodern metropolis, which behaves as a self-operating city-state, rather than a national center [225].

Certainly, urban centers are the primary interest and location of the majority of cyber texts, and often the cities are self-governing, as in the Parrish novels, rather than existing in a relationship to a country. Csicsery-Ronay, Jr., notes that cyberpunk positions business conglomerates in the place of nations: "the powers of the state have been usurped by profit-driven corporations, while the functions of communal solidarity have been reduced to the level of weak local and professional groups — gangs, squatters, hackers, black-marketeers, indentured laborers, and so on" (225).

Sponsler has suggested that the landscapes of cyberpunk are free from the anxieties evident in traditional apocalyptic landscapes, which were "hostile and forbidding, a no-man's land where humans must struggle to survive ... unfriendly, unyielding, and unforgiving ... the physical world must be battled *against*" ("Beyond the Ruins" 257). In contrast, she claims that in cyberpunk there is no nostalgia for the pre-apocalyptic past ("Beyond the Ruins" 257), but instead writers construct the wasteland now as exciting and full of potential, where characters are at home (261). To some extent, de Pierres's novels reflect these ideas. In contrast to the superficially perfect city or the suburbs where "you were little better than a drone in a hive" (*Nylon* 150), The Tert is apparently a space of authenticity and freedom; here Parrish finds "rebirth" (*Nylon* 151). Although she rejects the "freedom" of The Tert as an illusion (*Nylon* 151), there is no doubt that it functions as a place of "potential" as Sponsler writes of other cyberpunk narratives. There are, however, traces of nostalgia for the pre-apocalyptic time:

> Every now and then you'd come across a precious parcel of space; usually the gardens that had once served a hundred or so villas as a community meeting place. Occasionally you'd also find the concrete guts of an old swimming pool, legacy of the days when Australia was still a country of backyards and mortgages. Mostly, now, the pools were built over with who-knew-what living underneath [*Nylon* 52].

Elsewhere, Parrish reflects that The Tert "had been natural bush once. A glorious stretch of tropical exotics and lushness that unfurled down to a sparkling beach. At least so the archival holos said. Nothing much grew on it now, excepting a mud-coloured fungus" (*Nylon* 106).

Yet other critics write that cyberpunk creates localized and sometimes negative environments rather than generic spaces of optimism. Conn argues that there has been a shift in the way that authors have portrayed cyberspace, where earlier cyberspatial landscapes, such as in Gibsonian cyberpunk, were "spaces of rejection and oppression that alienate consciousness ... impenetrable" where the machine rejects the human mind, while recent examples eschew the mechanics for cyber environments that simulate the world, that "absorb" and "assimilate" the human mind (207). Conn suggests that the answer is to familiarize the unfamiliar — that the production of detailed descriptions of cyberspace is an attempt to impose familiarity, to inscribe something on what is otherwise a blank slate, in order to render it acceptable to the reader.

It is difficult here to ignore the parallels between Conn's descriptions of cyberspace and the common depictions of the Australian landscape, for there are connections to the ways that explorers and cartographers inscribed and encoded the tabula rasa of the *terra australis incognita* prior to European colonization. Conn's descriptions of Gibsonian cyberspace as "desolate and lifeless ... [a] nothingness" (211), a "dystopian and harsh frontier that rejects attempts to penetrate it" (217) are starkly reminiscent of countless descriptions of the Australian landscape. He suggests that the cyber landscapes of Gibson's work are *unheimlich* settings (213), places of "hidden information" (214) that resist and defend against "human intrusion" (211). Conn contrasts this with real-world landscapes that "cannot think," where any negative occurrences such as earthquakes are "random events and not deliberate or premeditated actions" (211–12). Similarly, authors have described the Australian landscape in gothic terms as *unheimlich*, resisting human interaction, and like cyberspace (but unlike Conn's real-life landscapes) deliberately, maliciously, consciously alienating humans, where the unrelenting flatness of the landscape — its "nothingness"— often conceals a darker reality.

As Chapter One suggested, we can read the work of Baudrillard on simulation and science fiction as a model for an idea of Australia as simulacra, the copy without an original. Baudrillard writes that "simulation threatens the difference between the 'true' and the 'false,' the 'real' and the 'imaginary'" (*Simulacra* 3). The distinction between what is real and what is fake is an ongoing preoccupation in many Australian apocalypses, including de Pierres's work, where the false illusion of a utopian image contrasts with the real, harsh wilderness. A similar interest in the real/imaginary dichotomy is evident in cyberpunk texts and often occurs in terms of anxieties about the dissolution of boundaries between real/image, human/machine, and natural/artificial.

One of the most popular texts to showcase this dichotomy is *The Matrix* and its sequels *The Matrix Reloaded* and *The Matrix Revolutions*. The films narrate the journey of the protagonist, Neo, as he discovers that the life he believed to be reality is, in fact, a construct, a simulation that malevolent artificial intelligence — machines — have designed, having enslaved the human race in the future in order to exploit them for power and energy. The machines have literally wired humans into the simulation, and people believe that they are living normal lives — normal in the context of late twentieth-century Western audiences[5]— but instead the world is a ruined and dark place. The few humans who seek more than this bland existence are given the chance, as is Neo, to abandon the world of illusion and instead enter the nightmarish reality to fight against the machines. *The Matrix* trilogy was filmed in Sydney, featuring the city as the unidentified location for the simulacra, the false reality. As Brian McFarlane has pointed out, despite the location of Sydney for filming, no "obvious landmarks, such as the Harbour Bridge or the Opera House" are present, giving the setting instead the appearance of being "any modern city" without specifically identifying a particular place ("Matrix" 106),[6] although others have suggested that Chicago was the intended location (Haslam 97, 110). Despite this apparently generic setting, there is nonetheless one point in the films that bears mentioning here: another character, Morpheus, tells Neo that this nameless, utopian city is merely a simulation of reality; the real world under the glossy metropolis is "the desert of the real" and the audience is shown a dark wilderness.[7]

"The desert of the real" quoted in *The Matrix* is, of course, Baudrillard's phrase, used in reference to maps and territories.[8] His discussion has proved to be a useful way to articulate how the early images of Australia determined an apocalyptic map of the country. As Chapter One noted, Baudrillard argues that the map "precedes the territory ... engenders the territory" (*Simulacra* 1). In *The Matrix*, the idea of the city (the unidentified, unintended Sydney) as a perfect simulation presenting a false image while a darker reality (a desert wilderness) hides underneath is appropriate, and a familiar theme in Australian apocalyptic works where utopian beach and city images ultimately are only illusions while the hostile desert, the outback, is a grim reality.

The Parrish novels reflect this idea. Even while the novels construct The Tert as a place of potential and freedom, a generic and global space, the environment is monstrous and menacing. If there is an apocalyptic map of Australia that continues to inform speculative fictions in the country, these novels suggest that it is a map of hell. Nature is dangerous to humans, a threat to bodies and buildings: "A mutated rainforest had sprung up around the empty villas. Upthrust roots nudged already subsiding buildings, and sharp-suckered vines pierced the porous walls. Brown-blood coloured groundcover clumped like fungus over pavement cracks, and ugly, squat, spiked date palms threatened to impale me if I brushed too close" (*Code* 117). Strange, grotesque creatures, such as canrats and bungarras, prowl the landscape, haunting and attacking people who journey through The Tert.

The name of The Tert's central area is Dis, a "dirty heart" (*Nylon* 25) and a "sinister heart" (*Code* 62) where "no people ever came out.... Rumour had it that Dis went far enough underground to hit lava; or hell; whichever came first" (*Nylon* 25). The name of Dis reinforces its monstrous state: "'Dis' had some obscure connection with hell" (*Code* 62)—that is, Dis appears to be a contraction of Hades (Ha-des — Dis). In Dis, thick barriers, webs, threaten to enclose people, giant mechanical spiders attack, and towers of wiring and cables grow from the ground and feed on human bodies. Soil poisoning and indiscriminate use of nanotechnologies have polluted the earth and created "wild-tek," an unnatural combination that grows from the blood of humans:

> I worked my way close to one of the mysterious towers and discovered they were bundles of fibre optics torn from underground and frozen in a glass haystack. Some pulsed with dying light, others jutted upward in blackened shards, leftovers of a one-time communication system that threaded underneath the villas. Something had eaten away the plas casings and forced the bundles upward in a series of bizarre tower-like structures. Compelled, I reached out to touch one and couldn't pull my hand away. A sting to my fingers, and my blood sprayed finely out from the tip. It pulsed up the length of the nearest fibre and glowed into life [*Code* 128–29].

The fusion of machine and nature creates a wild living technology that is menacing to humans and sustained by their flesh.

Dis is not the only dangerous landscape in the Parrish novels. In a similar way to the constructions of landscape discussed in Chapter Three, characters refer to the Australian interior as the Dead Heart, the Bitter Plains, and it is "barren. Hot in a way you can't imagine. Terrifying. Even underground. Too hot to breathe" (*Nylon* 133). People are captured and forced to work as slaves for the Dead Heart Mining Co-op in the Australian interior, and this environment is so bleak that it "made The Tert seem like a tropical paradise" in comparison (*Nylon* 57). The novels, then, not only explicitly reference the Dead Heart to describe the Australian outback but also suggest that other landscapes such as Dis have a dirty and sinister "heart" as if the land is full of death and decay rather than life.

As with the Indigenous fictions discussed in Chapter Five, the decaying landscape in the Parrish novels occurs in the context of an apocalyptic dream of a better world, because various groups see it in terms of restoration and healing. Dis is the target of a Cabal Coomera project to restore the poisoned land. The Cabal Coomera is a powerful group of men with clear links to Aboriginal traditions. They are "The Tert's real lawmakers. A mysterious, unaccountable sect who operated above the daily Tert politics. Some said they were descendants of the Kadaitcha, the feather feet police of the original indigenous tribes, but that sounded like romance to me" (*Nylon* 7–8). Parrish discovers the truth of this "romance" when she experiences a psychic connection with the Cabal and sees: "Ancient memories ... before me — dreamtime rituals of ochre-daubed faces. Wimmen's business — drinking dugong blood, dilly bags full of cramping berries.... Then newer ones of stolen lives, urban subsistence and lost stories" (*Code* 264).

The presence of Indigenous people in this imagined future contrasts with other Australian speculative fictions where Aboriginal groups are absent and suggests that they have an important role in the future. Yet as Csicsery-Ronay, Jr., points out, cyberpunk writers often mix Indigenous tribes and various mythologies in their work:

> Science fiction is fond of societies that operate by rules associated with primitive cultures — from lost races (isolated in the past as well as in space), quasi–Native Americans and frontier space stations, toga-clad utopians and Amazons in military societies, all the way to contemporary science fiction's fascination with aboriginal cultures and the voodoo deities that populate Gibson's cyberspace [231].

The presence of Indigenous peoples in de Pierres's novels, then, risks becoming merely another flavor *du jour* of the cosmopolitan society of cyberpunk, divorced from any real significance or meaning. As Parrish notes, "These days the tribes were pretty damn diluted, like all the other nations that lived in The Tert, but a flavour of tradition survived" (*Code* 7).

Yet the Cabal do have a significant role in de Pierres's trilogy. They ask Parrish to locate their Clever Men, the karadji, who are missing, along with shamans and other people with connections to the spirit world. In rescuing them, Parrish discovers a Cabal plan to "take back the Heart"—Dis—to heal the land that was once theirs (*Code* 213). This plot point works against cyberpunk's effacement of boundaries by articulating a self identity that characters explicitly link with place. For example, Daac, a member of the Cabal, says, "My *gens* have always lived in The Tert. It's our land.... Even though we don't exist as a tribe any more.... When people return to one place over generations, it becomes part of their soul's code" (*Nylon* 189–90). Daac's ancestry "maybe once" included Indigenous people (*Nylon* 190), and he is part of a project to restore the decaying lands to their former glory: "Our land is poisoned and sick. Our Task is to reclaim it, bring it to health, bring its people to health" (*Nylon* 189).

Parrish's reaction to this plan is ambivalent. The novels present the "Task" to restore the land with ambiguity, particularly in relation to nation and land rights. The Cabal plan is ostensibly to heal the land by seizing Dis, but Parrish calls them "colonialists. They just want more territory" (*Code* 261). Daac bases his scheme to win back The Tert for his people on racial birthright, and it includes the plan to eject "migrants," that is, anyone not of Daac's bloodlines (*Code* 224). Parrish also wishes to restore the land

and create a new, better place, but her desire is profoundly different to Daac's in that she hopes to make the land a place of refuge for all people, not just those with a particular ethnic heritage. Her attitude to land is fraught with contradictions. Essentially, Parrish appears to suspect the Cabal/Indigenous claim of land rights as colonialism and imperialism, ideologies that she rejects — incidentally while accruing a considerable fortune in finance and land in her own empire — and she is repeatedly shown to reject Daac's racial philosophies, yet her continued attraction to Daac as the (flawed) heroic ideal complicates and undercuts her denial of his own attitudes.

Chapter Five discussed Goldie's description of the dilemma that white Canadians face, in the double proposition of feeling "at home" while Indigenous people are the Other, and at the same time also feeling like outsiders, themselves the Other. As Gelder and Jacobs point out, this problem is evident in an Australian context in that after the Mabo and Wik court rulings (1993 and 1996) in favor of Aboriginal land rights, there was some concern on the part of white Australians who feared that the Indigenous population might now have "too much" (136), and that their land claims would eventually threaten to overtake all Australia. This reaction is, perhaps, one of the ways white people may solve the confusion of being both Australian and Other (not-native, not-Australian) by constructing Indigenous people as colonists. In the Parrish novels, Parrish's explicit linking of land-greedy colonizers and the Indigenous Cabal Coomera could be read in the sense of reverse colonization; the Cabal's plan to reclaim The Tert is, significantly, referred to as an "invasion" (*Code* 213).

Andrew Macrae has disputed the claim that cyberpunk has an objective, global perspective that eschews local and ethnic biases, and he argues that cyberpunk only "pretends to come from nowhere in particular" (34), a pretense that hides its "implicit xenophobia and isolationism" (31). He notes that "for a genre that constructs itself as being concerned with narrating the dissolution of boundaries, cyberpunk is very anxious about the effects this has" (41). For Macrae, North American cyberpunk in particular evidences fears about Asian technological supremacy as a threat to American power (35), effectively regurgitating traditional binaries of East/West, where East is always the Other (31).

If isolationism and fear of loss of power are recurrent themes in American cyberpunk, the Parrish novels demonstrate a similar concern that outside forces and a globalizing world will result in the loss of national identity:

> Australians had lost their twang sixty-odd years ago, along with their nationality, when refugees from southern Europe, forced away from their own contaminated territories, flooded their borders. The refugees tried Afreeka first, but the Freekans had their perimeter tied up tight with some advanced defence. Their conscience didn't blink at a horde of white Euros in trouble. Couldn't say I blamed them. Down here, we'd always thought the man-flood would come from the islands to the north, Indo and Malayland and the rest. But they'd got smart and cleaned up their countries [*Code* 135].

Describing the migrating foreigners as a "horde" and "man-flood" is reminiscent of invasion stories that narrate the dangers of the proximity of Asian nations; here, however, the migrants are white Europeans. This is a deft reversal of the notion of an Asian invasion, as seen in early campaigns to attract white Europeans to populate Australia against the threat of Asian or other non–European immigrants, evident in the Million Farms campaign discussed in Chapter One. The Asian invaders have become Europeans, and Africa is the new West, protected and superior. Despite this, the underlying theme again reminds us of the dangers to Australia's shield of distance: a weak defense force leaves Australia vulnerable to unwanted intruders. Australia is unable to protect itself against the immigrants who have "flooded their borders" and this invasion has led to the loss of Australian "nationality." "Afreeka," in this future, has an "advanced defence" system that Australia does not, and Asian nations are also dominant — "they'd got smart"— which suggests that the Asian Other has become superior to and stronger than Australia. The invasion of these newcomers, these Europeans, has irrevocably changed the nation.

De Pierres's series, then, initially seems to share in cyberpunk's dismissal of place and location and nation by incorporating a mix of cultures and ethnicities to create a global city, while also reproducing cyberpunk's cynicism about apocalypse. Yet ultimately the novels do not fully embrace these attitudes, for they adopt an apocalyptic discourse and paradigm of disaster and hope for a new world. This is therefore an ambiguous representation of apocalypse, with fears of the end of the world, the end of the human, undercut by wry nonchalance. The global setting is also challenged by the inclusion of several distinctively Australian representations of land; the novels align with other local apocalyptic texts that reproduce a dystopian map of nation. In de Pierres's approach to cyberpunk, she has adapted and rewritten the genre's anti-apocalyptic sentiments and globalized environments within the context of Australian attitudes to land and nation.

Yet de Pierres deviates from other Australian apocalyptic fictions by emphasizing the apocalyptic promise of a better world to come, for despite the bleak setting, the novels do suggest the utopian possibilities of apocalypse. The texts ultimately frame violence and battles in the service of a greater good, while Parrish's desire for a secure place for all people, irrespective of ethnicity or social status, is unquestionably utopian. Parrish's implied rejection of violence and war in the ambiguous conclusion of the third novel suggests that the ultimate goal is peace.

Conclusion

> Then I saw a new heaven and a new earth, for the first heaven and the first earth had passed away.
>
> Revelation 21:2

The paradigm of Biblical apocalypse in Revelation and other prophetic works offers a new perspective on the present by revealing future global catastrophe in the natural world. The ruling authorities are corrupt and hostile, oppressing the faithful minority. The promise of the "new heavens and the new earth," a new world that will be free from the pain and sorrow of the former one, follows the judgment and destruction of the present world. Biblical apocalypse always concludes with the promised salvation, restoration, and glorification of the oppressed people, with visions of a New Jerusalem, the holy city, in all its beauty and glory. The faithful will be secure, beloved of God and free from trials.

Secular apocalypse follows this paradigm. It reveals prophecies of future disasters that will occur unless societies make the necessary changes, and it envisages new worlds after the catastrophic event. As in Biblical apocalypse, minority groups can use disaster to comment on contemporary issues and articulate their judgment against corrupt and powerful groups in society. Yet secular apocalypse often focuses on the destruction, adapting the apocalyptic pattern to conclude with catastrophe. The end of the world is the focus of many modern apocalypses that evidence no interest in, or possibility of, a new and better world.

Apocalyptic themes and imagery are recurring and significant features of Australian writing. Contemporary writers and filmmakers of several of the most famous popular apocalyptic fictions have set their works in Australia, such as Nevil Shute's *On the Beach* and the *Mad Max* films. A significant number of apocalyptic works employs an Australian setting, demonstrating that the apocalyptic ethos is an enduring and appealing theme in the Australian context. Apocalyptic tropes have appeared in works for adults and children, in literature, film, television and comics, in speculative works rewriting the past and the present or imagining the near or distant future, and in works by male and female authors. The apocalyptic event might be invasion, nuclear war, or environmental catastrophe. Some fictions narrate the story of survivors; in other works there are no humans left after the destruction.

This book has suggested that we can understand the large number of apocalyptic and disaster fictions in Australian speculative literature and film in the context of the apocalyptic paradigm for the Australian national experience. Prior to European colonization of Australia, novelists, utopists, explorers, and cartographers created an apocalyptic map of the south land. This map inscribed the land in apocalyptic terms as a new world. Some texts imagined the new country as a utopia that was the literal New Jerusalem, the new heavens and new earth that Revelation promised, while others saw it as a secular paradise, a rich and abundant land offering wealth and fortune to its inhabitants. Yet alternative maps of the *terra australis incognita* delineated a dark place, a hell of nightmares and bleakness, a strange country of frightening and monstrous creatures in a hostile environment. This dystopian tradition has undermined and haunted the optimistic constructions, serving as a counterpoint to utopian expectations and renderings of the south land.

The endurance of this apocalyptic tradition in contemporary fictions is striking and significant. The recurring conflation of disaster and the nation both (re)produces and underscores an enduring relationship between Australia and apocalypse, effectively situating the land as an apocalyptic space. Apocalypse as a genre allows considerable scope for writers and filmmakers to articulate and address concerns and fears in the Australian cultural imagination. Australian speculative literature and films that invoke an apocalyptic discourse often reveal ambivalence about the land and anxieties about invasion, colonization, white existence, and Indigenous land rights. The case studies in this book highlight the ongoing appeal of apocalypse and its ability to critique a range of viewpoints and agendas in the genre of speculative fiction.

Conclusion

Australian apocalypse often emphasizes disaster and the bleak aspects, constructing the land as a terrifying space of destruction and chaos. For many apocalyptic texts set in the south land, there is either no new world after apocalypse or it is a dystopia. Greed, complacency, indifference and ignorance have caused humans to — accidentally, indirectly, deliberately — destroy the world, whether through nuclear weapons, environmental abuse and mismanagement, or race-targeted viruses. The "end of the world" does not result in a new and better one, but instead creates a dystopian post-apocalyptic wasteland or urban decaying environment, or the destruction is the final act in a series of tragedies that ultimately end in the extinction of all human life. This bleak picture is a popular one in Australian apocalyptic fictions, perhaps suggesting the early apocalyptic maps focusing on the dystopian aspects of the south land have retained a strong hold in the national culture. Other authors render the landscape of Australia as a space of punishment, in a secular parallel to Biblical depictions where the wilderness is outside the promised future blessing. These apocalyptic themes of exile, judgment, hostile landscapes and uncertainty over inhabitation of the south land are frequent concerns in Australian speculative fiction.

While there are many examples that evince anxieties about hostile forces both outside and inside the country, there are other texts that adapt apocalyptic tropes to envisage opportunities for new worlds, to warn against ecological mismanagement, or to reframe European colonization itself as a catastrophe for Indigenous people. Some present utopian dreams for new worlds. The authors often negotiate a path between dystopia and utopia, suggesting possibilities for ways forward. They do not celebrate destruction, but neither do they see it as definitive and final, for beyond catastrophe lies opportunities to remake the world. Indigenous writers, for instance, can highlight the disasters of European colonization while nonetheless presenting the potential for a better future for Australia where people can put aside the racial divides and injustices of the past and present and create a new world instead. Such visions offer the closest parallels to the traditional Biblical apocalypse, giving a voice to the oppressed and imagining new worlds that have banished the injustices of the present.

Apocalypse often proves irresistible to Australian speculative authors, its themes attractive for a range of perspectives and agendas. Countless local texts reproduce the imagery, themes and language of apocalypse —

punishment, judgment, exile and promised lands — by sometimes transferring the tropes from Biblical to secular accounts intact, while other times adapting and subverting them to suggest that the new world is, in fact, hell. In some fictions, the frequent associations of the Australian space and apocalyptic disaster reinforce perceptions of the nation as dystopia. Fears and incessant re-enactments of endings shadow hopes and expectations for a better world in *terra australis*. These narratives insist on an apocalyptic rendering of Australia as the land at the end(s) of the world, because of its geography and the circumstances under which Europeans colonized the land. Other texts offer more optimistic visions and the hope of heaven, exploring paths to new worlds and depicting utopian visions of potential and promise. The early maps of the country have exercised a powerful hold over the cultural imagination in Australia, leaving a lingering strand of apocalypse in the nation's speculative fictions.

Chapter Notes

Introduction

1. There is a significant amount of research devoted to exploring the definitions and boundaries of speculative fiction. See, for instance, Tzvetan Todorov, Rosemary Jackson, and Kathryn Hume for various approaches to the fantastic genre.

2. Others have, of course, discussed apocalypse at great length in various approaches (Cohn; Dellamora; Kermode; O'Leary, Quinby, among many others). For one longer discussion of apocalypse in Jewish and Christian traditions and popular culture, see Martens.

3. The Bible also shows the desert or wilderness in more positive terms, given its relationship with the affirmation of Jesus as the Christ in his time of testing, or its place as the home of John the Baptist, although the desert is more typically a place outside God's blessing.

4. For instance, severe snow storms in the U.S. in 2010 were described as "Snowmageddon" by President Obama (Mann). After the 2004 Asian tsunami catastrophe, *The Sydney Morning Herald* named its special edition "Tsunami Apocalypse" (1), and superimposed the headline over a picture of the debris and wreckage, while the back page had pictures of wounded and lost children accompanied by the headline "Children of the Apocalypse" (14). Inside the section, other headlines associated the disaster with religious imagery: "The earth shook, the sea rose up and there was death on a Biblical scale" (9) and "A deep-rooted psychological satisfaction in linking natural disaster with human excess" (13). In the weeks following the tsunami, newspaper letter pages contained debates about the disaster, the possible role of people in its cause (scientific, moral, political failures), and God's existence. Similar responses and debates occurred after the 9/11 terrorist attacks on the U.S., while people often refer to the attacks on Jews in World War II as the Holocaust — a term also denoting an apocalyptic event.

Chapter One

1. Donald Horne made the term "lucky country" famous in a book, also titled *The Lucky Country*. Horne's use of the term was ironic, referring to Australia as "a lucky country run mainly by second-rate people who share its luck" (220). Since then, however, the phrase has become a common way to describe Australia, although current popular usage tends to be more literal than ironic.

2. Ross Gibson's books *The Diminishing Paradise* and *South of the West* explore speculation about Australia, while other works that address the subject in various ways include Paul Longley Arthur's "Capturing the Antipodes," Robert Holden's

Bunyips, Richard White's *Images of Australia*, and Janeen Webb and Andrew Enstice's *Aliens and Savages*. In terms of literary utopias and dystopias, Lyman Tower Sargent has written a comprehensive bibliographic survey of the genre in Australia ("Australian Utopian Literature") as well as a piece on Australian utopia and dystopia ("Australia as Dystopia"), while Australian utopias have also been explored by Nan Bowman Albinski, Ralph Pordzik, and Robyn Walton, among others.

3. Others have defined and explored utopia and dystopia in some detail, including Lyman Tower Sargent ("Three Faces"), Baccolini and Moylan ("Dystopia"), and Moylan.

4. Perhaps this is why the other Antipodean country — New Zealand — was able to substitute for a fantasy Europe when *The Chronicles of Narnia: The Lion, The Witch and the Wardrobe* and *The Lord of the Rings* films were shot there, for its fjords, mountains and green valleys are far closer to the fantasized idyllic Europe C. S. Lewis and J. R. R. Tolkien immortalized than Australia could ever be.

5. For longer treatments of lost civilizations in the Australian interior, see Blackford, Ikin and McMullen, as well as the works of Ikin, Sargent, Albinski, and Walton.

6. See John Rieder's *Colonialism and the Emergence of Science Fiction* for a detailed discussion of the intersections of the genre and colonialism.

7. Early maps often joined up the lands now known as Australia and Antarctica (as well as New Zealand and some South Pacific islands) to form a supercontinent covering virtually half the globe. Antarctica, therefore, is also heir to the speculation about the south land. Albinski has pointed out that Australian utopists were more likely to choose "non–Earthly settings, the Arctic and the Antarctic" for their utopias than Australia itself (16). In fact, contemporary popular fictions often locate strange artifacts and alien or future technologies in the Antarctic continent, as if the writers have pushed the utopias or advanced civilizations of early European speculation further south to Antarctica after the disillusionment of Australia. For instance, in *Stargate SG-1* Antarctica is an outpost of the civilization of the race of the Ancients, and in *Stargate Atlantis* the Antarctic outpost is the original site of the city Atlantis that was later moved to another galaxy. Characters discover an ancient pyramid in Antarctica in *Alien vs. Predator*, Matthew Reilly's *Ice Station* imagines Antarctica as a location for futuristic technology, and Tess Williams's post-apocalyptic *Map of Power* uses the settings of Australia, Antarctica and space.

Chapter Two

1. Censors cut parts of the novel, written by Marjorie Barnard and Flora Eldershaw, but it was later published in full in 1983 as *Tomorrow and Tomorrow and Tomorrow*. See Ian Saunders for a discussion of the different versions.

2. Similar attitudes are evident in John Duigan's *One Night Stand*, which portrays four young adults trapped in Sydney Opera House while nuclear bombs detonate near the city. The film ends with survivors gathering together in an underground train station, presumably leaving the audience to draw the conclusion that the bombs have landed on the city and the world has effectively ended. As is the case in *On the Beach*, the characters know little of the reasons or cause of the war, and Brians has argued that in most nuclear fictions the cause of the nuclear war is either accidental or unknown (27).

3. The cultural and national symbolism of cities and landmarks around the world, not only in Britain, are why disaster films always show the destruction of global icons with great fervor, with a typical array of targets including the Statue of Liberty, Hollywood, the Golden Gate Bridge, the Eiffel Tower, Big Ben, the pyramids, and so on. The DVD for *The Day After Tomorrow* even comes with a feature

called "City Freeze — Famous Icons from Around the World" that allows viewers to choose their region and see the devastating effects of an ice age. For Australian viewers, a massive wave threatens the Sydney Opera House. Sontag has discussed the pleasures associated with destruction, and she argues that science fiction films are interested in the "aesthetics" of visual disaster and "the peculiar beauties to be found in wreaking havoc, making a mess. And it is in the imagery of destruction that the core of a good science fiction film lies" ("Imagination" 213).

4. Cities are, of course, an integral part of the American landscape and identity, hence the reading of the terrorist attacks on the World Trade Center in New York in 2001 as a symbolic strike at the financial heart of capitalist America. The fact that the attacks occurred in New York City, a city that people often read in terms of its history and hold on the American cultural imagination as a place of creativity and greatness, is also significant, and perhaps another reason why 9/11 is now virtually synonymous with the Twin Towers rather than the Pentagon or plane crash in Pennsylvania.

5. *Jericho* began screening in 2006, the same year as another American apocalyptic television program appeared, *Heroes*. *Heroes* was set in city and rural locations but the visions of apocalypse occurred in New York City. The post-apocalyptic *I Am Legend* was also set in a city. Meanwhile, suburban American apocalypse became the running plot on the television series *Buffy the Vampire Slayer*.

6. Survivalism seems to have found its way into all apocalyptic — not just nuclear — fictions over time; as time has passed, so too have fears of total nuclear wars that eliminate all human life. Instead, the nuclear explosion appears to have become less a thing of dread than merely a common plot point in thrillers such as *24*.

7. Journalist Neil Jillett has written that this line was his creation rather than Gardner's.

8. Buckrich notes that Turner believed he had Indigenous heritage (18, 185).

9. Despite this utopian conclusion, women do not generally fare well in Turner's works. They are almost entirely absent as either major or minor characters and those that do appear are usually defined and denigrated by male characters in terms of their sexuality. Turner's later female characters fare somewhat better in *Drowning Towers*, *The Destiny Makers*, and *Down There in Darkness*, although even Valda is unsympathetic, and male characters define her by her assertive sexuality and see her as perverse because of it. Others have commented on the flat characterization in Turner's works (Buckrich, D. Broderick, Kellaway), but it is worth noting that Turner's primary interest appears to be in describing future societies and their problems, not the people that populate them.

10. For instance, in the first decade of the twenty-first century, just some of the disaster or apocalyptic films released include *The Book of Eli*, *The Core*, *The Day After Tomorrow*, *Legion*, *Poseidon*, *Sunshine*, *Terminator Salvation*, *28 Days Later* and its sequel *28 Weeks Later*, *2012*, adaptations of novels such as *I Am Legend*, *I, Robot*, *War of the Worlds*, *The Road*, and telemovies including *Category 7: The End of the World*, *Category 6: Day of Destruction*, *Locusts: Day of Destruction*, *Oil Storm*, *Supervolcano*, *10.5*, and *10.5: Apocalypse*.

11. The expression "politics of fear" was made famous in the work of Frank Furedi, whose *Culture of Fear* and *Politics of Fear* have been influential in cultural studies. Furedi has used the phrase to describe the key characteristic of Western culture.

12. See Smith for a longer analysis of the novel; Smith's work discusses *Underground* as an example of dystopian works set in Canberra. The plot of *Underground* is complicated, and without going into some detail it is difficult to do justice to its multiple conspiracies and intercutting

scenes from past and present times. A previous work of mine ("Shadow") on literary apocalypses in general referred very briefly to *Underground* and its tone of warning about Australian and American politics that focus on fear and security, but did not fully explain the intricacies of the plot, particularly in regard to the repeated destruction of Canberra. The bombing of Canberra takes place on television (with faked footage showing the city's ruins), in reality (and limited only to the hills immediately outside the city), and in dreams (the protagonist dreams of its utter annihilation). Here the greater interest is probably the novel's positioning of Canberra as *imagined* apocalypse — real or otherwise — which again returns us to Chapter One's argument concerning the imaginary apocalyptic map of Australia, and the hyperreal.

Chapter Three

1. The disappearance of Tom and Eileen Lonergan in the Great Barrier Reef after being left behind by their dive boat in 1998 was the basis for the horror film *Open Water*, although the characters were different and the location was not Australia (Jinman 2). *Wolf Creek* has obvious connections to the Peter Falconio disappearance in 2001 as well as the "backpacker" serial murders by Ivan Milat in the 1990s, although the director has said that his film focuses on the general scenario rather than specific cases (McLean 16).

2. Although I briefly discuss some Australian horror films here and acknowledge their intersections with apocalypse, the larger field is outside the focus of this book. For more information, see Robert Hood for his extensive bibliography of the genre and Mark David Ryan for a discussion of the growth in horror films in Australia between 2000 and 2009.

3. McLean has his detractors, however, who are skeptical that he fulfilled his ambitions in *Wolf Creek*, with some reviews in particular suggesting the film failed to produce the "emotional tenor" and "haunting presence" that worked in films such as *Picnic* (Kakmi 77).

4. Rumors of a fourth *Mad Max* film have appeared in media reports for years. In 1999, the media widely reported plans for a fourth film (for example, Barra 9), with George Miller working on a script for *Fury Road*. Mel Gibson agreed to star in it, locations were scouted and pre-production progressed to the point that filming was to begin in early 2003. A short time later pre-production was put on hold indefinitely and Miller and Gibson moved on to other films; Miller, notably, to *Happy Feet*. Part of the reason for the film's delay was attributed to bad timing due to the war in Iraq (Brodesser and Groves 40). Politicians referred to the U.S.–Iraq conflict as the "war against terror" and commentators linked it to the control of oil in the region. This is ironic, given the *Mad Max* films' setting of oil wars and terrorist groups. However, in March 2007 Miller announced plans to make the film after he completes other projects, but Gibson is unlikely to star (Maddox 7). At the time of writing, the fourth film is reportedly in pre-production, again (Hildebrand).

5. Adams writes that he had previously warned investors against involving themselves in the Kennedy-Miller project because he considered Miller inexperienced, the film anachronistic, and the script immoral; thereafter he conceded the films were "doomed to make a great deal of money" (38).

6. Critics have often interpreted the films as post-nuclear (for example, Sharrett, Barbour, M. Broderick), yet George Miller has explicitly rejected a post-nuclear reading ("Directing" 281). Paul Brians has suggested that the idea of nuclear war is so pervasive in our society that we have a tendency to read every collapse in nuclear terms (55). Yet *Thunderdome* at least gives the nuclear theory credence when one character dismisses poisoned water as "what's a little fallout?"

7. Such fears of the future and oil shortages recur in the media. For example, a *Sydney Morning Herald* article "Running on Empty" outlined the grim possibilities of fuel shortages in the future: "The issue is Peak Oil, the theory that the world will face a sudden, cataclysmic decline in supplies after global production peaks in the next 20 years" (Kremmer 29).

8. The Latin phrase *terra nullius* means "land of no one" and in a legal sense it often signifies land that has no lawful owners or that no State governs. Commentators have used the phrase to explain Australia's colonization by European settlers, in that the way the British legitimized taking land was by a declaration of terra nullius because they did not acknowledge any prior inhabitation or form of government by the Indigenous people. Yet Michael Connor has argued that the British never actually used the term as a justification for colonization at the time of settlement (36) and that critics have erroneously used the phrase retrospectively and also without respect for its correct meaning. While usage may have diminished the correct meaning of terra nullius, the phrase is nonetheless common in popular discourse and contributes to a tradition that views Australia as a barren place, the land of nothing and no one. See Haynes for one in-depth study on the Australian desert.

9. This is a point that Paul Williams also recognizes in his discussion of *Thunderdome*, although he reads Aunty as "a figure opposed to essential identities, refusing to be governed by any destiny embodied in physical essence ... Aunty's future is hers to shape alone" (307).

10. This image of woman and child as well as Aunty's name as a familial title both suggest matriarchal societies, which is perhaps unusual in a film trilogy that until this point had marginalized women and focused almost exclusively on male characters. While *Thunderdome* suggests that Aunty's capitalist regime is amoral and explicitly shows Savannah's ideals as the preferred model — the baby represents future generations, the film concludes with images from their society in Sydney — the focus nonetheless remains on Max as he leaves both (matriarchal) societies behind. In general, George Miller has suggested that the loss of women is inevitable in the series: "We repeatedly asked ourselves what price sexuality would pay in this kind of medieval world. It certainly couldn't function as it does in our contemporary society.... It's very unlikely that a pregnant woman or a woman with a child could survive" ("Directing" 283).

11. The absence of Indigenous groups in the *Mad Max* films is not especially unusual given that many futuristic visions of the world do not include non-white characters. See Chapter Five for a discussion of novelists rewriting this absence.

Chapter Four

1. See Noga Applebaum's *Representations of Technology in Science Fiction for Young People* for one discussion of children, technology and nature.

2. *Stolen* is neither dystopian nor apocalyptic, nor even a work of speculative fiction, but it is worth mentioning here because of its use of the dual vision of the Australian landscape, referred to in Chapter One, and particularly the novel's use of the outback.

3. Pierce links the theme of missing children to both colonial apprehensions about the country and Aborigines and also to the stolen generations of Indigenous children in contemporary Australia.

4. See Hintz and Ostry, and also Bradford, Mallan, Stephens and McCallum, for two books exploring utopian and dystopian writing for children and young adults.

5. Critical contributions on Australian writing for children are often essays on particular novels or authors (for example, Michael Stone's edited collections) or general surveys of the field, although some longer works are available (for example, Scutter, Bradford).

6. Stephens suggests that although there are many disaster texts for children, catastrophe novels are "not a common genre in Australian adult fiction" (126), but this assertion appears to overlook the numerous apocalyptic texts for adults, such as those by Shute, Turner, and many others.

7. While this chapter offers a brief survey of some of the critical work on the subject of literary ghosts and postcolonial hauntings in Australian texts, for more in-depth analyses of the field see the work of Gelder and Jacobs, Crouch, Gelder, and Turcotte, to name only a few.

8. A film of the first *Tomorrow* book was released in late 2010, with potential sequels to follow.

Chapter Five

1. Indigenous activist and commentator Michael Dodson notes that stereotypes of Indigenous people have changed over time:
> We have been an ever-popular subject for portrayal in paintings or films. Initially, we appeared as the noble, well-built native, heroic, bearded, loin-clothed, one foot up, vigilant, with boomerang at the ready. Later, after we had fallen from grace, we appeared bent, distorted, overweight, inebriated, with bottle in hand. And more recently, we appear ochred, spiritual, and playing the didjeridu behind the heroic travels of a black Landcruiser [3].

2. Walliss also claims, however, that apocalyptic films instead uphold social order. See also John W. Martens's *The End of the World: The Apocalyptic Imagination in Film & Television* for a longer treatment of apocalypse in films.

3. For various approaches to and treatments of Biblical apocalypse, postcolonialism and empire, see Roland Boer's *Last Stop Before Antarctica: The Bible and Postcolonialism in Australia* and Leonard L. Thompson's *The Book of Revelation: Apocalypse and Empire*, among others.

4. Disaster and sacred sites seems to be a theme in *Prey*, one of the horror films briefly mentioned in Chapter Three, which uses Aboriginal motifs throughout. The promotional tagline is "Dreamtime's over" and the storyline frequently alludes to Indigenous elements. The (white, American, Australian) travelers criticize Indigenous artwork early on and are terrorized by a (white) man who seems to be called "the kadaitcha" and who paints the captive protagonist's skin in Aboriginal dot art, for no explained reason. The behind-the-scenes DVD documentary explains that he has cursed them and drawn them to a sacred site for revenge. Any idea that this might be a critique of white attitudes to Indigenous culture should probably be abandoned because the film's use of Indigeneity seems highly problematic, if not inexplicable. The documentary explains numerous problems with the film (the original director left the project, they were not allowed to film at a sacred site, and Indigenous actors were dissatisfied with Aboriginal elements, resulting in characters being re-written as white), so it seems safer to simply contextualize *Prey* as another horror film using the trope of tourists in danger in the hostile Australian outback rather than attempt serious analysis with it.

5. Paul Sharrad has suggested that the magic realist form allows Wright to engage effectively with real-life problems: "Wright employs her own mode of 'magic realism' not as an escapist entertainment, nor as an indigenist essentialist romanticism, but 'to create a truer replica of reality' that holds out some promise for freedom" (57).

6. Parts of this chapter were published in an earlier version ("Smudged") that included a treatment of Wright's use of apocalypse in *Plains of Promise* alongside Watson and Weller.

7. B. Wongar is the pen name of Sreten Bozic, whose novels deal with Indigenous themes and characters.

8. As others have noted, questions over authorship and Indigenous identity remain contentious. Authors of texts deal-

ing with Indigenous issues can face suspicion and attempts to (dis)prove their identity as Indigenous people. This is no doubt prompted by previous hoaxes and aggravated by a long tradition of dominant groups refusing Indigenous peoples the right to speak for themselves. Various groups have questioned and discounted Archie Weller's Indigenous identity; however, I have not excluded him from my case studies on this basis. His work meets my criteria of an Australian setting and apocalyptic events and his work identifies with Indigenous people. Weller is not the only writer who has experienced challenges to identity; see Nolan and Dawson for one analysis of the issue of author identity and literary works. Mudrooroo, for instance, was a high-profile Indigenous writer celebrated for his works such as *Wild Cat Falling*. Yet he became the subject of public scrutiny over the authenticity of his Indigenous heritage in the mid-1990s, with his Aboriginal identity since rejected. Maureen Clark's work surveys the circumstances in some detail. Similarly, Wongar was the subject of scrutiny over his identity; Nolan is one critic who has discussed this more closely.

9. In Australia, the earlier practice of removing children from their families to place them in missions or institutions or with white families is commonly known as "the stolen generations." In 1997, the Human Rights and Equal Opportunity Commission published "'Bringing Them Home'— The Report of the National Inquiry into the Separation of Aboriginal and Torres Strait Islander Children from their Families." This report examined the policies and practices that resulted in the "stolen generations" of Indigenous families separated by force. See Moran, and also Chesterman and Douglas, for more analysis of assimilation in the Australian context. The loss of children also recalls Chapter Four's discussion of children and the Australian environment, and, as Kay Torney Souter points out, Indigenous children in Australia were in danger from the governing bodies rather than their own land:

> The children of indigenous Australia didn't wander off because someone stopped thinking about them: they were violently ripped from their mothers' arms in living memory. Since the eighteenth century, non–Indigenous Australia has readily tolerated the kidnapping and resettlement of many thousands of human beings of all ages precisely because it has metaphorised the land as empty, with what is ambiguously called a Dead Heart as its centre.... My claim is that the image of the Dead Heart of Australia — with its implications of sterility and murder — should be understood as a guilty response to the experience of living on the site of innumerable massacres [n.p.].

10. See H. L. Malchow for a discussion of colonial racist attitudes to non-white people, which saw them as having "bad blood" (39), monstrous beings outside the natural order. See also Terry Goldie's *Fear and Temptation* for one explanation of the two key ways in which white people have viewed Indigenous peoples in the world. He describes these in terms of violence and sex, or fear and temptation: "poles of attraction and repulsion, temptation by the dusky maiden and fear of the demonic violence of the fiendish warrior" (15). For an analysis of how Mudrooroo's works interrogate such concepts using vampire motifs, see Gerry Turcotte's "Vampiric Decolonization: Fanon, 'Terrorism' and Mudrooroo's Vampire Trilogy."

11. Eva Rask Knudsen suggests that Watson's message more effectively reaches Indigenous, not white, groups (308). *Kadaitcha*'s graphic scenes of violence and rape may alienate readers, although Marion Halligan claims that the "awful prose" of the novel is "the right vehicle for his message" (11).

Chapter Six

1. Slavoj Žižek's memorable opening comments in his essay suggest he finds little in *The Matrix* worthy of discussion: "When I saw *The Matrix* at a local theatre

in Slovenia, I had the unique opportunity of sitting close to an ideal spectator of the film — namely, to an idiot. A man in his late twenties at my right was so immersed in the film that he continuously disturbed the other spectators with loud exclamations, like 'My God, wow, so there is no reality!' I definitely prefer such naive immersion to pseudo-sophisticated intellectualist readings that project into the film refined philosophical or psychoanalytic conceptual distinctions" (11).

2. In a response to McMullen and Dowling's essay surveying Australian cyberpunk, Greg Egan rejects the suggestion that Australian fiction is different to writing elsewhere, believing such a difference implies inferiority, that local authors cannot "compete on equal terms with writers elsewhere" ("Miracle Ingredient A" n.p.). He also dismisses literary criticism that reads fiction as examples of a specifically "Australian" tradition. Egan's rejection of this critical approach reappears in his novel *Distress*— set on an artificial island called Stateless — with characters who satirize the critical establishment's attempts to define an Australian national identity (121). Egan's other works, such as *Permutation City*, despite being set in Sydney, do not seem particular to Australia and perhaps offer a more truly global perspective than many other cyber-themed novels.

3. Although the open-ended conclusion of the third novel suggests the series will continue, which de Pierres has also confirmed ("Message"), the series remains at three novels at the time of writing.

4. While some critics have read cyberpunk's interest in posthuman issues as opening a way for writers to challenge and subvert traditional gender stereotypes (for example, Donna Haraway, Lauraine Leblanc), others are less convinced, instead insisting that the genre demonstrates little more than a reconfirmation of masculinist ideologies. Sharon Stockton, for instance, has suggested that cyberpunk essentially reworks the adventure story, importing that genre's themes of a (male) hero journeying into new lands and territories. She argues that the cyberpunk hero conquers, colonizes, and exploits others for profit in cyberspace, enacting a masculinist and imperialist discourse. Outside cyberpunk, Ildney Cavalcanti similarly suggests that a "masculine economy" informs quest narratives (57); we can apply this to cyberpunk. In this reading, authors thus encode cyberpunk with ideologies that are hostile to feminist agendas. As Gwyneth Jones puts it: "We feminists of sf read the dazzling *Neuromancer* perhaps with much the same feelings as those unfortunate elvensmiths in *The Lord of the Rings*, when the Dark Lord unveiled his new creation. We knew that the One Ring had been forged, and there wasn't a thing we could do to save ourselves, and what's more, *we had helped him to do it*" (247–48). While analyzing gender in cyberpunk is outside the scope of this book, de Pierres's series does appear to promote Parrish as a feminist icon.

5. The audience learns that the AI, the machines, originally chose a perfect world without suffering as the virtual reality to enslave human consciousness, but this utopian illusion proved to be a "disaster. No one would accept the program" and so the AI changed the program to an illusion satisfying enough to discourage the enslaved humans to seek a different life. The new program chosen "was redesigned to the peak of your civilization," that is, late twentieth-century Western culture. Despite the films being set in the future, apparently life does not get better than it is now, for Western audiences. This perhaps confirms Fukuyama's proposition that we can no longer imagine an alternative society to the one we have now, where liberal democracy signals the end of history. In the schema of *The Matrix*, life does not improve — nor would humans wish for a utopian life.

6. It is, of course, possible for audiences familiar with Sydney to identify locations such as Martin Place and buildings and signs such as the Commonwealth

Bank, which the film does not disguise. While one should not read too much into *The Matrix* in terms of its setting, the film nonetheless reflects the anxieties about the utopian façade hiding a darker reality that are so prevalent in Australian fiction.

7. *The Matrix* is replete with Judeo-Christian apocalyptic imagery, symbolism and themes, such the City of Zion, Neo's messianic role as "the one," and the character name of Trinity. Critics have read the films in terms of their parallels — and differences — to Christianity (for example, Dark, Witherington, Faller), although as Žižek points out, the abundance of philosophical and religious symbols in the films operates as a "kind of Rorschach test, setting in motion a universalized process of recognition" (11) where any interpretation may appear valid.

8. David Detmer notes that Baudrillard criticized *The Matrix* for (mis)appropriating his terminology (102).

Bibliography

Adams, Phillip. "The Dangerous Pornography of Death." *The Bulletin* 1 May 1979: 38+.
Albinski, Nan Bowman. "A Survey of Australian Utopian and Dystopian Fiction." *Australian Literary Studies* 13.1 (1987): 15–28.
Alien vs. Predator. Dir. Paul W. S. Anderson. Twentieth Century–Fox, 2004.
Applebaum, Noga. *Representations of Technology in Science Fiction for Young People.* 2009. Taylor & Francis e-Library. Web. 2 June 2010.
Arthur, Paul Longley. "Capturing the Antipodes: Imaginary Voyages and the Romantic Imagination." *Journal of Australian Studies* 67 (2001): 186+.
Attebery, Brian. "Aboriginality in Science Fiction." *Science Fiction Studies* 32.3 (2005): 385–404.
_____. "But Aren't Those Just ... You Know, Metaphors? Postmodern Figuration in the Science Fiction of James Morrow and Gwyneth Jones." In Hollinger and Gordon, eds., 90–107.
Baccolini, Raffaella, and Tom Moylan, eds. *Dark Horizons: Science Fiction and the Dystopian Imagination.* New York: Routledge, 2003.
_____, and _____. "Dystopia and Histories." Introduction. In Baccolini and Moylan, eds., 1–12.
Barbour, Dennis H. "Heroism and Redemption in the *Mad Max* trilogy." *Journal of Popular Film and Television* 27.3 (1999): 28–34.
Barnett, P. Chad. "Reviving Cyberpunk: (Re)Constructing the Subject and Mapping Cyberspace in the Wachowski Brothers' Film *The Matrix*." *Extrapolation* 41.4 (2000): 359–74.
Barra, Allen. "A Road Warrior Is Still on a Roll." *New York Times* 15 Aug. 1999, late ed. east coast ed., sec. 2: 9.
Baudrillard, Jean. "The Anorexic Ruins." *Looking Back on the End of the World.* Ed. Dietmar Kamper and Christoph Wulf. Trans. David Antal. New York: Semiotext(e), 1989, 29–45.
_____. *Simulacra and Simulation.* Trans. Sheila Faria Glaser. Ann Arbor: University of Michigan Press, 1994. Trans. of *Simulacres et Simulation.* 1981.
Bellanta, Melissa. "Fabulating the Australian Desert: Australia's Lost Race Romances, 1890–1908." *Philament* 3 (2004). Web. 2 June 2010.
Bendle, Mervyn F. "The Apocalyptic Imagination and Popular Culture." *Journal of Religion and Popular Culture* 11 (2005). Web. 2 June 2010.

Berger, James. *After the End: Representations of Post-Apocalypse*. Minneapolis: University of Minnesota Press, 1999.
Bernard, Patricia. *The Outcast*. The Outcast Trilogy 1. Sydney: Harper, 1997.
_____. *The Punisher*. The Outcast Trilogy 2. Sydney: Harper, 1997.
_____. *The Rule Changer*. The Outcast Trilogy 3. Pymble: Harper, 1998.
Bibby, Paul. "Between the Flags." *Sydney Morning Herald: The Guide* 9–15 July 2007: 4.
Biber, Katherine. "The Threshold Moment: Masculinity at Home and on the Road in Australian Cinema." *Limina* 7 (2001): 26–46.
Bird, Delys. "The 'Settling' of English." *The Oxford Literary History of Australia*. Ed. Bruce Bennett, Jennifer Strauss, and Chris Wallace-Crabbe. Melbourne: Oxford University Press, 1998, 21–43.
Black Water. Dir. Andrew Traucki and David Nerlich. AV, 2007.
Blackford, Russell. "Glass Reptile Breakout." 1985. *Glass Reptile Breakout and Other Australian Speculative Stories*. Ed. Van Ikin. Western Australia: Centre for Studies in Australian Literature–University of Western Australia, 1990, 11–22.
_____. "Mutants, Cyborgs, AI & Androids." *Meanjin* 63.1 (2004): 14–21.
_____. "The Soldier in the Machine." In Dann and Webb, eds., 63–86.
Blackford, Russell, Van Ikin, and Sean McMullen. *Strange Constellations: A History of Australian Science Fiction*. Westport, Conn.: Greenwood, 1999.
Blackmore, Leigh. "The Uneasy Chair." Introduction. *Terror Australis: The Best of Australian Horror*. Ed. Blackmore. Rydalmere: Coronet-Hodder & Stoughton, 1993. vii–xii.
Blade Runner. Dir. Ridley Scott. Warner Bros., 1982.
Blainey, Geoffrey. *A Land Half Won*. Rev. ed. South Melbourne: Macmillan, 1982.
_____. *The Tyranny of Distance: How Distance Shaped Australia's History*. 1966. Rev. ed. Sydney: Pan Macmillan: 2001.
Boer, Roland. *Last Stop Before Antarctica: The Bible and Postcolonialism in Australia*. 2nd ed. Atlanta: Society of Biblical Literature, 2008.
The Book of Eli. Dir. the Hughes Brothers. Warner Bros., 2010.
Border Security: Australia's Frontline. Channel Seven. 2004–2010.
Botero, Giovanni. *Relations of the Most Famous Kingdomes and Common-wealths thorowout the World: Discoursing of Their Situations, Religions, Languages, Manners, Customes, Strengths, Greatnesse and Policies*. London, 1630. Trans. of *le Relationi Universali*, 1618.
Bowen, Emanuel. "A Complete Map of the Southern Continent." 1744. MAP NK 4185. National Library of Australia.
Boyd, Hannah Villiers. *A Voice from Australia; or An Inquiry into the Probability of New Holland Being Connected with the Prophecies Relating to the New Jerusalem and the Spiritual Temple*. Sydney: Robert Barr, 1851.
Bradford, Clare. *Reading Race: Aboriginality in Australian Children's Literature*. Carlton South: Melbourne University Press, 2001.
Bradford, Clare, Kerry Mallan, and John Stephens. "New World Orders and the Dystopian Turn: Transforming Visions of Territoriality and Belonging in Recent Australian Children's Fiction." *Journal of Australian Studies* 32.3 (2008): 349–59.
Bradford, Clare, Kerry Mallan, John Stephens, and Robyn McCallum. *New World Orders in Contemporary Children's Literature: Utopian Transformations*. Basingstoke: Palgrave Macmillan, 2008.
Braithwaite, Elizabeth. "'When I Was a Child I Thought as a Child...': The Importance of Memory in Constructions of Childhood and Social Order in a Selection of

Post-Disaster Fictions." *Papers: Explorations into Children's Literature* 15.2 (2005): 50–57.
Brennan, Peter. *Razorback*. London: Fontana, 1981.
Brians, Paul. *Nuclear Holocausts: Atomic War in Fiction 1895–1984*. Kent: Kent State University Press, 1987.
Broderick, Damien. "George Turner's Critical Reception in Australia." *Panterraweb.com*. 18 Jan. 2001. Web. 2 June 2010.
Broderick, Mick. "Heroic Apocalypse: *Mad Max*, Mythology and the Millennium." In Sharrett, ed., 251–72.
_____. "Surviving Armageddon: Beyond the Imagination of Disaster." *Science Fiction Studies* 20.3 (1993). Web. 2 June 2010.
Brodesser, Claude, and Don Groves. "Threat of War Stalling 'Max.'" *Variety* 3 Mar. 2003: 40.
Brown, Simon. *Winter*. Pymble: Harper, 1997.
Bruno, Giuliana. "Ramble City: Postmodernism and *Blade Runner*." In Sharrett, ed., 237–49.
Bryson, Bill. *Down Under*. London: Doubleday-Transworld, 2000.
Buckrich, Judith Raphael. *George Turner: A Life*. Carlton South: Melbourne University Press, 1999.
Buffy the Vampire Slayer. WB-UPN. 1997–2003.
Bukatman, Scott. "Cybersubjectivity and Cinematic Being." In Sharrett, ed., 77–102.
Bull, Malcolm, ed. *Apocalypse Theory and the Ends of the World*. Oxford: Blackwell, 1995.
_____. "On Making Ends Meet." In Bull, ed., 1–17.
_____. *Seeing Things Hidden: Apocalypse, Vision and Totality*. London: Verso, 1999.
Caesar, Adrian. "Invasions of the Mind: John Marsden and the Threat from Asia." *Overland* 157 (1999): 46–50.
Campbell, Joseph. *The Hero with a Thousand Faces*. 1949. 2nd ed. Princeton: Princeton University Press, 1972.
Campbell, Patty. "The Sand in the Oyster." *The Horn Book Magazine* 71.5 (1995): 634–39.
Carey, John, ed. *The Faber Book of Utopias*. London: Faber and Faber, 1999.
Carmody, Isobelle. *Ashling*. The Obernewtyn Chronicles 3. Ringwood, Vic.: Viking-Penguin, 1995.
_____. *The Farseekers*. The Obernewtyn Chronicles 2. Ringwood, Vic.: Viking, 1990.
_____. *The Keeping Place*. The Obernewtyn Chronicles 4. Ringwood, Vic.: Viking-Penguin, 1999.
_____. *Obernewtyn*. The Obernewtyn Chronicles 1. Ringwood, Vic.: Puffin-Penguin, 1987.
_____. *Scatterlings*. Ringwood, Vic.: Penguin, 1991.
_____. *The Stone Key*. The Obernewtyn Chronicles 5. Camberwell, Vic.: Penguin, 2008.
The Cars That Ate Paris. Dir. Peter Weir. BEF, 1974.
Category 7: The End of the World. Dir. Dick Lowry. CBS, 2005.
Category 6: Day of Destruction. Dir. Dick Lowry. CBS, 2004.
Caterson, Simon. "The Best Australian Film You've Never Seen." *Quadrant* 50.1–2 (2006): 86–88.
Cavalcanti, Ildney. "The Writing of Utopia and the Feminist Critical Dystopia: Suzy McKee Charnas's Holdfast Series." In Baccolini and Moylan, eds., 47–67.
The Chain Reaction. Dir. Ian Barry. Hoyts, 1980.

Chapman, Jennie. "Selling Faith Without Selling Out: Reading the *Left Behind* Novels in the Context of Popular Culture." In Walliss and Newport, eds., 148–72.
Chesterman, John, and Heather Douglas. "'Their Ultimate Absorption': Assimilation in 1930s Australia." *Journal of Australian Studies* 81 (2004): 47+.
Children of Men. Dir. Alfonso Cuarón. Universal, 2006.
Christopher, Lucy. *Stolen*. Frome: Chicken House, 2009.
The Chronicles of Narnia: The Lion, the Witch and the Wardrobe. Dir. Andrew Adamson. Buena Vista, 2005.
Clark, C. M. H. [Manning]. *A History of Australia. II. New South Wales and Van Diemen's Land 1822–1838*. Carlton: Melbourne University Press, 1968.
_____. *Manning Clark's History of Australia*. Ed. Michael Cathcart. Abr. ed. Carlton: Melbourne University Press, 1993.
Clark, Maureen. "Mudrooroo and the Death of the Mother." *New Literatures Review* 40 (2003): 83–102.
_____. "Mudrooroo: Crafty Impostor or Rebel with a Cause?" *Australian Literary Studies* 21.4 (2004): 101–10.
Clark, Stephen R. L. "The End of the Ages." In Seed, ed., 27–44.
Clarke, I. F. "The Tales of the Last Days, 1805–3794." In Seed, ed., 15–26.
Cohn, Norman. *The Pursuit of the Millennium: Revolutionary Millenarians and Mystical Anarchists of the Middle Ages*. 1957. Rev. ed. London: Pimlico-Random, 1993.
Collins, Paul. *Cyberskin*. Melbourne: Hybrid, 2000.
_____. *The Earthborn*. The Earthborn Wars 1. New York: Tor, 2003.
_____. *The Hiveborn*. The Earthborn Wars 3. Andover: Bohemian Ink, 2006.
_____. *The Skyborn*. The Earthborn Wars 2. New York: Starscape–Tom Doherty, 2005.
_____. "Wired Dreaming." In Dann and Webb, eds., 142–51.
_____, ed. *The M.U.P. Encyclopaedia of Australian Science Fiction and Fantasy*. Carlton South: Melbourne University Press, 1998.
Collins, Suzanne. *The Hunger Games*. London: Scholastic, 2008.
Coman, B. J. "La Austrialia Del Espiritu Santo: Captain Quirós and the Discovery of Australia in 1606." *Quadrant* 50.5 (2006): 60–64.
Conn, Matthew. "The Cyberspatial Landscapes of William Gibson and Tad Williams." *AUMLA: Journal of the Australasian Universities Language and Literature Association* 96 (2001): 207–19.
Connor, Michael. *The Invention of Terra Nullius: Historical and Legal Fictions on the Foundation of Australia*. Sydney: Macleay, 2005.
Conrad, Joseph. *The Heart of Darkness, and the Secret Sharer*. 1899. New York: Signet, 1950.
Cook, Kenneth. *Wake in Fright*. 1961. Sydney: Angus & Robertson, 1981.
Cooper, Ken. "The Whiteness of the Bomb." In Dellamora, ed., 79–106.
The Core. Dir. John Amiel. Paramount, 2003.
Cousins, A. D. "Barron Field and the Translation of Romanticism to Colonial Australia." *Southerly* 58.4 (1998): 157–74. Academic OneFile. Web. 2 June 2010.
Cox, Erle. *Out of the Silence*. Melbourne: E. A. Vidler, 1925.
Creed, Barbara. *Media Matrix: Sexing the New Reality*. Crows Nest: Allen & Unwin, 2003.
Crocodile Dundee. Dir. Peter Faiman. Paramount, 1986.
Crocodile Dundee 2. Dir. John Cornell. Paramount, 1988.
Crouch, David. "National Hauntings: The Architecture of Australian Ghost Stories." *Spectres, Screens, Shadows, Mirrors*. Spec. issue of *JASAL* (2007): 94–105.
Csicsery-Ronay, Istvan, Jr. "Dis-Imagined Communities: Science Fiction and the Future of Nations." In Hollinger and Gordon, eds., 217–37.

Dann, Jack, and Janeen Webb, eds. *Dreaming Down Under*. 1998. New York: Tor–Tom Doherty, 2001.
Dark, David. *Everyday Apocalypse: The Sacred Revealed in Radiohead, The Simpsons and Other Pop Culture Icons.* Grand Rapids: Brazos-Baker, 2002.
Dark City. Dir. Alex Proya. New Line, 1998.
Davison, Graeme. "Images of Modern Melbourne, 1945–1970." *Journal of Australian Studies* 57 (1998): 145–61.
The Day After. Dir. Nicholas Meyer. American Broadcasting Corporation–Buena Vista, 1983.
The Day After Tomorrow. Dir. Roland Emmerich. DVD. Two-Disc Special Edition. Twentieth Century–Fox Home Entertainment, 2004.
Dead End Drive-In. Dir. Brian Trenchard-Smith. Greater Union, 1986.
de Foigny, Gabriel. *La Terre Australe Connue*. 1676. Geneva: Slatkine, 1981.
de Jode, Cornelius. "Novae Guineae forma, & situs." 1593. MAP RM 389. National Library of Australia.
Dellamora, Richard. *Apocalyptic Overtures: Sexual Politics and the Sense of an Ending.* New Brunswick: Rutgers University Press, 1994.
_____. Introduction. In Dellamora, ed., 1–14.
_____. Preface. In Dellamora, ed., xi–xiii.
_____, ed. *Postmodern Apocalypse: Theory and Cultural Practice at the End.* Philadelphia: University of Pennsylvania Press, 1995.
de Pierres, Marianne. *Code Noir*. Parrish Plessis 2. London: Orbit–Time Warner, 2004.
_____. *Crash Deluxe*. Parrish Plessis 3. London: Orbit–Time Warner, 2005.
_____. Message to the author. 20 Mar. 2007. Email.
_____. *Nylon Angel*. Parrish Plessis 1. London: Orbit–Time Warner, 2004.
Dermody, Susan, and Elizabeth Jacka. *The Screening of Australia: Anatomy of a National Cinema.* Sydney: Currency, 1988.
Derrida, Jacques. "No Apocalypse, Not Now (Full Speed Ahead, Seven Missiles, Seven Missives)." Trans. Catherine Porter and Philip Lewis. *Diacritics* 14.2 (1984): 20–31.
_____. "Of an Apocalyptic Tone Recently Adopted in Philosophy." Trans. John P. Leavey, Jr. *Oxford Literary Review* 6.2 (1984): 3–37.
Detmer, David. "Challenging *Simulacra and Simulation*: Baudrillard in *The Matrix*." In William Irwin, ed., 93–108.
Dillon, Matthew. "Summertime Blues." *Metro* 133 (2002): 30+.
Dixon, Robert. *Writing the Colonial Adventure: Race, Gender and Nation in Anglo-Australian Popular Fiction, 1875–1914.* Cambridge: Cambridge University Press, 1995.
Dobson, Jill. *The Inheritors*. St. Lucia: University of Queensland Press, 1988.
Dodson, Michael. "The Wentworth Lecture: The End in the Beginning: Re(de)finding Aboriginality." *Australian Aboriginal Studies* 1 (1994): 2–12.
"Doomsday Clock Moves Closer to the End." *The Age* 19 Jan. 2007. Web. 2 June 2010.
Douglas, J. D., ed. *The New Bible Dictionary*. London: Inter-Varsity Fellowship, 1962.
DuPrau, Jeanne. *The City of Ember*. New York: Random, 2003.
Dutton, Jacqueline. "Three French Futures: Australia, Antarctica and Ailleurs." *Arena* 25–26 (2006): 278–94.
Ebert, Roger. Rev. of *Mad Max: Beyond Thunderdome*, dir. George Miller and George Ogilvie. *Chicago Sun-Times* 10 July 1985. Web. 2 June 2010.
Egan, Greg. *Distress*. London: Millennium-Orion, 1995.
_____. *Luminous*. London: Millennium, 1998.
_____. *Permutation City*. London: Millennium-Orion, 1994.
_____. *Quarantine*. London: Legend, 1992.

_____. "A Report on the Origins & Hazardous Effects of Miracle Ingredient A." *Eidolon* 17–18 (1995): 32–38. Web. 2 June 2010.
Eldershaw, M. Barnard. *Tomorrow and Tomorrow*. Melbourne: Georgian, 1947.
Escape from Absalom. Dir. Martin Campbell. Columbia Tristar, 1994.
Esmonde, Margaret P. "After Armageddon: The Post Cataclysmic Novel for Young Readers." *Children's Literature* 6 (1977): 211–20.
Falconer, Delia. "We Don't Need to Know the Way Home: Selling Australian Space in the *Mad Max* Trilogy." *Southern Review* 27.1 (1994): 28–44.
Faller, Stephen. *Beyond the Matrix: Revolutions and Revelations*. St. Louis: Chalice, 2004.
Farscape. Channel Nine. 1999–2003.
Fitting, Peter. "Unmasking the Real? Critique and Utopia in Recent SF Films." In Baccolini and Moylan, eds., 155–66.
Fortress. Dir. Stuart Gordon. Village Roadshow, 1993.
Freud, Sigmund. "The Uncanny." 1919. Trans. Alix Strachey. *An Infantile Neurosis and Other Works*. London: Hogarth–Institute of Psycho-Analysis, 1964. 217–56. Vol. 17 of *The Standard Edition of the Complete Psychological Works of Sigmund Freud*.
Frye, Northrop. *Anatomy of Criticism: Four Essays*. 1957. New York: Atheneum, 1969.
Fukuyama, Francis. *The End of History and the Last Man*. 1992. New York: Bard-Avon, 1998.
Furedi, Frank. *Culture of Fear: Risk-taking and the Morality of Low Expectation*. Rev. ed. London: Continuum, 2003.
_____. *Politics of Fear*. London: Continuum, 2005.
Galbreath, Robert. "Ambiguous Apocalypse: Transcendental Visions of the End." In Rabkin, Greenberg and Olander, eds., 53–72.
Gale, Peter. *The Politics of Fear: Lighting the Wik*. Frenchs Forest: Pearson, 2005.
Gannon, Charles E. "Silo Psychosis: Diagnosing America's Nuclear Anxieties Through Narrative Imagery." In Seed, ed., 103–17.
Gelder, Ken. Introduction. *The Oxford Book of Australian Ghost Stories*. Ed. Gelder. Melbourne: Oxford University Press, 1994, ix–xviii.
_____, and Jane M. Jacobs. *Uncanny Australia: Sacredness and Identity in a Postcolonial Nation*. Melbourne: Melbourne University Press, 1998.
Ghosts ... of the Civil Dead. Dir. John Hillcoat. Correctional Services Inc., 1988.
Gibson, Ross. *The Diminishing Paradise: Changing Literary Perceptions of Australia*. Sydney: Sirius-Angus & Robertson, 1984.
_____. *South of the West: Postcolonialism and the Narrative Construction of Australia*. Bloomington: Indiana University Press, 1992.
_____. "Yondering: A Reading of *Mad Max Beyond Thunderdome*." *Art & Text* 19 (1985): 25–33.
Gibson, William. *Burning Chrome*. New York: Ace, 1987.
_____. "Johnny Mnemonic." 1981. In *Burning Chrome*, 1–22.
_____. *Neuromancer*. 1984. London: Voyager-Harper, 1995.
The Girl from Tomorrow: Tomorrow's End. Channel Nine. 1991.
Goldie, Terry. *Fear and Temptation: The Image of the Indigene in Canadian, Australian, and New Zealand Literatures*. Montreal: McGill-Queen's University Press, 1989.
Goldman, Marlene. *Rewriting Apocalypse in Canadian Fiction*. Montreal: McGill-Queen's University Press, 2005.
Gone. Dir. Ringan Ledwidge. Universal, 2006.
Gordon, Joan. "Utopia, Genocide, and the Other." In Hollinger and Gordon, eds., 204–16.

Grace, Helen. "The Persistence of Culture: Recovering *On the Beach*." *Continuum: Journal of Media & Cultural Studies* 15.3 (2001): 289–301.
Haggard, H. Rider. *King Solomon's Mines*. London, 1885.
Hall, Penny. *The Catalyst*. 1989. Pymble: Collins-Angus & Robertson, 1993.
_____. *The Paperchaser*. Glebe: Walter McVitty, 1987.
Hall, Sandra. "On a Road to Hell Paved with Gold." *Sydney Morning Herald* 12 Dec. 2002. Web. 2 June 2010.
Halligan, Marion. "About Books." *National Library of Australia News* 1.1 (1990): 8–11.
Hamilton, M. Lynn. *The Hidden Kingdom*. Melbourne: N. Wentworth Evans, 1932.
Hanson, Donna Maree. *Australian Speculative Fiction: A Genre Overview*. Murrumbateman: Aust Speculative Fiction, 2005.
Happy Feet. Dir. George Miller. Warner Bros., 2006.
Haraway, Donna. *Simians, Cyborgs and Women: The Reinvention of Nature*. New York: Routledge, 1991.
Harding, Lee. *Displaced Person*. Melbourne: Hyland, 1979.
_____. *Waiting for the End of the World*. Melbourne: Hyland, 1983.
_____. *The Web of Time*. Stanmore: Cassell, 1980.
Harland, Richard. *Ferren and the Angel*. The Heaven and Earth Trilogy 1. Ringwood, Vic.: Penguin, 2000.
_____. *Ferren and the Invasion of Heaven*. The Heaven and Earth Trilogy 3. Ringwood, Vic.: Penguin, 2003.
_____. *Ferren and the White Doctor*. The Heaven and Earth Trilogy 2. Ringwood, Vic.: Penguin, 2002.
Haslam, Jason. "Coded Discourse: Romancing the (Electronic) Shadow in *The Matrix*." *College Literature* 32.3 (2005): 92–115.
Haynes, Roslynn D. *Seeking the Centre: The Australian Desert in Literature, Art and Film*. Cambridge: Cambridge University Press, 1998.
Heffernan, Teresa. "Can the Apocalypse Be Post?" In Dellamora, ed., 171–81.
Henning, Rachel. *The Letters of Rachel Henning*. Ed. David Adams. Ringwood, Vic.: Penguin, 1988.
Heroes. NBC. 2006–2010.
Hewlett, Jamie, and Alan Martin. *Tank Girl*. 1990. London: Titan, 2002.
Hildebrand, Joe. "Mad Max 4: Fury Road Gets Green Light; Sam Worthington Tipped to Star." *The Daily Telegraph* Oct. 24, 2009. Web. 7 Jan. 2010.
Hintz, Carrie, and Elaine Ostry. Introduction. *Utopian and Dystopian Writing for Children and Young Adults*. Ed. Hintz and Ostry. New York: Routledge, 2003. 1–20.
Holden, Robert. *Bunyips: Australia's Folklore of Fear*. Canberra: National Library of Australia, 2001.
Hollinger, Veronica. "Apocalypse Coma." In Hollinger and Gordon, eds., 159–73.
_____. "Cybernetic Deconstructions: Cyberpunk and Postmodernism." *Mosaic* 23.2 (1990): 29–44.
_____. "Future/Present: The End of Science Fiction." In Seed, ed., 215–29.
_____, and Joan Gordon, eds. *Edging Into the Future: Science Fiction and Contemporary Cultural Transformation*. Philadelphia: University of Pennsylvania Press, 2002.
The Holy Bible. New International Version: The NIV Study Bible. Grand Rapids: Zondervan, 1995.
Hood, Robert. "Killer Koalas: Australian (and New Zealand) Horror Films: A History." *Tabula Rasa*. 1994. Web. 2 June 2010.
Hook. Dir. Steven Spielberg. Columbia TriStar, 1991.

Horne, Donald. *The Lucky Country*. 1964. 3rd Rev. ed. Ringwood, Vic.: Penguin, 1984.
Hughes, Robert. *The Fatal Shore: A History of the Transportation of Convicts to Australia, 1787–1868*. London: Collins, 1987.
Human Rights and Equal Opportunity Commission. "'Bringing Them Home'— Report of the National Inquiry into the Separation of Aboriginal and Torres Strait Islander Children from Their Families." *Australian Human Rights Commission*. April 1997. Web. 27 June 2010.
Hume, Kathryn. *Fantasy and Mimesis*. New York: Methuen, 1984.
I Am Legend. Dir. Francis Lawrence. Warner Bros., 2007.
I, Robot. Dir. Alex Proyas. Twentieth Century–Fox, 2004.
Ikin, Van. "Dreams, Visions, Utopias." *The Penguin New Literary History of Australia*. Ed. Laurie Hergenhan. Ringwood, Vic.: Penguin, 1988, 253–66.
_____. "The History of Australian Science Fiction." Introduction. *Australian Science Fiction*. Ed. lkin. St. Lucia: University of Queensland Press, 1982. ix–xl.
_____, and Terry Dowling. Introduction. *Mortal Fire: Best Australian SF*. Eds. lkin and Dowling. Rydalmere: Coronet-Hodder & Stoughton-Hodder Headline, 1993, vii–xviii.
An Inconvenient Truth. Dir. Davis Guggenheim. United Intl, 2006.
Irvine, Ian. *The Last Albatross*. The Human Rites Trilogy 1. 2000. East Roseville: Earthlight-Simon, 2001.
_____. *The Life Lottery*. The Human Rites Trilogy 3. Pymble: Pocket-Simon, 2004.
_____. *Terminator Gene*. The Human Rites Trilogy 2. East Roseville: Earthlight-Simon, 2003.
Irwin, William, ed. *More Matrix and Philosophy: Revolutions and Reloaded Decoded*. Chicago: Open Court, 2005.
Irwin, W. R. *The Game of the Impossible: A Rhetoric of Fantasy*. Urbana: University of Illinois Press, 1976.
Jackson, Rosemary. *Fantasy: The Literature of Subversion*. London: Methuen, 1981.
Jacobs, Naomi. "Posthuman Bodies and Agency in Octavia Butler's *Xenogenesis*." In Baccolini and Moylan, eds., 91–111.
James, Caryn. "A Distinctive Shade of Darkness." *The New York Times* 28 Nov. 1993. Academic OneFile. Web. 2 June 2010.
James, Edward. "Rewriting the Christian Apocalypse as a Science-Fictional Event." In Seed, ed., 45–61.
Jameson, Fredric. *Archaeologies of the Future: The Desire Called Utopia and Other Science Fictions*. London: Verso-New Left, 2005.
_____. *Postmodernism, or, The Cultural Logic of Late Capitalism*. 1991. Durham: Duke University Press, 2003.
Jericho. CBS. 2006–2008.
Jillett, Neil. "We Were All Wrong, Ava." *The Age* 14 Jan. 1982. Web. 23 June 2010.
Jinman, Richard. "Loved Your Work in *Jaws*, Actor Tells Co-Stars." *Sydney Morning Herald* 9–10 Oct. 2004, sec. 1: 2.
Johinke, Rebecca. "Manifestations of Masculinities: *Mad Max* and the Lure of the Forbidden Zone." *Journal of Australian Studies* 67 (2001): 118–25.
Johnston, Rosemary Ross. "Summer Holidays and Landscapes of Fear: Toward a Comparative Study of 'Mainstream' Canadian and Australian Children's Novels." *CCL: Canadian Children's Literature* 109–110 (2003): 87–104.
Jones, Gwyneth. "*Kairos*: The Enchanted Loom." In Hollinger and Gordon, eds., 174–89.
Jorgensen, Darren. "The Utopian Imagination of Aboriginalism." *Arena Journal* 25–26 (2006): 178–90.

Kakmi, Dmetri. "The Hideous Blank at *Wolf Creek*." *Metro* 148 (2006): 72–77.
Kellaway, Frank. "Visions of Conflict: The Novels of George Turner." *Overland* 87 (1982): 9+.
Kelleher, Victor. *The Makers*. Ringwood, Vic.: Penguin, 1987.
_____. *Parkland*. Ringwood, Vic.: Viking, 1994.
_____. *Red Heart*. Ringwood, Vic.: Viking-Penguin, 2001.
_____. *Taronga*. Ringwood, Vic.: Puffin-Penguin, 1986.
Keller, Catherine. *Apocalypse Now and Then: A Feminist Guide to the End of the World*. Boston: Beacon, 1996.
Kennon, Patricia. "'Belonging' in Young Adult Dystopian Fiction: New Communities Created by Children." *Papers: Explorations into Children's Literature* 15.2 (2005): 40–49.
Kermode, Frank. *The Sense of an Ending: Studies in the Theory of Fiction with a New Epilogue*. 1967. New York: Oxford University Press, 2000.
Ketterer, David. *New Worlds for Old: The Apocalyptic Imagination, Science Fiction, and American Literature*. Garden City, NY: Anchor-Doubleday, 1974.
Kiernan, Brian. *Images of Society and Nature: Seven Essays on Australian Novels*. Melbourne: Oxford University Press, 1971.
Kitson, Michael. "Adrian Martin: The *Mad Max* Movies: *Mad Max, Mad Max 2/The Road Warrior, Mad Max Beyond Thunderdome*." *Metro* 138 (2003): 199–200.
Knudsen, Eva Rask. *The Circle & the Spiral: A Study of Australian Aboriginal & New Zealand Māori Literature*. Amsterdam: Rodopi, 2004.
Kotlowski, Elizabeth Rogers. *Stories of Australia's Christian Heritage: Explorers, Colonial Times, Pioneers, Statesmen*. Sydney: Strand, 2006.
Kremmer, Christopher. "Running on Empty." *Sydney Morning Herald* 2–3 Apr. 2005, sec. 2: 29+.
Kumar, Krishan. "Apocalypse, Millennium and Utopia Today." In Bull, ed., 200–24.
La Forgia, Rebecca. "Truth: But Still Waiting for Justice." *Alternative Law Journal* 22.4 (1997): 192–95.
Land of the Apocalypse. Dir. Bob Plasto and Ruth Berry. Videocassette. Video Educ. Australasia, 1991.
The Last Wave. Dir. Peter Weir. United Intl, 1977.
Lawrence, Carmen. *Fear and Politics*. Melbourne: Scribe, 2006.
Leblanc, Lauraine. "Razor Girls: Genre and Gender in Cyberpunk Fiction." *Women and Language* 20.1 (1997): 71+. ProQuest. Web. 2 June 2010.
Legion. Dir. Scott Stewart. Screen Gems, 2010.
Lewis, C. S. *The Horse and His Boy*. Chronicles of Narnia 3. 1954. London: Lions-Collins, 1987.
_____. *The Last Battle*. Chronicles of Narnia 7. 1956. London: Lions-Collins, 1987.
_____. *The Lion, the Witch and the Wardrobe*. Chronicles of Narnia 2. 1950. London: Lions-Collins, 1987.
_____. *The Magician's Nephew*. Chronicles of Narnia 1. 1955. London: Lions-Collins, 1987.
_____. *Prince Caspian*. Chronicles of Narnia 4. 1951. London: Lions-Collins, 1987.
_____. *The Silver Chair*. Chronicles of Narnia 6. 1953. London: Lions-Collins, 1987.
_____. *The Voyage of the Dawntreader*. Chronicles of Narnia 5. 1955. London: Lions-Collins, 1987.
Lindsay, Joan. *Picnic at Hanging Rock*. 1967. Ringwood, Vic.: Viking-Penguin, 1987.
Locusts: Day of Destruction. Dir. David Jackson. CBS, 2005.

Loder, Kurt. "The Heroes of Thunderdome: On the Road with *Mad Max*." *Rolling Stone* 29 Aug. 1985: 40+.
Long Weekend. Dir. Colin Eggleston. Australian Film Commission, 1978.
Long Weekend. Dir. Jamie Blanks. Roadshow, 2008.
Lord, Gabrielle. *Salt*. Ringwood, Vic.: McPhee Gribble-Penguin, 1990.
The Lord of the Rings: The Fellowship of the Ring. Dir. Peter Jackson. New Line, 2001.
The Lord of the Rings: The Return of the King. Dir. Peter Jackson. New Line, 2003.
The Lord of the Rings: The Two Towers. Dir. Peter Jackson. New Line, 2002.
Maack, Annagret. "'It's All Contrary': Utopian Projections in the Antipodes." *Antipodes* 14.2 (2000): 123–28.
Macdonald, Caroline. *The Eye Witness*. 1991. Sydney: Starlight-Hodder & Stoughton, 1993.
_____. *The Lake at the End of the World*. Ringwood, Vic.: Viking-Kestrel-Penguin, 1988.
Macrae, Andrew. "Looking Awry at Cyberpunk Through Antipodean Eyes: Reading Neal Stephenson and Greg Egan from the Margins." *Australian Studies* 13.1 (1998): 31–43.
Mad Max. Dir. George Miller. Roadshow, 1979.
Mad Max: Beyond Thunderdome. Dir. George Miller and George Ogilvie. Warner Bros., 1985.
Mad Max 2: The Road Warrior. Dir. George Miller. Warner Bros., 1981.
Maddox, Garry. "Max Will Be Back — After a Few Detours." *Sydney Morning Herald* 15 Mar. 2007: 7.
Malchow, H. L. *Gothic Images of Race in Nineteenth-Century Britain*. Stanford: Stanford University Press, 1996.
Mann, Simon. "Snowmageddon: How America Is Battling a Real Cold War." *Sydney Morning Herald* 8 Feb. 2010. Web. 7 June 2010.
Marsden, John. *Burning for Revenge*. Tomorrow Ser. 5. 1997. Sydney: Pan Macmillan, 2005.
_____. *Circle of Flight*. Ellie Chronicles 3. Sydney: Pan Macmillan, 2006.
_____. *Darkness, Be My Friend*. Tomorrow Ser. 4. 1996. Sydney: Pan Macmillan, 2000.
_____. *The Dead of the Night*. Tomorrow Ser. 2. 1994. Sydney: Pan Macmillan, 1997.
_____. *Incurable*. Ellie Chronicles 2. Sydney: Pan Macmillan, 2005.
_____. "John Marsden." Interview with George Negus. *George Negus Tonight*. ABC, Sydney. 4 Nov. 2004. Transcript. Web. 2 June 2010.
_____. *The Night Is for Hunting*. Tomorrow Ser. 6. 1998. Sydney: Pan Macmillan, 1999.
_____. *The Other Side of Dawn*. Tomorrow Ser. 7. Sydney: Pan Macmillan, 1999.
_____. "PW Talks with John Marsden: Bestseller Down Under." Interview with Elizabeth Devereaux. *Publishers Weekly* 26 Aug. 2002: 70.
_____. *The Third Day, The Frost*. Tomorrow Ser. 3. 1995. Sydney: Pan Macmillan, 2000.
_____. *Tomorrow, When the War Began*. Tomorrow Ser. 1. 1993. Sydney: Pan Macmillan, 1994.
_____. *While I Live*. Ellie Chronicles 1. Sydney: Pan Macmillan, 2003.
_____, and Shaun Tan. *The Rabbits*. Melbourne: Lothian, 1998.
Martens, John W. *The End of the World: The Apocalyptic Imagination in Film & Television*. Winnipeg: J. Gordon Shillingford, 2003.
Martin, Adrian. *The Mad Max Movies*. Sydney: Currency, 2003.
The Matrix. Dir. the Wachowski Brothers. Village Roadshow, 1999.

The Matrix Reloaded. Dir. the Wachowski Brothers. Village Roadshow, 2003.
The Matrix Revolutions. Dir. the Wachowski Brothers. Village Roadshow, 2003.
Mayers, Rhonda. "'As If This Were Narnia or Somewhere': What's Real(ly) Fantasy? An Exploration of John Marsden's *Tomorrow, When the War Began* and Isobelle Carmody's *Greylands*." *Papers: Explorations into Children's Literature* 8.1 (1998): 18–24.
McCarthy, Cormac. *The Road*. London: Picador, 2006.
McFarlane, Brian. *Australian Cinema 1970–1985*. Richmond: William Heinemann, 1987.
_____. "The Australian Literary Adaptation: An Overview." *Film Literature Quarterly* 21.2 (1993): 90–101.
_____. "*The Matrix*: Cult Classic or Computerized Con?" *Australian Screen Education* 41 (2006): 105–9.
McFarlane, Peter. *The Enemy You Killed*. Ringwood, Vic.: Penguin, 1996.
McGahan, Andrew. *Underground*. Crows Nest: Allen & Unwin, 2006.
_____. *Wonders of a Godless World*. Crows Nest: Allen & Unwin, 2009.
McGuire, Ann. Editorial. *Papers: Explorations into Children's Literature* 15.2 (2005): 3–5.
McLean, Greg. "Australian Gothic: Greg McLean on the Genesis of *Wolf Creek*." Interview with Raffaele Caputo. *Metro* 145 (2005): 10–19.
McMullen, Sean. *Eyes of the Calculor*. The Greatwinter Trilogy 3. 2001. New York: Tor-Tom Doherty, 2003.
_____. *The Miocene Arrow*. The Greatwinter Trilogy 2. 2000. New York: Tor-Tom Doherty, 2003.
_____. *Souls in the Great Machine*. The Greatwinter Trilogy 1. 1999. New York: Tor-Tom Doherty, 2002.
_____, and Terry Dowling. "A Lateral Leading Edge: Australian SF and Cyberpunk." *Eidolon* 14 (1994): 14–21. Web. 2 June 2010.
McNab, Andrew. "I Peter: Commentary." *The New Bible Commentary*. Ed. F. Davidson. 2nd ed. London: Inter-Varsity Fellowship, 1962. 1130–43.
Meyer, Stephenie. *Breaking Dawn*. New York: Little, Brown, 2008.
_____. *Eclipse*. London: Atom, 2007.
_____. *New Moon*. 2006. London: Atom, 2007.
_____. *Twilight*. 2005. London: Atom, 2006.
Michaels, Wendy. "The Realistic Turn: Trends in Recent Australian Young Adult Fiction." *Papers: Explorations into Children's Literature* 14.1 (2004): 49–59.
Miller, George. "The Apocalypse and the Pig: or, The Hazards of Storytelling." *The Sydney Papers* 8.4 (1996): 38–49.
_____. "Directing *Mad Max* and the *Road Warrior*: An Interview with George Miller by Danny Peary." *Screen Flights, Screen Fantasies: The Future According to Science Fiction Cinema*. Ed. Danny Peary. Garden City, NY: Dolphin-Doubleday, 1984. 279–86.
Miller, Walter M., Jr. *A Canticle for Leibowitz*. 1959. New York: Bantam Spectra-Random, 1997.
Million Farms Campaign. 1921–1922. National Archives of Australia: A457, I400/5 Part 2.
Mills, Alice, ed. *Seriously Weird: Papers on the Grotesque*. New York: Peter Lang, 1999.
Milner, Andrew. "Apocalypse Australia." *ABR: Australian Book Review* 153 (1993): 36–37.
Moran, Anthony. "White Australia, Settler Nationalism and Aboriginal Assimilation." *Australian Journal of Politics and History* 51.2 (2005): 168–93.

Morris, L. L. "Book of Revelation." In Douglas, ed., 1093–95.
Morris, Meaghan. "Fate and the Family Sedan." *Senses of Cinema* 19 (2002). Web. 5 Apr. 2004.
_____. "White Panic, or, *Mad Max* and the Sublime." *Senses of Cinema* 18 (2002). Web. 16 Apr. 2004.
Moylan, Tom. *Scraps of the Untainted Sky: Science Fiction, Utopia, Dystopia*. Boulder: Westview, 2000.
Mudrooroo [Colin Johnson]. *Doctor Wooreddy's Prescription for Enduring the Ending of the World*. 1983. Melbourne: Hyland, 1994.
_____. *Master of the Ghost Dreaming*. Sydney: Collins-Angus & Robertson-Harper, 1991.
_____. *The Undying*. Sydney: Angus & Robertson-Harper, 1998.
_____. *Wild Cat Falling*. 1965. Sydney: Angus & Robertson, 1995.
Ness, Patrick. *The Knife of Never Letting Go*. London: Walker, 2008.
Nimon, Maureen, and John Foster. *The Adolescent Novel: Australian Perspectives*. Wagga Wagga: Centre for Information Studies, 1997.
Nolan, Maggie. "The Absent Aborigine." *Antipodes* 12.1 (1998): 7–13.
_____, and Carrie Dawson. "Who's Who? Mapping Hoaxes and Imposture in Australian Literary History." *Australian Literary Studies* 21.4 (2004): v–xx.
Oil Storm. Dir. James Erskine. Wall to Wall, 2005.
O'Leary, Stephen D. *Arguing the Apocalypse: A Theory of Millennial Rhetoric*. 1994. New York: Oxford University Press, 1998.
On the Beach. Dir. Russell Mulcahy. Southern Star, 2000.
On the Beach. Dir. Stanley Kramer. United Artists, 1959.
One Night Stand. Dir. John Duigan. Hoyts, 1984.
Oo-a-deen; or, The Mysteries of the Interior Unveiled. Geelong, 1847.
Open Water. Dir. Chris Kentis. Lions Gate, 2004.
O'Regan, Tom. "The Enchantment with Cinema: Film in the 1980s." *The Australian Screen*. Ed. Albert Moran and Tom O'Regan. Ringwood, Vic.: Penguin, 1989, 118–45.
Ortelius, Abraham. *Typus orbis terrarum*. 1570. MAP NK 10001. National Library of Australia.
Pask, Kevin. "Cyborg Economies: Desire and Labor in the *Terminator* Films." In Dellamora, ed., 182–98.
Pearce, Sharyn. "Messages from the Inside: Multiculturalism in Contemporary Australian Children's Literature." *The Lion and the Unicorn* 27 (2003): 235–50.
Person, Lawrence. "Notes Toward a Postcyberpunk Manifesto." *Slashdot.org*. Web. 2 June 2010.
Peter Pan. Dir. P. J. Hogan. Columbia Tristar, 2003.
Phipson, Joan. *Keep Calm*. 1978. Melbourne: Sunbird-Macmillan, 1988.
Picnic at Hanging Rock. Dir. Peter Weir. Greater Union, 1975.
Pierce, Peter. *The Country of Lost Children: An Australian Anxiety*. Cambridge: Cambridge University Press, 1999.
Pirate Islands. Channel Ten. 2002.
Pirate Islands 2: The Lost Treasure of Fiji. Channel Ten. 2007.
Pitch Black. Dir. David Twohy. United Intl. 2000.
Plank, Robert. "The Lone Survivor." In Rabkin, Greenberg and Olander, eds., 20–52.
Pordzik, Ralph. *The Quest for Postcolonial Utopia: A Comparative Introduction to the Utopian Novel in the New English Literatures*. New York: Peter Lang, 2001.

Poseidon. Dir. Wolfgang Peterson. Warner Bros., 2006.
The Postman. Dir. Kevin Costner. Warner Bros., 1997.
Potter, Robert. *The Germ Growers.* Melbourne, 1892.
Prey. Prod. Robert Lewis Galinsky and Elizabeth Howatt-Jackman. Top Cat-Paramount, 2009.
Quest Beyond Time. Dir. Stephen Wallace. Australian Children's Television Foundation, 1985.
Quinby, Lee. *Anti-Apocalypse: Exercises in Genealogical Criticism.* Minneapolis: University of Minnesota Press, 1994.
_____. "'The Days Are Numbered': The Romance of Death, Doom, and Deferral in Contemporary Apocalypse Films." In Walliss and Newport, eds., 97–119.
Rabkin, Eric S., Martin H. Greenberg, and Joseph D. Olander, eds. *The End of the World.* Carbondale: Southern Illinois University Press, 1983.
Rayner, Jonathan. *Contemporary Australian Cinema: An Introduction.* Manchester: Manchester University Press, 2000.
Razorback. Dir. Russell Mulcahy. Greater Union, 1984.
Reilly, Matthew. *Ice Station.* Sydney: Pan Macmillan, 1998.
Rieder, John. *Colonialism and the Emergence of Science Fiction.* Middletown, Conn.: Wesleyan University Press, 2008.
_____. "Science Fiction, Colonialism, and the Plot of Invasion." *Extrapolation* 46.3 (2005): 373–94.
The Road. Dir. John Hillcoat. Dimension, 2009.
Road Train. Dir. Dean Francis. Polyphony, 2010.
Rogue. Dir. Greg McLean. Roadshow, 2007.
Ross, Catriona. "Prolonged Symptoms of Cultural Anxiety: The Persistence of Narratives of Asian Invasion within Multicultural Australia." *JASAL* 5 (2006): 86–99.
Ross, Robert L. "The Track to Armageddon in B. Wongar's Nuclear Trilogy." *World Literature Today* 64.1 (1990). EBSCOhost. Web. 8 June 2010.
Rowland, Christopher. "'Upon Whom the Ends of the Ages Have Come': Apocalyptic and the Interpretation of the New Testament." In Bull, ed., 38–57.
Rowling, J. K. *Harry Potter and the Chamber of Secrets.* Harry Potter 2. London: Bloomsbury, 1998.
_____. *Harry Potter and the Deathly Hallows.* Harry Potter 7. London: Bloomsbury, 2007.
_____. *Harry Potter and the Goblet of Fire.* Harry Potter 4. London: Bloomsbury, 2000.
_____. *Harry Potter and the Half-Blood Prince.* Harry Potter 6. London: Bloomsbury, 2005.
_____. *Harry Potter and the Order of the Phoenix.* Harry Potter 5. London: Bloomsbury, 2003.
_____. *Harry Potter and the Philosopher's Stone.* Harry Potter 1. London: Bloomsbury, 1997.
_____. *Harry Potter and the Prisoner of Azkaban.* Harry Potter 3. London: Bloomsbury, 1999.
Rubinstein, Gillian. *Beyond the Labyrinth.* South Yarra, Vic.: Hyland, 1988.
_____. *Shinkei.* Norwood, S. Aust.: Omnibus-Scholastic, 1996.
_____. *Skymaze.* Norwood, S. Aust.: Omnibus-Puffin, 1989.
_____. *Space Demons.* 1986. Norwood, S. Aust.: Omnibus-Scholastic, 2000.
Ryan, Mark David. "Australian Cinema's Dark Sun: The Boom in Australian Horror Film Production." *Studies in Australasian Cinema* 4.1. (2010).

Ryan, Simon. "Inscribing the Emptiness: Cartography, Exploration and the Construction of Australia." *De-Scribing Empire: Post-Colonialism and Textuality.* Ed. Chris Tiffin and Alan Lawson. London: Routledge, 1994, 115–30.
Said, Edward. *Culture and Imperialism.* New York: Vintage-Random, 1994.
Salute of the Jugger. Dir. David Peoples. Kings Road Entertainment, 1989.
Sambell, Kay. "Carnivalizing the Future: A New Approach to Theorizing Childhood and Adulthood in Science Fiction for Young Readers." *The Lion and the Unicorn* 28.2 (2004): 247–67.
Sargent, Lyman Tower. "Australia as Dystopia and Eutopia." *Arena Journal* 31 (2008): 109–25.
_____. "Australian Utopian Literature: An Annotated, Chronological Bibliography 1667–1999." *Utopian Studies* 10.2 (1999): 138–73.
_____. "The Three Faces of Utopianism Revisited." *Utopian Studies* 5.1 (1994): 1–37.
Saunders, Ian. "The Texts of *Tomorrow and Tomorrow and Tomorrow*: Author, Agent, History." *Southern Review* 26 (1993): 239–61.
Saxby, Maurice. "Fantasy in Australia." *Classroom* 5 (2000): 17–19.
Scott, G. Firth. *The Last Lemurian: A Westralian Romance.* London, 1898.
Scutter, Heather. *Displaced Fictions: Contemporary Australian Books for Teenagers and Young Adults.* Carlton South: Melbourne University Press, 1999.
_____. "A Very Long Way from Billabong." *Papers: Explorations into Children's Literature* 2.1 (1991): 30–35.
Sea Patrol. Channel Nine. 2007–2010.
Seed, David. "Aspects of Apocalypse." Introduction. In Seed, ed., 1–14.
_____. "Cyberpunk and Dystopia: Pat Cadigan's Networks." In Baccolini and Moylan, eds., 69–89.
_____. "The Dawn of the Atomic Age." In Seed, ed., 88–102.
_____, ed. *Imagining Apocalypse: Studies in Cultural Crisis.* Hampshire: Macmillan, 2000.
Shapiro, Jerome F. "Atomic Bomb Cinema: Illness, Suffering, and the Apocalyptic Narrative." *Literature and Medicine* 17.1 (1998): 126–48.
Sharrad, Paul. "Beyond Capricornia: Ambiguous Promise in Alexis Wright." *Australian Literary Studies* 24.1 (2009): 52–65.
Sharrett, Christopher, ed. *Crisis Cinema: The Apocalyptic Idea in Postmodern Narrative Film.* Washington: Maisonneuve, 1993.
_____. "The Hero as Pastiche: Myth, Male Fantasy and Simulacra in *Mad Max* and *The Road Warrior*." *Journal of Popular Film and Television* 13.2 (1985): 80–91.
Sheckels, Theodore F. "Do We Need Another Schema? 'New Wave' Cinema's Redefinition of Australian Heroism." *Antipodes* 12.1 (1998): 29–36.
Sheriffs, R. J. A. "Har-Magedon." In Douglas, ed., 505.
Shute, Nevil. *On the Beach.* London: Heinemann, 1957.
Simpson, Helen. *The Woman on the Beast: Viewed from Three Angles.* London: William Heinemann, 1933.
Slusser, George. "Pocket Apocalypse: American Survivalist Fictions from *Walden* to *The Incredible Shrinking Man*." In Seed, ed., 118–35.
Smith, Russell. "The Literary Destruction of Canberra: Utopia, Apocalypse and the National Capital." *Australian Literary Studies* 24.1 (2009): 78–94.
Sontag, Susan. *AIDS and Its Metaphors.* New York: Farrar, 1989.
_____. "The Imagination of Disaster." 1965. *Against Interpretation and Other Essays.* New York: Anchor-Doubleday-Bantam, 1990. 209–25.
Souter, Kay Torney. "Lost in Culture: A Response to John Boots's Paper." *Psychoanalysis*

Downunder: The Online Journal of the Australian Psychoanalytical Society 3 (2003). Web. 2 June 2010.
Sponsler, Claire. "Beyond the Ruins: The Geopolitics of Urban Decay and Cybernetic Play." *Science-Fiction Studies* 20.2 (1993): 251–65.
_____. "William Gibson and the Death of Cyberpunk." *Modes of the Fantastic: Selected Essays from the Twelfth International Conference on the Fantastic in the Arts.* Ed. Robert A. Latham and Robert A. Collins. Westport, Conn.: Greenwood, 1995. 47–55.
Stableford, Brian. "Man-Made Catastrophes." In Rabkin, Greenberg and Olander, eds., 97–138.
Stargate: Atlantis. Syfy. 2004–2009.
Stargate: SG-1. Showtime-Syfy. 1997–2007.
Stephens, John. "Post-Disaster Fiction: The Problematics of a Genre." *Papers: Explorations into Children's Literature* 3.3 (1992): 126–30.
Sterling, Bruce. "Cyberpunk in the Nineties." *Streettech.com.* 1991. Web. 2 June 2010.
_____. Preface. *Burning Chrome,* by William Gibson. ix–xii.
_____. Preface. *Mirrorshades: The Cyberpunk Anthology.* Ed Sterling. 1988. London: Harper, 1994. vii–xiv.
Stockton, Sharon. "The Self Regained: Cyberpunk's Retreat to the Imperium." *Contemporary Literature* 36.4 (1995): 588–612.
Stone, Graham. *Australian Science Fiction Bibliography.* Sydney: Graham Stone, 2004.
_____. *Notes on Australian Science Fiction.* Sydney: Graham Stone, 2001.
Stone, Michael, ed. *Australian Children's Literature: Finding a Voice.* Wollongong: New Literatures Research Centre–University of Wollongong, 1993.
_____, ed. *Children's Literature and Contemporary Theory.* Wollongong: New Literatures Research Centre, 1991.
Stratton, Jon. "What Made *Mad Max* Popular? The Mythology of a Conservative Fantasy." *Art & Text* 9 (1983): 37–56.
Sullivan, Andrew. *A Sunburnt Country.* Charnwood, ACT: Ginninderra, 2003.
Sunshine. Dir. Danny Boyle. Fox, 2007.
Supervolcano. Dir. Tony Mitchell. BBC, 2005.
Surf Patrol. Channel Seven. 2007–2010.
"Tape 'Shows Irwin's Last Moments.'" *BBC News* 5 Sep. 2006. Web. 2 June 2010.
Telotte, J. P. "*The Terminator, Terminator 2,* & the Exposed Body." *Journal of Popular Film and Television* 20.2 (1992): 26–34.
10.5. Dir. John Lafia. NBC, 2004.
10.5: Apocalypse. Dir. John Lafia. NBC, 2006.
The Terminator. Dir. James Cameron. Orion, 1984.
Terminator Salvation. Dir. McG. Warner Bros., 2009.
Terminator: The Sarah Connor Chronicles. Fox. 2008–2009.
Terminator 3: Rise of the Machines. Dir. Jonathan Mostow. Warner Bros., 2003.
Terminator 2: Judgment Day. Dir. James Cameron. Tristar, 1991.
Thompson, Leonard L. *The Book of Revelation: Apocalypse and Empire.* Oxford: Oxford University Press, 1990.
Thunderstone. Channel Ten. 1999–2000.
The Time Guardian. Dir. Brian Hannant. Hemdale, 1987.
Todorov, Tzvetan. *The Fantastic: A Structural Approach to a Literary Genre.* 1970. Trans. Richard Howard. Cleveland: Case Western Reserve University, 1973.
Tolkien, J. R. R. *The Fellowship of the Ring.* The Lord of the Rings 1. 1954. London: Grafton-Harper, 1991.

———. *The Return of the King*. The Lord of the Rings 3. 1955. London: Grafton-Harper, 1991.
———. *The Two Towers*. The Lord of the Rings 2. 1954. London: Grafton-Collins, 1991.
"Tsunami Apocalypse." *Sydney Morning Herald* 1–2 Jan. 2005, weekend special ed.: 1–14.
Turcotte, Gerry. "Australian Gothic." *The Handbook to Gothic Literature*. Ed. Marie Mulvey-Roberts. Basingstoke: Macmillan, 1998, 10–19.
———. "'A Fearful Calligraphy': De/scribing the Uncanny Nation in Joy Kogawa's *Obasan*." *Reconfigurations: Canadian Literatures and Postcolonial Identities*. Ed. Marc Maufort and Franca Bellarsi. Brussels: Peter Lang, 2002. 123–42.
———. "Footnotes to an Australian Gothic Script." *Antipodes* 7.2 (1993): 127–34.
———. "'Generous, Refined, and Most Self-Denying Fiends': Naming the Abomination in James de Mille's *Strange Manuscript*." In Mills, ed., 77–88.
———. "Ghosts of the Great South Land." *The Global South* 1.1 (2007): 109–16.
———. "Vampiric Decolonization: Fanon, 'Terrorism' and Mudrooroo's Vampire Trilogy." *Postcolonial Whiteness: A Critical Reader on Race and Empire*. Ed. Alfred J. López. Albany: State University of New York Press, 2005. 103–18.
Turkey Shoot. Dir. Brian Trenchard-Smith. Hemdale, 1982.
Turner, George. *Beloved Son*. London: Faber and Faber, 1978.
———. *The Destiny Makers*. New York: Avon, 1993.
———. *Down There in Darkness*. New York: Tor-Tom Doherty, 1999.
———. *Drowning Towers*. New York: Arbor-Morrow, 1987.
———. "Some Unreceived Wisdom." *Overland* 87 (1982): 14–19.
———. *Vaneglory*. London: Faber and Faber, 1981.
———. *Yesterday's Men*. London: Faber and Faber, 1983.
Turner, Graeme. *National Fictions: Literature, Film and the Construction of Australian Narrative*. 1986. 2nd ed. St. Leonards: Allen & Unwin, 1993.
28 Days Later. Dir. Danny Boyle. Twentieth Century–Fox, 2002.
28 Weeks Later. Dir. Juan Carlos Fresnadillo. Twentieth Century–Fox, 2007.
24. Fox. 2001–2010.
2012. Dir. Roland Emmerich. Columbia, 2009.
Undead. Dir. the Spierig Brothers. Spierigfilm, 2002.
Until the End of the World. Dir. Wim Wenders. Village Roadshow, 1991.
Wagar, W. Warren. "The Rebellion of Nature." In Rabkin, Greenberg and Olander, eds., 139–72.
———. *Terminal Visions: The Literature of Last Things*. Bloomington: Indiana University Press, 1982.
Wake in Fright. Dir. Ted Kotcheff. United Artists, 1971.
Walliss, John. "Apocalypse at the Millennium." In Walliss and Newport, eds., 71–96.
———, and Kenneth G. C. Newport, eds. *The End All Around Us: Apocalyptic Texts and Popular Culture*. London: Equinox, 2009.
Walton, Robyn. "Utopian and Dystopian Impulses in Australia." *Overland* 173 (2003): 5–20.
War of the Worlds. Dir. Steven Spielberg. Paramount, 2005.
Waterworld. Dir. Kevin Reynolds. Universal, 1995.
Watson, Sam. "Aboriginal Activists Speak Out: It's Time for a Treaty." Interview with Simon Butler. *Green Left Weekly* 430 (2000): 12–13. Web. 2 June 2010.
———. "I Say This to You." Interview. *Meanjin* 53.4 (1994): 589–96.
———. *The Kadaitcha Sung*. Ringwood, Vic.: Penguin, 1990.

_____. "Our Dreaming Stilled." Interview with Florence Spurling. *Encounter*. ABC, Sydney. 14 Mar. 2010. Transcript. Web. 9 June 2010.
_____. "Treaty or Ghost Dance — One Time." *Indigenous Law Bulletin* 5.21 (2002): 15.
Weaver, Roslyn. "'The Shadow of the End': The Appeal of Apocalypse in Literary Science Fiction." In Walliss and Newport, eds., 173–97.
_____. "'Smudged, Distorted and Hidden': Apocalypse as Protest in Indigenous Speculative Fiction." *Science Fiction, Imperialism and the Third World: Essays on Postcolonial Literature and Film*. Ed. Ericka Hoagland and Reema Sarwal. Jefferson, NC: McFarland, 2010, 99–114.
Webb, Janeen, and Andrew Enstice. *Aliens and Savages: Fiction, Politics and Prejudice in Australia*. Sydney: Harper, 1998.
_____, and _____. "Domesticating the Monster." In Mills, ed., 89–103.
Wegner, Phillip E. "Where the Prospective Horizon Is Omitted: Naturalism and Dystopia in *Fight Club* and *Ghost Dog*." In Baccolini and Moylan, eds., 167–85.
Weller, Archie. *Land of the Golden Clouds*. St. Leonards: Allen & Unwin, 1998.
Wevers, Lydia. "Globalising Indigenes: Postcolonial Fiction from Australia, New Zealand and the Pacific." *JASAL* 5 (2006): 121–32.
Where the Green Ants Dream. Dir. Werner Herzog. Orion, 1985.
Whitcomb, J. C., Jr. "Book of Daniel." In Douglas, ed., 290–93.
White, Richard. *Inventing Australia: Images and Identity 1688–1980*. Sydney: Allen & Unwin, 1981.
Willey, Keith. *When the Sky Fell Down: The Destruction of the Tribes of the Sydney Region 1788–1850s*. Sydney: Collins, 1979.
Williams, Paul. "Beyond *Mad Max III*: Race, Empire, and Heroism on Post-Apocalyptic Terrain." *Science-Fiction Studies* 32.2 (2005): 301–15.
Williams, Sean. *Metal Fatigue*. Sydney: Harper, 1996.
Williams, Sue. "A Long Way from Here." *Sydney Morning Herald: Spectrum* 21–22 July 2007: 18–19.
Williams, Tess. *Map of Power*. Milsons Point: Arrow-Random, 1996.
Witherington, Ben, III. "Neo-Orthodoxy: Tales of the Reluctant Messiah, or 'Your Own Personal Jesus.'" In William Irwin, ed., 165–74.
Wolf Creek. Dir. Greg McLean. Roadshow, 2004.
Wolfe, Gary K. "The Remaking of Zero: Beginning at the End." In Rabkin, Greenberg and Olander, eds., 1–19.
Wongar, B. *Karan*. 1985. Melbourne: Macmillan, 1986.
_____. *Manhunt*. Carnegie: Dingo, 2008.
Wright, Alexis. "Breaking Taboos." *Australian Humanities Review* 11 (1998). Web. 2 June 2010.
_____. "An Interview with Alexis Wright." Interview with Jean-François Vernay. *Antipodes* 18.2 (2004): 119–22.
_____. *Plains of Promise*. St. Lucia: University of Queensland Press, 1997.
Wright, Judith. *Preoccupations in Australian Poetry*. Melbourne: Oxford University Press, 1965.
Wrightson, Patricia. *The Ice Is Coming*. Richmond: Hutchinson, 1977.
Zamora, Lois Parkinson. *Writing the Apocalypse: Historical Vision in Contemporary U.S. and Latin American Fiction*. Cambridge: Cambridge University Press, 1989.
Žižek, Slavoj. "*The Matrix*, or, Malebranche in Hollywood." *Philosophy Today* 43 (1999): 11–26.

Index

Numbers in **_bold italics_** indicate pages with photographs.

Aboriginal peoples *see* Indigenous peoples (Australia; Canada; U.S.)
Adams, Phillip 89, 194*n*
adolescent literature *see* young adult literature
adventure 48, 96, 128
adventure narratives 47–49, 113, 129, 133–134, 198*n*
adventure romance *see* adventure narratives
adventurers 35, 84, 154
aesthetics of destruction 57, 193*n*
Africa 30, 34, 46, 49, 75, 125–126, 150, 184
aged groups in apocalypse 76
AI 175, 198*n*; *see also* artificial intelligence
AIDS 60
Albinski, Nan Bowman 41, 47, 49, 192*n*
Alien vs. Predator 192*n*
alienation 41–42, 44, 112, 114, 172
America *see* United States
American apocalypse 1, 5, 29–30, 66–68, 193*n*; *see also* America
American cyberpunk 183
American film noir 45
American gothic 45
Americans in danger 84, 86–87, 196*n*
Antarctica 51, 63, 192*n*
anti-authority 4, 45, 114–115, 134, 140, 162; *see also* authority
Antichrist 9, 13, 15
Antipodes 23, 31, 35, 45, 68, 83, 117, 192*n*
apocalypse: after World War II 18, 55, 58–62, 65, 80, 83; definition of 7–17; flexibility of meanings of 6, 16, 55, 136–138; and race *see* race and apocalypse; resilience of 55–56
apocalypse, uses of: as conservative 20, 136–139, 196*n*; as critique 14–15, 18, 20, 57–58, 62–63, 66, 76, 80–81, 104, 115, 124, 139–141, 150, 157, 187; as encourage-

ment 11–12, 14; as political 20, 137, 139–140, 142; as positive 17, 95, 116; as protest 2, 63, 146; as radical 20, 136, 139–140, 157; as renewal 9, 19, 150, 156, 158; as revelation 1, 7–8, 12–13, 15–16, 82, 91–92, 96, 115, 136–137, 142–143, 152, 186–187; as subversive 139–143, 157; as voice for suffering and oppressed 12, 188; as warning 2, 8, 12–15, 55, 58, 63–64, 79–80, 82, 91–92, 127, 146, 165, 168–169, 188, 194*n*
apocalyptic dialectic 23–24, 42, 61
apocalyptic map 2, 18, 23–54, 61, 83, 145, 159, 176, 180, 184, 187–189, 194*n*; *see also* cartography; maps
apocalyptic paradigm 6, 8–9, 12–13, 19, 27, 65, 72, 77, 88, 95–96, 116, 136, 150, 152, 157, 184, 186–187
apocalyptic rhetoric 14, 25, 57, 137, 140
appeal of apocalypse 55–58, 187
Applebaum, Noga 108–109, 195*n*
Armageddon 13, 15, 41, 152
Arthur, Paul Longley 31, 35, 44, 46, 191*n*
artificial intelligence 169, 175, 179; *see also* AI
artificial, suspicion of 74, 169–173, 179; *see also* authenticity, threat to
Asian invasion 48–51, 129–132, 184
Asian peoples 73, 125, 130, 156, 183
Asian power 48, 183–184
Asian tsunami 16, 191*n*
assimilation 144, 148, 157, 197*n*; and cyberspace 178
atomic weapons *see* nuclear
Attebery, Brian 25, 77, 136, 150, 155
Australia: as blank slate 24, 31; expectations of 23–53; geographical position 6, 48–49, 52, 66, 68; *see also* south land; *terra australis*
Australian gothic 44–45, 90
Australian horror 44, 86–87, 194*n*, 196*n*

219

Australian identity 3, 26, 48, 77, 84, 90, 102–103, 107, 113–114, 125–126, 130, 133, 144, 183–184, 198*n*
Australian landscape: ambivalence about 19, 131, 187; as barren 39, 41, 100, 136, 152, 181, 195*n*; as beautiful 42, 96–97, 109–110; compared to Europe 12, 24, 45–46, 96, 109, 118, 192*n*; as harsh 36, 73, 84, 97, 99–100, 102, 110, 160; and healing 149, 151, 181–182, 196*n*; as hostile 19, 46, 72, 83–85, 88, 93, 101–102, 109–110, 131, 134, 145, 150, 160, 180, 187–188, 196*n*; as punishment 2, 12, 19, 27, 40, 53, 83, 88, 92, 94–96, 99, 107, 188; romanticized 45–46, 118; as sacred 20, 48, 136, 143, 149–150, 157, 196*n*; as spiritual status 40, 94, 99; as uncanny 43, 133; *see also* dead heart; desert; outback; wasteland; wilderness
Australian science fiction 5, 46, 48, 83, 155, 163, 182
Australian speculative fiction 4–6, 12, 17–18, 46, 52, 66, 136, 145, 180, 182, 188–189
Austrialia del Espiritu Santo 33, 47
authenticity, threat to 160, 169, 172, 174, 177; *see also* artificial, suspicion of
authority 4, 45, 57, 74–76, 93, 114, 124, 126, 134, 140, 149, 154, 186; *see also* antiauthority
Ayers Rock *see* Uluru

Baccolini, Raffaella 160, 192*n*
backpacker murders 194*n*
Banks, Joseph 39
Barbour, Dennis H. 89, 194*n*
Barnard, Marjorie *see* Eldershaw, M. Barnard
Barnett, P. Chad 162–163
Bartlett, John 156
Baudrillard, Jean 18, 23–26, 31, 35, 43, 59–60, 172, 179–180, 199*n*
beaches 19, 66, 70, 85, 100–101, 159, 167, 178, 180
Bellanta, Melissa 50–51
belonging 19, 44, 87, 102, 104, 107, 113–114, 116–119, 122, 126, 128, 131, 133–135, 148–149, 151
Beloved Son 4, 72–76
Bendle, Mervyn F. 57
Berger, James 5, 16, 29–30, 56, 123–124, 139–140, 150
Bernard, Patricia 112
Beyond the Labyrinth 112
Biber, Katherine 89
Bible 8–12, 14, 28, 33, 40, 83, 85, 88, 94, 127, 145, 156, 188, 191*n*; *see also* Biblical apocalypse; Biblical attitudes to land

Biblical apocalypse 1, 8–15, 27–28, 41, 47, 52, 62, 68, 88, 95, 123–124, 128, 140–142, 146, 186, 188–189, 196*n*; *see also* Bible; Biblical attitudes to land
Biblical attitudes to land 11–12, 27, 40–41, 83, 88, 94, 145, 188, 191*n*; *see also* Bible; Biblical apocalypse
Big Ben 192*n*
Bird, Delys 30
Black Water 87
Blackford, Russell 5, 46–47, 49, 163, 172, 192*n*
Blackmore, Leigh 86
Blade Runner 160–161
Blainey, Geoffrey 38–39, 69
blank slate 24, 31, 97, 178
blessing 11, 14, 28, 41–42, 188, 191*n*
boat people 80
Boer, Roland 196*n*
The Book of Eli 67, 193*n*
Book of Revelation *see* Revelation
Border Security 80
borders 29, 36, 80, 85, 121, 125, 133, 159, 167, 176, 184
Botero, Giovanni 30–31
Bowen, Emanuel 33–36
Boyd, Hannah Villiers 47
Bozic, Sreten *see* Wongar, B.
Bradford, Clare 5, 111, 124, 126, 132, 134, 154, 195*n*
Brathwaite, Elizabeth 111, 116
Brennan, Peter 86
Brians, Paul 13, 58, 62, 64–65, 67, 192*n*, 194*n*
"Bringing Them Home" 197*n*
Brisbane 149
Britain 38, 40, 43, 45, 48–49, 66–67, 73, 85, 99, 104, 116–118, 130, 132, 192*n*
British apocalypse 66–67
British Empire 48, 68, 130, 134
Broderick, Damien 193*n*
Broderick, Mick 57, 89–90, 95, 194*n*
Broken Hill 97
Brown, Simon 3
Bruno, Giuliana 161
Bryson, Bill 84
Buckrich, Judith Raphael 72, 193*n*
Buffy the Vampire Slayer 193*n*
Bukatman, Scott 169, 172
Bull, Malcolm 5, 16, 136–137
Burning for Revenge 127, 132

Cadigan, Pat 160
Caesar, Adrian 129
Calcutta 75
Campbell, Joseph 90
Campbell, Patty 111

Index

Canada 1, 5, 130, 149, 183; *see also* Canadian apocalypse
Canadian apocalypse 1, 5, 103, 141; *see also* Canada
Canberra 4, 5, 33, 70, 81, 193n-194n
A Canticle for Leibowitz 67
capitalism 24, 27, 62, 95, 160, 162, 167, 193n, 195n
Carmody, Isobelle 112
Carruthers, Joseph 49-51
The Cars That Ate Paris 44, 87
Carstenz, Jan 39
cartography 1, 26, 30-31, 35-36, 52, 154-155, 157, 178, 187; *see also* apocalyptic map; maps
The Catalyst 112
Category 7: The End of the World 193n
Category 6: Day of Destruction 193n
Caterson, Simon 86
Cavalcanti, Ildney 198n
Central America 49
The Chain Reaction 4, 63
Chamberlain, Azaria 84, 110
Chamberlain, Neville 127
Chapman, Jennie 13
chemical weapon 16
Chesterman, John 197n
Chicago 67, 179
children and nature 41, 106, 108-111, 122, 131, 195n; *see also* nature
Children of Men 67
children, Romantic ideas about 108-110
children's literature 1, 3, 5-6, 19, 49, 69, 107-134, 140, 159, 163, 187, 195n-196n; *see also* lost children; young adult literature
children's tribe in *Mad Max* 91, 96, 98, 100-102, 104-106, 108
Chinese healing 156
Christ *see* Jesus Christ
Christianity 13, 56, 95, 168, 191n, 199n
Christians 10, 40, 140
Christopher, Lucy 109
The Chronicles of Narnia: The Lion, the Witch, and the Wardrobe (film) 192n
Circle of Flight 127, 129
cities 5, 11, 15, 19, 33, 41, 48, 55, 62, 66-67, 70, 72-75, 81, 88, 91, 93-96, 98, 100-101, 105, 108-109, 114-115, 119, 122, 130, 139, 152, 162, 164-165, 177, 179-180, 192n-194n
city (heavenly) 11, 15, 95, 124, 186, 199n
The City of Ember 111
Civil War (American) 16
Clark, C.M.H. *see* Clark, Manning
Clark, Manning 35-36
Clark, Maureen 197n
Clark, Stephen R.L. 63
Clarke, I.F. 58, 63-64
class 72-73, 75-77, 105, 130, 139, 163-164
Code Noir 20, 159, 164-185
Cohn, Norman 5, 9, 137, 191n
the Cold War 55, 58-59, 69, 111
Coleridge, Samuel Taylor 46
Collins, Paul 5, 112, 163
Collins, Suzanne 111
colonization 1-2, 4, 6, 11, 18-21, 23-53, 105, 108, 110, 112-118, 123-126, 129, 132-136, 140-159, 178, 182-183, 187-189, 192n, 195n-198n; reverse 183; and violence 20, 113, 119, 121, 123-126, 134, 136, 145-146, 154
Columbus, Christopher 29
Coman, B.J. 33
communism 73
complacency 2, 6, 19, 55, 62-63, 66, 75-76, 78-80, 82, 127, 130, 173, 188
"A Complete Map of the Southern Continent" 33-34
concentration camps 16
Conn, Matthew 174, 178-179
Connor, Michael 195n
Conrad, Joseph 124
conservativism 66, 89, 160
convicts 35, 40, 43-44, 145
Coober Pedy 97
Cook, Kenneth 4, 84-86
Cooper, Ken 139
The Core 61, 193n
Cousins, A.D. 46
Cox, Erle 4
Crash Deluxe 20, 164-185
Creed, Barbara 172, 176
Crocodile Dundee 84
Crocodile Dundee 2 84
Crouch, David 117, 196n
Csicsery-Ronay, Istvan, Jr. 49, 177, 182
cyberpunk 6, 8, 20, 140, 159-185; as adventure narrative 198n; as anti-authority 162; as anti-nation 20, 159; and apocalypse 159-160, 164-165, 167, 169-170, 177, 184; Australian 163-164, 198n; and capitalism 160, 162; and colonization 198n; and dystopia 161-163; end of 162-163; and feminism 198n; as globalized 20, 159-161, 163-164, 176-177, 183-184, 198n; and 1980s 160-161, 169; as political protest 161-162; as quest narrative 198n; setting of 162, 177; style of 161, 163-164
Cyberskin 163
cyberspace 172-175, 178-179, 182, 198n
cyborgs 24, 169, 171-173

Dampier, William 39
Daniel 8-10, 12, 141

222 Index

Dark, David 199*n*
Dark City 4, 174
Darkness, Be My Friend 127, 131
Davison, Graeme 66, 69–70
Dawson, Carrie 197*n*
The Day After 67
The Day After Tomorrow 14, 61, 192*n*-193*n*
day of the Lord 3, 9
dead center 95
Dead End Drive-In 4
dead heart 19–20, 41, 48, 85, 88, 95, 100, 107, 135–136, 145, 149–150, 152–153, 181, 197*n*; *see also* Australian landscape; desert; outback; wasteland; wilderness
The Dead of the Night 127–129, 131–133
de Foigny, Gabriel 38
de Jode, Cornelius 36–37
Dellamora, Richard 5, 59, 80, 137–138, 191*n*
de Pierres, Marianne 20, 159–160, 164–185, 198*n*
de Quiros, Pedro Fernandez 33–35, 47
Dermody, Susan 44, 90, 103
Derrida, Jacques 13, 16, 59–60, 137–138
desert 11, 19, 23, 27, 41, 45, 47, 51, 67, 83–84, 86–87, 90–107, 110, 135–136, 144, 180, 191*n*, 195*n*; as dead center 95; as hideous blank 95; and Indigenous peoples 135–136; as nameless blank 102; as the never-never 95; as the nothing 19, 83, 99, 101–104, 107, 135, 150; as the nothingness 95, 103; nuclear wilderness 96; as spiritual 95, 191*n*; *see also* Australian landscape; dead heart; outback; wasteland; wilderness
desert of the real 23, 180
The Destiny Makers 4, 72, 76–78, 193*n*
Detmer, David 24, 199*n*
Deuteronomy 40–41, 94
dialectic 23–24, 42, 61
didactic writing 63–64, 79, 112, 151
Dillon, Matthew 90
Displaced Person 112
displacement 104, 114, 126, 144
Distress 198*n*
Dixon, Robert 47–50, 102, 113, 125, 127, 129–130
Dobson, Jill 112
Doctor Wooreddy's Prescription for Enduring the Ending of the World 143–144
Dodson, Michael 142, 196*n*
doomsday 15, 80, 165
Doomsday Clock 59
the double 22, 26, 43
double aspect 42
Douglas, Heather 197*n*
Dowling, Terry 7, 160, 163, 198*n*
Down There in Darkness 70, 71, 72, 77–79, 193*n*

Down Under 84
dreaming 131–132, 148–149
dreamtime 143, 182, 196*n*
Drowning Towers 54, 72–73, 75–76, 78–80, 193*n*
drugs 74, 77, 114–115, 174
dual vision 42, 45, 52, 96, 110, 195*n*
Duigan, John 192*n*
DuPrau, Jeanne 111
Dutton, Jacqueline 51
dystopia 1–2, 4–5, 12–13, 15, 17–19, 21, 23, 30, 36, 38, 40, 42, 52–53, 55, 58, 62–63, 65, 72, 77, 81–82, 88, 91, 93–94, 97, 108, 111–113, 115, 118, 121, 134, 145, 153, 155, 159–165, 167, 178, 184, 187–189, 192*n*-193*n*, 195*n*; and apocalypse 27–28; definition of 27–28

The Earthborn Wars 112
East/West 183
Ebert, Roger 90
ecological disaster *see* environment: and disaster
Eden 29–30, 94, 119, 145
edge of the world 68, 82
Egan, Greg 163–164, 198*n*
Eiffel Tower 192*n*
Eldershaw, Flora *see* Eldershaw, M. Barnard
Eldershaw, M. Barnard 62, 192*n*
Eliot, T.S. 65
The Ellie Chronicles 127–133
empires 9, 11, 23, 35, 48, 68, 105, 123–124, 129–130, 138, 183; and apocalypse 140–141, 196*n*; British 48, 68, 130, 134; Roman 10, 141
end of evil 11
end of the human 20, 167–168, 170, 173, 184
The Enemy You Killed 112
England *see* Britain
England as home 104, 116; *see also* home, concept of
Enstice, Andrew 39, 47–48, 192*n*
environment: and disaster 1–2, 10, 16, 53, 61, 73, 111, 143, 159, 187; fears about 59; mismanagement 82, 188; policies for 18, 63; problems 4, 14, 19, 60–61
Escape from Absalom 99
eschatology 25, 139, 160, 164, 167–168
Esmonde, Margaret 111
Ethical Culture series 4
ethnicity 77, 159, 184–185
European gothic 45
European imagination 24, 26, 31, 38, 52, 110
European proximity to conflict 69
exile 2, 11–12, 27, 40, 42, 52, 83, 94, 99, 107, 188–189
Exodus 30, 94

Index

experimentation 63, 76, 173; genetic 74, 164, 175
extrapolation 7–8, 57–58, 63, 88, 91–92
The Eye Witness 4, 112

façade 62, 66, 72, 109, 173, 199*n*; *see also* false image
faith 56–57
the faithful 9–12, 27, 94, 107, 126, 141, 186
Falconer, Delia 90, 104
Falconio, Peter 84, 194*n*
Faller, Stephen 199*n*
false image 19–20, 69, 75, 83, 88, 96, 101, 175, 179–180; *see also* façade
the fantastic 7, 58, 191*n*
fantasy 1, 6–7, 44, 47, 112, 159, 162; definition of 7
Farscape 4, 84
fascism 55, 76
First Fleet 39, 155
First Nation 126
First People 116
Fitting, Peter 175
Fortress 99
Foster, John 42, 45, 69, 110, 114, 116
French Revolution 16
Freud, Sigmund 43–44
the frontier 29, 68, 178, 182
fruitful land 11–12, 27, 41, 45, 94, 96, 100–102, 104, 106–107, 145; *see also* promised land
Frye, Northrop 13
fuel 91–92, 195*n*; *see also* oil wars
Fukuyama, Francis 28, 198*n*
Furedi, Frank 193*n*
Furphy, Joseph 41
Fury Road 194*n*

Galbreath, Robert 13–14, 173
Gale, Peter 81
Gannon, Charles E. 66–68, 70
gardens 46–47, 63, 178; of Eden 94, 119, 145; in heavenly city 15; *see also* parks
Gardner, Ava 62, 70, 193*n*
Gelder, Ken 43, 49, 117, 148–150, 183, 196*n*
gender 76, 78, 105, 113, 137, 172, 198*n*
Genesis 94
genetics 164, 168–169; experimentation in 74, 175; manipulation of 4, 72, 171–172
genocide 55, 63, 73, 148
geographical end of the world 2, 23
The Germ Growers 4
German power 48
ghosts 43, 114, 116–118, 154, 196*n*
Ghosts ... of the Civil Dead 4, 99
Gibson, Mel 83, 89, **98**, 194*n*
Gibson, Ross 31, 33, 36, 39–40, 46, 90, 99, 106, 154–155, 191*n*
Gibson, William 160, 163, 165, 176, 178, 182
The Girl from Tomorrow: Tomorrow's End 70, 112
"Glass Reptile Breakout" 163
global warming 14, 75, 80; *see also* greenhouse effect
God 3, 9–12, 15–16, 27, 33, 40–41, 56, 94–95, 100, 127, 186, 191*n*
Golden Gate Bridge 192*n*
Goldie, Terry 149, 183, 197*n*
Goldman, Marlene 5, 103, 137, 141
Gone 87
Gordon, Joan 148
gothic 6, 19, 42, 44–45, 47, 85, 90, 113, 179; American 45; Australian 44–45, 90; European 45
government, failure of 66, 76, 79–80, 112, 114, 127–129
Grace, Helen 66
Great Barrier Reef 194*n*
Great Britain *see* Britain
The Greatwinter Trilogy 4
greed 16, 77, 79, 134, 167, 183, 188
greenhouse effect 79, 123; *see also* global warming
guilt 61, 116–117, 146, 197*n*
Gulag 99

hackers 175, 177
Hades 180
Haggard, H. Rider 46
Hall, Penny 4, 112
Hall, Sandra 89–90
Halligan, Marion 197*n*
Hamilton, M. Lynn 46
Hanson, Donna Maree 5
Happy Feet 194*n*
Haraway, Donna 198*n*
Harding, Lee 3, 19, 108, 112, 114–119, 126
Harland, Richard 112
Har-magedon 41
Harry Potter 5
Haslam, Jason 179
Haynes, Roslynn D. 46, 90, 95, 135, 195*n*
Heart of Darkness 124
heaven 3, 10–11, 15, 24, 26–30, 33–34, 41, 52, 62, 94–95, 186–187, 189
Heaven and Earth Trilogy 112
hedonism 65–66
Heffernan, Teresa 24
hell 15, 23–24, 26, 39, 42, 52, 74, 83, 85, 95, 123, 127, 131, 141, 180, 187, 189
Henning, Rachel 46
Heroes 193*n*
Herzog, Werner 143

Hewlett, Jamie 4
The Hidden Kingdom 46
hideous blank 95
Hintz, Carrie 108, 111, 115, 195n
Hiroshima 16, 55, 58–60, 65
Hitler, Adolf 55, 74, 137
Hobbes, Thomas 93–94
Holden, Robert 31, 38, 40, 110, 191n–192n
Hollinger, Veronica 24–26, 58, 159–160, 162, 165, 167, 171
Hollywood 61, 192n
holocaust 64, 67, 114, 138–139, 151–152, 162, 167–168
the Holocaust 16, 55, 191n
holographs 172
Holt, Harold 84
home, concept of 3, 11, 24, 38, 40, 43, 45–46, 83, 94, 101–105, 110–111, 118, 122, 126, 131, 133, 177, 183, 191n; *see also* England as home
Hood, Robert 86, 194n
Hook 105
hope and apocalypse 2, 9, 11–12, 15, 28, 33, 56, 83, 100, 116, 152, 184, 189
Horne, Donald 191n
horror *see* Australian horror
horsemen of the apocalypse 15, 79
Howard, John 84
Hughes, Robert 93–94, 99
Human Rights and Equal Opportunity Commission 197n
the Human Rites series 4, 164
humans as cause of disaster 15–16, 57, 63, 79, 188
Hume, Kathryn 7, 191n
The Hunger Games 111
hyperreal 23–25, 35, 194n; *see also* models; simulacra; simulation

I Am Legend 193n
I, Robot 193n
The Ice Is Coming 112, 132
Ice Station 192n
identity *see* Australian identity
ignorance 66, 106, 132, 150, 188
Ikin, Van 5, 7, 46–49, 192n
immigration 50–51, 79–81, 121, 125, 128–129, 184
imperialism 6, 20, 28, 49, 105, 113, 116, 122–126, 155, 183; and apocalypse 126, 141; and violence 20, 113, 124, 154
An Inconvenient Truth 14, 61
Incurable 127, 131–133
India 30
Indians *see* Indigenous peoples
Indigenous peoples (Australia) 4, 18–20, 36, 44, 77–78, 101–102, 105–107, 116, 122–123, 126, 131–158, 181–183, 195n–197n; and apocalypse 135–158; and authorship 196n–197n; colonial attitudes towards 197n; as colonists 183; land rights 21, 43, 81, 108, 114, 116–118, 132, 183, 187; lifestyle 73; lore 38, 132, 156; loss of culture and language 146, 148; as migrants 123; and minority groups 150; and national identity 48, 77; and nature 132; racist attitudes towards 47; and the right to speak 142, 197n; in science fiction 136, 155, 182, 195n; stereotypes of 104, 132, 155, 196n; stolen generations of 195n, 197n; and stories 122, 133, 151, 181; treaty 151; whites as 19, 131–132
Indigenous peoples (Canada) 149, 183
Indigenous peoples (U.S.) 29, 49, 123, 139, 150, 182
industrial revolution 16
The Inheritors 112
interior *see* Australian landscape; dead heart; desert; outback
invasion 1, 5, 9, 11–12, 18–19, 21, 27, 41, 48–53, 55, 65, 108, 127–134, 141, 145, 183–184, 187; Asian 48–51, 129–132, 184; narratives of 48–49, 113, 130, 184; *see also* vulnerability to outside
Iraq war 194n
Irvine, Ian 4, 164
Irwin, Steve 84
Irwin, W.R. 7
Isaiah 8, 11, 28–29, 94, 127, 141
Islam 76, 81, 95
islands 51, 66, 121
isolation 6, 40, 49, 69, 73, 75, 82–83, 86, 108, 121, 128, 130, 183
Israel 11, 19, 27, 29, 40–41, 47, 110, 127; modern state of 76

Jacka, Elizabeth 44, 90, 103
Jackson, Rosemary 58, 191n
Jacobs, Jane M. 43, 49, 117, 148–150, 183, 196n
Jacobs, Naomi 171–172
James, Caryn 45
James, Edward 15, 64, 138–139
Jameson, Fredric 27–28, 93, 104, 125, 160, 162, 170–171, 174
Japan as threat to Australia 50, 130
Jeremiah 94
Jericho 67, 193n
Jerusalem 28
Jesus Christ 9–10, 28, 33, 56, 141, 191n; *see also* Messiah
Jillett, Neil 193n
Joel 9
Johinke, Rebecca 89

John the Baptist 191*n*
"Johnny Mnemonic" 160
Johnson, Colin *see* Mudrooroo
Johnston, Rosemary Ross 130, 132
Jones, Gwyneth 198*n*
Jorgensen, Darren 136
judgment 9–12, 14, 16, 21, 27, 95, 99, 123, 126, 146, 152, 186, 188–189
Judgment Day 13, 68, 159, 167–168

kadaitcha 146, 181, 196*n*; *see also* kurdaitcha
The Kadaitcha Sung 4, 20, 135, 144–153, *147*, 155, 157–158, 197*n*
Kakmi, Dmetri 194*n*
karadji 182
Karan 144
Keep Calm 109, 112
Kellaway, Frank 72, 193*n*
Kelleher, Victor 19, 108, 112, 116, 118–126, 154
Keller, Catherine 137
Kennedy, Byron 88–90, 194*n*
Kennon, Patricia 115, 121
Kermode, Frank 5, 55–56, 64, 137, 140–141, 191*n*
Ketterer, David 5, 7, 13–15, 27–28, 30, 57, 61
Kiernan, Brian 41–42
King Solomon's Mines 46
Kitson, Michael 90
The Knife of Never Letting Go 111
Knudsen, Eva Rask 150, 197*n*
Kokoda Trail 55
Kotlowski, Elizabeth Rogers 33
Kumar, Krishan 15, 28
kurdaitcha 78; *see also* kadaitcha

La Forgia, Rebecca 148
The Lake at the End of the World 112
Land of the Apocalypse 143
Land of the Golden Clouds 20, 144, 152–158
land rights 43, 81, 108, 132–135, 149, 182–183; Indigenous (Australia) 21, 43, 81, 108, 114, 116–118, 132, 183, 187
landscape, Australian *see* Australian landscape
The Last Albatross 164
The Last Lemurian 46
The Last Wave 143
Latin America *see* South America
Lawrence, Carmen 81
Leblanc, Lauraine 165, 198*n*
Legion 193*n*
Lenin, Vladimir 137
Lewis, C.S. 192*n*
The Life Lottery 164
Lindsay, Joan 4, 84–85
Locusts: Day of Destruction 193*n*

London 67, 86
Lonergan, Eileen 84, 194*n*
Lonergan, Tom 84, 194*n*
Long Weekend (1978 film) 87
Long Weekend (2008 film) 87
Lord, Gabrielle 3
The Lord of the Rings (book) 5, 192*n*, 198*n*
The Lord of the Rings (films) 5, 192*n*
Los Angeles 67
lost children 41, 84–85, 98, 105, 108–110, 126, 134, 148, 191*n*, 195*n*, 197*n*; *see also* children's literature; removal of children; vanishing
lost civilizations 104, 192*n*
lost race narratives 18, 46–48, 50–52, 102, 113, 154, 182
lost tribes of Israel 29, 46
lucky country 23, 30, 54, 62, 75, 191*n*
Luminous 163

Maack, Annagret 35
Mabo 183
Macdonald, Caroline 4, 112
machines 68, 78, 91, 164, 168–173, 175, 178–179, 181, 198*n*
Mackellar, Dorothea 42
Macrae, Andrew 183
Mad Max 40–41, 72, 85, 88–107
Mad Max: Beyond Thunderdome 5, 70, 83, 88–108, *98*, 194*n*-195*n*
Mad Max 4 194*n*
the *Mad Max* series 1, 4, 19, 72, 83–86, 88–107, 187, 194*n*-195*n*
Mad Max 2: The Road Warrior 88–107
magic realism 6, 144, 196*n*
The Makers 112
Malchow, H.L. 197*n*
Mallan, Kerry 5, 111, 124, 126, 154, 195*n*
man-made disaster *see* humans as cause of disaster
Manhunt 144
Map of Power 3, 192*n*
maps 18, 23–26, 31, 33–38, 46, 49–50, 52–53, 124, 154, 172, 180, 187; *see also* apocalyptic map; cartography
Marley, Bob 156
Marsden, John 3, 19, 108, 112, 118, 127–134
Martens, John W. 11, 56, 191*n*, 196*n*
Martin, Adrian 90, 104
Martin, Alan 4
Master of the Ghost Dreaming 143
The Matrix 4, 160, 162–163, 174–175, 179–180, 197*n*-199*n*
The Matrix Reloaded 179
The Matrix Revolutions 179
Mayers, Rhonda 127
McCallum, Robyn 195*n*

McCarthy, Cormac 67
McFarlane, Brian 86, 96, 179
McFarlane, Peter 112
McGahan, Andrew 4, 81
McGuire, Ann 115
McLean, Greg 87, 194*n*
McMullen, Sean 4–5, 46–47, 49, 160, 163, 192*n*, 198*n*
McNab, Andrew 10
media 18, 161, 164–165, 169, 175–176
medievalism 4, 104, 195*n*
Megiddo 41
Melbourne 63, 65–66, 70, 74–75, 97, 152
mercy 14
Messiah 9, 12; *see also* Jesus Christ
messianic discourse 169
messianic figures 13, 20, 68, 95, 168, 199*n*; *see also* savior figures
Metal Fatigue 163
Meyer, Stephenie 5
Michaels, Wendy 128
Middle of Nowhere 87
migrants 123, 144, 150, 182, 184
Milat, Ivan 194*n*
millennium 13, 15, 28, 92, 165, 167
Miller, George 88–92, 96–98, 104, 194*n*–195*n*
Miller, Walter M., Jr. 67
Million Farms campaign 49–51, **50–51**, 184
Milner, Andrew 5, 65, 73
minority groups 2, 14, 136–137, 139, 150, 186
models 23–25, 31, 177, 179; *see also* hyperreal; simulacra; simulation
Moran, Anthony 197*n*
Morris, L.L. 8, 10
Morris, Meaghan 89, 96–97, 101–102
Moylan, Tom 58, 160, 192*n*
Mudrooroo 143, 197*n*
multiculturalism 6, 126, 152, 176
Mussolini, Benito 55
"My Country" 42

Nagasaki 55, 58
nameless blank 102
names *see* place names
nanotechnology 180
national identity *see* America: national identity; Australian identity
Native Americans *see* Indigenous peoples (U.S.)
natural disasters 4, 10, 15–16, 36, 75, 123
nature: as against civilization 109; as dangerous 93, 110–111, 122, 131, 180; as refuge 42, 109, 122, 131; and technology 181; *see also* children and nature
Nature's Grave 87

Ness, Patrick 111
the Net 164
Neuromancer 160, 198*n*
the never-never 95
New Caledonia 29
New England 29, 67
New Guinea 34, **37**
New Hampshire 28
new heaven and new earth 3, 11, 15, 27–29, 33–34, 41, 62, 186–187
New Holland 29, 47
New Jerusalem 1, 11, 27–29, 47, 103, 124, 186–187
new Jews 29
New South Wales 29, 36
New Testament 8–11, 141
new world 1–2, 8, 11, 13–15, 17–19, 21, 26, 28–29, 31, 33–34, 42, 44, 47, 52, 62, 65, 69–70, 72, 74, 76–78, 81–83, 88, 94–95, 101, 103, 106–107, 115, 123–124, 136, 143, 150–151, 154, 156–157, 174, 184, 186–189; and Australia 23–53
New York 28, 73
New York City 67, 86, 193*n*
New Zealand 29, 45, 63, 76, 192*n*
The Night Is for Hunting 127, 132
Nimon, Maureen 42, 45, 69, 110, 114, 116
9/11 16, 191*n*, 193*n*
Nolan, Maggie 197*n*
nostalgia 104–105, 171, 177–178
the nothing (desert) 19, 83, 99, 101–104, 107, 135, 150
the nothingness (desert) 95, 100, 103, 179
Nova Scotia 29
"Novae Guineae forma, & situs" 36, **37**
nuclear: age 18, 165; proliferation 18, 60; protests over 109; setting 5, 91, 111–112, 152, 193*n*–194*n*; testing 59, 135, 144; war 1, 13, 53, 57–67, 73, 79–80, 96, 112, 139, 152, 159, 187, 194*n*; weapons 4, 16, 55, 57–60, 65, 70, 81, 139, 188, 192*n*
Nylon Angel 20, 164–185, **166**

Obama, Barack 191*n*
The Obernewtyn Chronicles 112
Ogilvie, George 89
Oil Storm 193*n*
oil wars 88, 92, 103, 194*n*; *see also* fuel
Old Testament 8–9, 19, 100, 141
O'Leary, Stephen D. 5, 57, 60, 136, 191*n*
On the Beach (book) 3, 18, 55, 61–73, 78, 80–81, 88, 187, 192*n*
On the Beach (film) 4, 62, 64
On the Beach (telemovie) 62
One Night Stand 61, 63, 70, 192*n*
Oo-a-deen 46
Open Water 194*n*

oppression 9, 11, 14, 28, 44, 81, 114–115, 138–140, 144, 170, 178, 186, 188
optimism 2–3, 36, 39, 41, 50–51, 58, 67–70, 72, 77, 93, 121, 150, 162–163, 178, 187, 189
O'Regan, Tom 44, 89–90
Ortelius, Abraham 31, 33
Ostry, Elaine 108, 111, 115, 195n
the Other 125, 129, 149, 183–184
The Other Side of Dawn 127
Out of the Silence 4
outback 4, 12, 19, 41, 46, 70, 86–88, 96, 100, 104, 106–107, 110, 135–136, 144, 181, 195n; as amoral 99; as apocalypse 93; as beautiful 109; as hostile 72, 83–84, 86–88, 101, 109, 180, 196n; as lawless 99, 107; as refuge 109; as sacred 149–150; *see also* Australian landscape; dead heart; desert; wasteland; wilderness
Outback see *Wake in Fright* (film)
The Outback see *Prey*
The Outcast Trilogy 112
overpopulation 60–61, 73, 76, 79

The Paperchaser 4, 112
Papua New Guinea 33–34
paradigm of apocalypse *see* apocalyptic paradigm
Parkland 112
parks 109; *see also* gardens
Parrish Plessis novels 20, 160, 164–185, 198n
Pask, Kevin 161
peace 28, 62, 155–156, 185
Peak Oil 195n
Pearce, Sharyn 126
Pearl Harbor 55
penal colony 4, 12, 40, 99
Pentagon 193n
Permutation City 164, 198n
persecution 9–11, 14, 28, 74, 137, 140
Person, Lawrence 163
pessimism 14, 62, 121
Peter Pan 105
Phipson, Joan 109, 112
Picnic at Hanging Rock (book) 4, 84–85, 110
Picnic at Hanging Rock (film) 84, 87, 194n
Pierce, Peter 41, 110, 195n
Pirate Islands 163
Pirate Islands 2 163
Pitch Black 4, 84
place names: and colonization 124, 154; and new worlds 28–29
Plains of Promise 144, 148, 196n
Plank, Robert 137
politics of fear 81, 193n
Pordzik, Ralph 192n
Poseidon 193n
postcolonial haunting 154, 196n

posthumanism 160, 171–173, 198n
The Postman 67
Potter, Robert 4
prairie lands 67
Prey 87, 196n
prison films 4, 99
promised land 12, 15, 19, 27, 30, 33, 40–41, 62, 94, 100, 102, 106, 115, 123–126, 131, 145, 189; *see also* fruitful land
prophecy 8, 15, 29, 47, 58, 79, 91, 141, 143
prophets 14, 68, 79, 169, 173
protectionism 119, 121, 123
Psalms 68
punishment in apocalypse 12, 27, 52, 146, 189
punk 140, 161

Quarantine 164
Queensland 84, 100
Quest Beyond Time 112
Quinby, Lee 15, 137, 191n

The Rabbits 133–134
race 18, 48, 73, 76–78, 105, 130, 132, 172, 182–183; and apocalypse 4–5, 20, 133, 135–159, 188
racism 47–48, 76–77, 105, 123, 129, 138–140, 197n
Rayner, Jonathan 45
Razorback (book) 86–87
Razorback (film) 86
reconciliation 43, 126, 134, 143–144, 150–152, 155–158
red center 95
red heart 95
Red Heart 19, 112, 119, 122–126, 128, 154
refugees 80–81, 119, 121, 125, 128–129, 184
Reilly, Matthew 192n
Le Relationi Universali 30–31
removal of children 148, 157, 197n; *see also* lost children; stolen generations
Revelation 8–15, 28–29, 52–53, 94, 137, 140–141, 146, 186–187
revelation, apocalypse as *see* apocalypse: as revelation
reverse colonization 183
reward from God 10–11
Rieder, John 48, 154, 192n
The Road (book) 67, 193n
The Road (film) 67, 193n
Road Kill 87
Road Train 87
The Road Warrior see *Mad Max 2: The Road Warrior*
roads 88, 91, 93, 95, 98, 101
robots 74, 169–170
Rogue 87
Roman Empire 10, 141

228 Index

romanticism 45–46, 108–110, 118, 196n
Ross, Catriona 129, 131–132
Ross, Robert L. 144
Rowland, Christopher 139
Rowling, J.K. 5
Rubinstein, Gillian 112, 163
rural locations 46, 67, 70, 96, 193n
Russian: power 48; prison labor camps 99
Ryan, Mark David 194n
Ryan, Simon 154–155

sacred heart 20, 149, 151
sacred sites 143, 196n
Said, Edward 154
Salt 3
Salute of the Jugger 4, 84
Sambell, Kay 115
Sargent, Lyman Tower 5, 27, 36, 153, 155, 192n
Saunders, Ian 192n
savior figures 95–96, 146, 168; *see also* messianic figures
Saxby, Maurice 5, 111
Scatterlings 112
science 7, 13, 17, 31, 63–64, 72, 74, 76–78, 139, 161–162, 191n
science fiction 6–7, 13, 24–26, 49, 57–58, 72–73, 91–93, 109, 112, 137, 140, 155, 161–163, 165, 171, 175, 177, 179, 182, 192n–193n, 198n; Australian 5, 46, 48, 83, 155, 163, 182; definition of 7; and Indigenous groups 136, 155, 182, 195n; *see also* speculative fiction
Scott, G. Firth 46
Scott, Ridley 160
Scutter, Heather 111, 115, 122, 129, 195n
The Sea and Summer see *Drowning Towers*
Sea Patrol 80
secular apocalypse 1, 8, 11–15, 17, 27–28, 41, 52, 62, 103, 127, 137, 142–143, 186–189
Seed, David 5, 59, 136, 160
settlement of Australia 18, 26, 31, 38, 113, 117, 123, 135–136, 144, 195n
settlers 24, 36, 39–41, 43, 45–46, 104, 110, 131, 145, 195n
SF *see* science fiction
shamans 176, 182
Shapiro, Jerome F. 64
Sharrad, Paul 196n
Sharrett, Christopher 89, 194n
Sheckels, Theodore F. 89
Sheriffs, R.J.A. 41
shield of distance 18, 54–82, 121, 184; *see also* vulnerability to outside
Shinkei 112, 163
Shute, Nevil 1, 3, 18–19, 54–55, 61–72, 88, 173, 187, 196n

Simpson, Helen 4
simulacra 23–26, 31, 35, 179–180; *see also* hyperreal; models; simulation
simulation 4, 23–26, 34, 173–174, 178–180; *see also* hyperreal; models; simulacra
Skymaze 112, 163
slavery (American) 16, 29–30
Slusser, George 67
small towns 44, 86–87, 96
Smith, Russell 5, 33, 61, 70, 193n
snow storms (2010), U.S. 16, 191n
Snowmageddon 191n
social criticism 57, 63, 140
"The Soldier in the Machine" 163
Sontag, Susan 57–61, 193n
Souter, Kay Torney 197n
South America 31, 49, 75
South American apocalypse 5
south land 24, 47, 145, 188; expectations of 1–2, 18, 27, 30–40, 44, 52, 62, 187, 192n; *see also* Australia; *terra australis*
south land of the Holy Spirit 33, 47
South Pacific 33, 192n
Space Demons 112, 163
speculation about new lands 1, 18, 21, 23–53, 61, 191n–192n
speculative fiction 1, 49, 58, 88, 111, 113, 159, 177, 187, 191n; Australian 4–6, 12, 17–18, 46, 52, 66, 136, 145, 180, 182, 188–189; definition of 6–7; and relationship to apocalypse 7–8; *see also* science fiction
Sponsler, Claire 159, 161–163, 165, 170–171, 176–178
Stableford, Brian 13, 60, 170
Stargate: Atlantis 192n
Stargate: SG-1 192n
Statue of Liberty 192n
Stephens, John 5, 111, 124, 126, 154, 195n–196n
Stephenson, Neal 160
Sterling, Bruce 159–162, 165, 169–170, 174, 176
Stockton, Sharon 198n
Stolen 109, 195n
stolen generations 195n, 197n; *see also* removal of children
Stone, Graham 5
Stone, Michael 195n
Stratton, Jon 89–90, 93–94, 105–106
Sullivan, Andrew 4
A Sunburnt Country 4
Sunshine 193n
Sunshine Coast 100
Supervolcano 193n
Surf Patrol 80
survivalism 64, 67–68, 72, 165, 193n
Sydney 4, 62, 70, 85, 93, 98, 100–102, 109,

Index 229

119, 121–122, 174, 179–180, 195*n*, 198*n*; Harbour 98; Harbour Bridge *71*, 98, 179; Opera House *71*, 119, 179, 192*n*-193*n*
tabula rasa 24, 31, 36, 97, 104, 154, 178
Tan, Shaun 133
Tank Girl 4, 72, 84
Taronga 19, 112, 116, 119–123, **120**, 125–126, 128–129
technology 8, 16, 18, 20, 26, 53, 63–64, 77, 79, 92–93, 105, 109, 140, 151, 161, 164, 168–173, 175–176, 180–181, 183, 192*n*, 195*n*
Telotte, J.P. 169
10.5 193*n*
10.5: Apocalypse 193*n*
The Terminator 68
Terminator Gene 164
Terminator Salvation 68, 193*n*
Terminator: The Sarah Connor Chronicles 68
Terminator 3: Rise of the Machines 68
Terminator 2: Judgment Day 68
terra australis 30–31, 33–34, 44, 61, 189; incognita 1, 23, 30–33, **32**, 178, 187; *see also* Australia; south land
terra nullius 95, 136, 195*n*
La Terre Australe Connue 38
terrorism 16, 55, 80–81, 115, 191*n*, 193*n*-194*n*
The Third Day, The Frost 127, 129–130, 132
Third Reich 55
Thompson, Leonard L. 10, 196*n*
Thunderstone 4, 84, 112
The Time Guardian 84
time travel 112
Todorov, Tzvetan 191*n*
Tolkien, J.R.R. 192*n*
Tomorrow and Tomorrow 62, 70, 192*n*
Tomorrow and Tomorrow and Tomorrow see *Tomorrow and Tomorrow*
Tomorrow, When the War Began (book) 3, 19, 112, 127–128, 130–132
Tomorrow, When the War Began (film) 196*n*
totalitarianism 4, 74, 112
tourists in danger 84, 87–88, 196*n*
tropics 101–102, 125, 181
tsunami *see* Asian tsunami
Turcotte, Gerry 44, 110, 113, 117–118, 196*n*-197*n*
Turkey Shoot 4, 99
Turner, George 4, 7, 18–19, 54–55, 61–62, 70–82, 173, 193*n*, 196*n*
Turner, Graeme 41–42
28 Days Later 67, 193*n*
28 Weeks Later 67, 193*n*
24 193*n*
2012 61, 193*n*

Twilight series 5
Twin Towers 193*n*
2 Peter 3
2 Thessalonians 9
Typus orbis terrarum 31–33, **32**
tyranny 9, 108
tyranny of distance 18, 69, 86

Uluru 149–150
uncanny 42–44, 113, 133, 149; *see also* unheimlich
Undead 87
Underground 4, 81, 193*n*-194*n*
The Undying 143
unheimlich 43, 178–179; *see also* uncanny
United Kingdom *see* Britain
United States 16, 47, 59, 63, 69–70, 73, 75–76, 84, 86–87, 89, 101, 123, 128, 140, 150, 160, 183, 191*n*, 193*n*-194*n*; Civil War 16; disappointment with 29–30, 36; expectations of 29–30, 36; national identity 49, 67–68; as New World 29; and nuclear bomb 67–68, 70; politics 81, 194*n*; proximity to conflict 69–70; slavery 16, 29–30; war on terror 81, 194*n*; *see also* American apocalypse
unknown south land *see terra australis*: *incognita*
Until the End of the World 3
utopia 1–2, 5–6, 12, 15, 18–21, 24, 27–31, 33, 35–36, 38, 41, 46–47, 50–54, 58, 61–62, 66, 69–70, 72–75, 78, 82–83, 85, 93–94, 103, 107, 111–112, 115, 126, 136, 138, 145, 155–158, 161, 167, 172, 175, 179–180, 182–183, 185, 187–189, 192*n*-193*n*, 195*n*, 198*n*-199*n*; and apocalypse 27–28

vampires 143, 197*n*
Vaneglory 4, 72–75
vanishing: in the bush 85, 110; in the outback 19, 84, 87, 110, 194*n*; at sea 84, 194*n*; *see also* lost children
Vanuatu 33
Vietnam 129, 144
Vietnam War 16, 29, 129, 144
violence 45, 60, 88–89, 91–92, 95, 99–100, 112, 114, 165; and apocalypse 61, 64, 67, 103, 137, 141, 185; of colonization 20, 113, 119, 121, 123–126, 134, 136, 145–146, 154; and white people 148–149, 153
virtual media 176
virtual reality 161, 163, 169, 172, 174–176, 198*n*
virus weapons 16, 67, 76–77, 188
A Voice from Australia 47
voodoo 168, 176, 182

vulnerability to outside 2, 11, 19, 21, 27, 36, 49–50, 54, 65, 72, 82, 113, 128, 130, 133, 184; *see also* invasion; shield of distance

Wagar, W. Warren 5–6, 10, 13, 15–16, 56, 58, 65, 80, 93, 139, 169–170
Waiting for the End of the World 19, 108, 112, 114–119, 122
Wake in Fright (book) 4, 84–86
Wake in Fright (film) 44, 84, 86–87, 96
Walliss, John 140, 196*n*
Walton, Robyn 192*n*
war against terror *see* war on terror
War of the Worlds 193*n*
war on terror 81, 194*n*
wasteland 41, 72, 94–95, 98, 100, 106–107, 145, 152, 177, 188; *see also* Australian landscape; dead heart; desert; outback; wilderness
Waterworld 67
Watson, Sam 4, 20, 135–136, 144–153, 155, 157–158, 196*n*-197*n*
The Web of Time 112
Webb, Janeen 39, 47–48, 192*n*
Wegner, Phillip E. 162
Weir, Peter 143
Weller, Archie 20, 136, 144, 152–158, 196*n*-197*n*
the West 8, 26, 56, 59, 65, 73, 76–77, 95, 105, 179, 184, 193*n*, 198*n*
Wevers, Lydia 142, 150
When the Sky Fell Down 143
Where the Green Ants Dream 3, 143
While I Live 127
Whitcomb, J.C., Jr. 141
White, Patrick 41
White, Richard 31, 38–40, 42, 192*n*
white people: as Indigenous 19, 131–132; and the nuclear bomb 139; and violence 148–149, 153
Wik 183

Wild Cat Falling 197*n*
wilderness 11–12, 19, 27, 29, 41, 52, 70, 84, 94, 96, 98, 100–101, 105, 107, 122, 127, 179–180, 188, 191*n*; *see also* Australian landscape; dead heart; desert; outback; wasteland
Willey, Keith 143
Williams, Paul 5, 47, 96, 105, 195*n*
Williams, Sean 163
Williams, Tess 3, 192*n*
Winter 3
"Wired Dreaming" 163
Witherington, Ben, III 199*n*
Wolf Creek 87, 194*n*
The Woman on the Beast 4
Wonders of a Godless World 4
Wongar, B. 4, 144, 196*n*-197*n*
Wordsworth, William 46
World Trade Center 193*n*
World War I 113
World War III 62
World War II 16, 18, 55, 58–59, 61–62, 65, 80, 83, 91, 130, 177, 191*n*
world wars 58, 68
Wright, Alexis 142, 144, 148, 196*n*
Wright, Judith 42
Wrightson, Patricia 112, 132

xenophobia 183

YA literature *see* young adult literature
Yesterday's Men 4, 72
young adult literature 4, 108, 110–116, 121, 128, 195*n*; *see also* children's literature

Zamora, Lois Parkinson 5, 29, 140
Zechariah 8–9
Zion 11, 199*n*
Žižek, Slavoj 163, 173, 197*n*-199*n*
zombies 74, 87

www.ingramcontent.com/pod-product-compliance
Ingram Content Group UK Ltd.
Pitfield, Milton Keynes, MK11 3LW, UK
UKHW041943140426
5217IPUK00014B/636

9 780786 460519